Y0-BCE-403

THE PRINCIPLES OF RELIGIOUS DEVELOPMENT

MACMILLAN AND CO., Limited
LONDON . BOMBAY . CALCUTTA
MELBOURNE

THE MACMILLAN COMPANY
NEW YORK . BOSTON . CHICAGO
ATLANTA . SAN FRANCISCO

THE MACMILLAN CO. OF CANADA, Ltd.
TORONTO

THE PRINCIPLES OF RELIGIOUS DEVELOPMENT

A Psychological and Philosophical Study

BY

GEORGE GALLOWAY, M.A., B.D., D.PHIL.

AUTHOR OF "STUDIES IN THE PHILOSOPHY OF RELIGION"
FORMERLY EXAMINER IN PHILOSOPHY IN THE UNIVERSITY OF ST. ANDREW'S

MACMILLAN AND CO., LIMITED
ST. MARTIN'S STREET, LONDON
1909

Richard Clay and Sons, Limited,
bread street hill, e.c., and
bungay, suffolk.

PREFACE

THE generous recognition accorded by well qualified critics to a former work by the author (*Studies in the Philosophy of Religion*, W. Blackwood and Sons, 1904) has encouraged him to submit to the public the further fruit of his studies in the same field. The present volume, despite its shortcomings, will perhaps help to draw attention to a point which has been somewhat overlooked by English writers. I mean the indispensable function of psychology in constructing a theory of religious development. The reader, however, is referred to the Introduction for an indication of the scope and purpose of the book.

It is not easy, nor is it necessary, to state all one's intellectual obligations. In process of time a student finds he has learned much, the sources of which he can no longer clearly trace. But the instructed reader will perceive that, in philosophical matters, I have profited greatly by the study of Lotze. Among writers on religious philosophy I owe not a little to the late Prof. Pfleiderer, whose lectures I was privileged to hear a good many years ago, and who first stimulated my interest in the subject. Prof. H. Siebeck's *Religionsphilosophie* I have also found very suggestive.

The first chapter of the book has already appeared in *Mind*, and is reprinted with a few verbal alterations. I have to thank the editor for permission to republish the article. The Rev. D. Frew, B.D., has again given me valued help in revising the proofs, and Mr. David Morrison, M.A., kindly read Chapter IX, and made some suggestions.

G. G.

CASTLE-DOUGLAS, N.B.

CONTENTS

INTRODUCTION

CHAPTER I

THE IDEA OF DEVELOPMENT AND ITS APPLICATION TO HISTORY

CHAPTER II

THE DEVELOPMENT OF RELIGION

CHAPTER V

THE FUNCTION OF THOUGHT IN RELIGION

CHAPTER VI

THE WILL IN RELIGION: THE DEVELOPMENT OF THE CULT

CHAPTER VII

INTERACTION IN RELIGIOUS DEVELOPMENT

CHAPTER VIII

THE MORAL IDEAL AND THE RELIGIOUS CONSCIOUSNESS

CHAPTER IX

THE ULTIMATE GROUND OF EXPERIENCE

CHAPTER X

SOME FINAL PROBLEMS OF RELIGIOUS DEVELOPMENT

“ Es sagen’s aller Orten
Alle Herzen unter dem himmlischen Tage,
Jedes in seiner Sprache.”

—*Goethe.*

“ Gott ist zunächst etwas ganz Unbestimmtes ; in dem Gange der Entwickelung bildet sich aber das Bewusstseyn dessen, was Gott ist, allmälig weiter aus, verliert immer mehr die anfängliche Unbestimmtheit und damit schreitet auch die Entwickelung des wirklichen Selbstbewusstseyns weiter fort.”

—*Hegel.*

εἰ δή τις ἐξ ἀρχῆς τὰ πράγματα φυόμενα βλέψειεν, ὥσπερ ἐν τοῖς ἄλλοις, καὶ ἐν τούτοις κάλλιστ’ ἂν οὕτω θεωρήσειεν·

—*Aristotle.*

INTRODUCTION

Though opinions vary in regard to the truth of religion, no one doubts the deep importance of the study of religion at the present day. For the temper and ideals of peoples are expressed in their religions, and a man's religious faith is the revelation of his deepest thoughts on life and destiny. In the great religions of the past we behold, as in a mirror, the strivings and aspirations of the races that have gone before, and a reflexion of the meaning they read into the world. Despite vast differences in culture, a spiritual unity is traceable in humanity; and in studying the rise and decay of religions men attain a profounder knowledge of themselves and the spiritual forces which have helped to mould them. They learn how rich and varied is their inheritance from the past, and see 'writ large' the principles at work which are still active in shaping their own spiritual experience. And the vogue of the evolutionary method has broken down an ancient prejudice. Any hard and fast grouping of religions into true and false is generally felt to be inadmissible, and the tendency is rather to adopt the idea of 'degrees of truth' or to fall back on the conception of 'working value.' Under the guidance of modern ideas of development, the study of the whole subject has been taken up in a catholic and sympathetic spirit which recognises nothing human as foreign to it. As the speech of the grown man is prefigured in the lispings of the child, so in the vague and confused Spiritism of primeval races we acknowledge the faint stirrings of that religious impulse which finds expression to-day in the exalted language of spiritual religion. But if the successful application of the developmental method is largely a recent thing, it may be well to remember that the old world had some glimpses of its value. In the opening of his *Politics*, Aristotle pointed out that a sound political philosophy should be based on a study of the growth of human institutions. It was reserved for the nineteenth century to follow up this hint with far-reaching results.

Within the last few decades the materials available for the study of religious development have been increased on every side. Histories both of religion in general and of particular religions have been written, and students of Comparative Religion have been busy trying to bring out the points of correspondence and difference as well as the links of connexion between the various religions.[1] The process is still far from complete; but even as it is, the individual who seeks to reach a philosophical conception of religion "on the ground of its history" has a great body of materials before him, more, indeed, than he can thoroughly master. And the abundance and complexity of the facts make it difficult to form any comprehensive theory which will do justice to them all. Hegel, writing in the third decade of last century, could use the material

[1] Of general Histories of Religion the best at present is probably the *Lehrbuch der Religionsgeschichte*, edited by Chantepie de la Saussaye, with the co-operation of a number of distinguished scholars. The third edition appeared in 1905 In his *Orpheus: Histoire générale des Religions*, M. Salomon Reinach has condensed a remarkable amount of information into a rapid survey, though the work is not free from bias.

at his disposal to show, in a powerful and impressive way, that the different historical religions are determinate stages by which the Absolute Religion is realised. But no one now supposes that historic religions can be characterised by a phrase and fitted into a scheme in this way: in the face of our greatly extended knowledge of the subject an attempt of the kind is no longer practicable. Yet Hegel's great influence in the sphere of spiritual development, taken along with his neglect of psychology, has in some ways hindered rather than helped the progress of sounder ideas on the development of religion. The prejudice in favour of a purely philosophical interpretation lingered on. For example, Dr. Edward Caird's *Evolution of Religion* is a very thoughtful and suggestive book, and no one will read it without profit. But he clings to the notion that you can rightly construe the development of the religious consciousness by the generalised categories of object and subject, and their higher synthesis. In truth, you can only do so by neglecting a great deal, by judiciously selecting your material, and by treating it with some ingenuity.

A point strongly and repeatedly urged in the following pages, is that a speculative theory cannot be applied straight away to the interpretation of the materials which the History and Science of Religion set before us. The mediation of psychology is indispensable to a right understanding of facts which are primarily psychical, and of the movements of the human mind which give the facts the form of development. It is true, I think, that the backward state of the social sciences at the present day is not a little due to the defective psychological training of those who have treated of them. Think, for instance, how the theory of economic value suffered from neglect of psychological analysis. In this connexion I am glad to quote a couple of sentences from a recent work by a psychologist of distinction. "A certain number, perhaps the majority, of recent writers on social topics recognise the true position of psychology, but in practice are content to take as their psychological foundations the vague and extremely misleading psychology embodied in common speech, with the addition of a few hasty assumptions about the mind made to suit their particular purposes. There are signs, however, that this regrettable state of affairs is about to pass away, that psychology will before long be accorded in universal practice the position at the base of the social sciences which the more clear-sighted have long seen that it ought to occupy."[1] It may be added that it is a hopeful sign for the future study of religious phenomena that the value of psychology in this regard is coming to be widely recognised.

On the other hand, the reader will find the view is frankly accepted here that psychology must hand over the final interpretation of religious development to a Philosophy of Religion. The latter completes the work of the former by attempting to show the ultimate ground and meaning of the process, and the validity which attaches to religion. One has to admit, however, that there will always be something provisional and tentative in the final unification; and it is foolish to cherish enthusiastic hopes about what metaphysics can accomplish. Yet a study of religious development which eschews metaphysics can only reach an ambiguous and unsatisfying conclusion. An exposition of the function and value of religion in the individual and social life can never be taken as settling the question of its truth; and it would be a desperate expedient to accord validity to any belief which you found

[1] *An Introduction to Social Psychology*, by W. McDougall. Methuen & Co., 1908, p. 2.

practically useful. Spiritual experience, in fact, has its postulates, and the coherency of these with the body of knowledge is a question which is pressed upon us. It is just on this point that the late Professor Tiele's excellent work entitled *Elements of the Science of Religion* will be found defective. One has the feeling after reading it, that much has been wisely said about the place of religion in culture and the want it supplies, but that the problem of its rational justification has been left undecided. Accordingly I have not tried to evade this ultimate question ; with what success it has been treated the reader must determine.

It may be well, in order to avoid possible misapprehension, to say a word on the scope and purpose of this volume. It is not to be regarded as a History of the Development of Religion. This is a task of another kind wnich the present writer has not attempted to discharge. What is offered here is a study of the principles which underlie and are disclosed in the development of religion. Facts are used to illustrate principles. Of course it was only possible to execute such an undertaking by drawing freely and constantly on the materials supplied by the History and Science of Religions. But at the same time it was necessary to exercise a selection upon the materials, to single out facts which were relevant to the point under consideration, and to sacrifice anything like completeness of historical exposition. The purpose has been to bring out in this way the characteristic features of religious development, and to set forth the principles, psychological and philosophical, which help to explain it. It is impossible to deal satisfactorily with this subject in a merely critical spirit ; effective criticism must proceed from a positive standpoint, and a constructive theory is implied in adequately carrying out the work of selection and valuation. At the same time, I can only hope that the subject is treated in a calm and dispassionate way, and that, whatever the defects of the book, no attempt is made to wrest facts to suit a preconceived opinion.

It only remains to point out briefly the plan followed in the succeeding chapters. I have thought it well to begin with an examination of the idea of development which seeks to bring out the distinctive character of spiritual as contrasted with natural evolution. The concluding part of the chapter contains a discussion of certain ultimate postulates which seem to be involved in the interpretation of historical development. In the second chapter the main facts in regard to the development of religion are set forth. The next five chapters deal with the psychological basis of religion, the psychical factors implicated, and their interaction in religious development. A special chapter is devoted to the relation of morality and religion, and it leads naturally up to the speculative theory of experience outlined in the ninth chapter. This theory is applied to aid in solving some ultimate problems of religious development in the concluding chapter. I am conscious that the philosophical discussion of the subject may be considered rather rapid and condensed ; and some may think a more extended treatment was called for. But I would ask the reader to remember that it was no part of my purpose to offer an elaborate essay in metaphysics. The intention has rather been to show the kind of speculative theory to which the psychology of religion points, and to indicate the interpretation it gives to problems that are involved in the development of religion. And, as I have already said, it seems better to deal with this question, even if shortly, than to leave it wholly in abeyance.

THE PRINCIPLES OF RELIGIOUS DEVELOPMENT

CHAPTER I

THE IDEA OF DEVELOPMENT AND ITS APPLICATION TO HISTORY.

This chapter does not pretend to answer the large questions which belong to the province of the Philosophy of History. It is meant to be a discussion of the applicability of the notion of development in the sphere of historic phenomena, which may prepare the way for a detailed examination of the principle in the domain of religion. Our purpose will be realised if we succeed in setting the idea in a clearer light, in showing with what qualifications we must employ it in the region of human culture, and in suggesting the postulates which this use involves.

The word development is popularly used with a slender appreciation of its connotation. And even in scientific circles the term is applied without reflexion : it has in fact become one of the *idola fori*, a stock-phrase of the scientific market-place which it is not thought needful to justify. Speaking of words like "latent," "potential," and "tendency," Mr. Bradley cuttingly remarks, "It would be hard to overestimate the service rendered by these terms to some writers on philosophy."[1] And the same is precisely true of development. But the facility with which the word is predicated of objects so diverse as a plant, a man, a nation, and a type of culture, should suffice to give the critically minded pause. It is only natural to ask whether the idea has the same significant content in each of these examples. These are matters about which we must be clear, ere we can decide on the validity of the conception of development when applied to historical phenomena.

At the outset it may be of advantage to consider the origin of the idea and its introduction into modern thought. Like most of our philosophical ideas we inherit it from Greece, and it was first definitely formulated by Aristotle. The χωρισμός of Plato's ideas seemed to make process and becoming unintelligible, and Aristotle sought to solve the problem by his theory of a vital relation of form and matter which is realised in the constant transition from the possible to the actual. An object which is a concrete whole can be analysed into a form and a matter, and the fact that it passes through definite phases or stages must find its explanation in the form or τὸ τί ἦν εἶναι. Change and movement are the outcome of the innate striving of matter after form, but it is the form which ποιεῖ καὶ γεννᾷ ἐκ τοῦδε τοιόνδε.[2] Here Aristotle sets over against a mechanical (ἐξ ἀνάγκης) a final and immanent causality (οὗ ἕνεκα) which explains the process of unfolding in things. The form is at once the τέλος as it is also the universal by means of which we know the object.[3] Aristotle thus read the meaning of becoming as a transition from potential to actual existence,—a transition which is based on the presence even in natural

[1] *Appearance and Reality*, first ed., p. 384. [2] *Meta.* vii., 8, 1033 b, 12.
[3] κατὰ τὸ εἶδος ἅπαντα γιγνώσκομεν, *Meta.* iv., 5, 1010 a, 25.

organisms of an intelligible form or constitutive idea. With the difficulties and inconsistencies in which the carrying out of this thought involved Aristotle we are not at present concerned. But it is hard to overestimate the influence of this great conception on all later thought. The point we have to note is that Aristotle never seems to have considered history in the light of this theory of development. Indeed the classical world, when it thought of history, thought of a cycle and not of a progressive movement towards some far-off goal: and Aristotle himself threw out the hypothesis that the fruits of culture might more than once have been lost and found again.

The spread of the idea that human history is a process towards a divinely appointed end was directly due to Christianity. Eschatological notions flourished greatly in the primitive Church; and if some of these notions were crude, the whole movement had the effect of bringing the wide field of human life under the scope of a comprehensive teleology. Men were made familiar with the thought that the world and its inhabitants were moving forward to some end appointed by God. The view of history as the unfolding of a divinely ordained plan gradually fulfilling itself received an impressive expression at the hands of Augustine. In all this, however, we have history broadly treated on the basis of certain religious postulates rather than a deliberate and reflecting endeavour to interpret it through the principle of development. We must come well down into modern times ere we find the steps taken which led towards such an attempt.

The first significant treatment of the idea of development in modern philosophy is that of Leibniz. From Aristotle he derived the conception of a continuous inner process teleologically not mechanically determined. The complete idea of the organism implicitly existed in the germ and directed its unfolding. Leibniz applied the same idea to the striving of the monad through the different stages of mental life towards completed self-knowledge. Then the system of monads has its Sufficient Reason in God, who must thus be the ground of that orderly development of their inner lives which stands for experience to each of them. Under the figure of the Choice of the best Possible World Leibniz expressed the thought that the ground both of the world's existence and development is a highest Ethical Value. To apply his conception of development to history would perforce have been very difficult for Leibniz, inasmuch as the evolution of each member of the system must be rigidly determined from within, and his philosophy excluded the notion of fruitful interaction of elements with one another.

Both in the theoretical and practical philosophy of Kant, in many ways under the influence of the eighteenth century, the notion of development is notably in the background. Still in his *Lectures on History* we find him putting forward the idea, often to be repeated by others, that the aim of history is the development of all the natural capacities of man. For a more striking exposition and enforcement of this idea we must turn to the work of Herder. A new and deeper view of history had already been given by Lessing, who applied in the historic sphere the notion of development learned from Leibniz. But it was Herder who first, in an impressive and comprehensive manner, treated historical phenomena from this point of view. Both in nature and human life he saw the tokens of a great process of growth; and even those who (like the present writer) have only a slight knowledge at first hand of the *Ideen zur Philosophie der Geschichte der Menschheit* are struck by the boldness and confidence with which he carries the idea of development from the organic into the spiritual world. In both spheres a similar drama is advancing to its goal. History for Herder is just the development of human nature towards a perfect humanity which achieves the form of freedom. The movement unfolds after the fashion of a natural organism, and the religious optimism of the writer enabled him to pass somewhat lightly over the failures and the ruin brought about by conflicting human wills. Despite the suggestiveness of Herder's theory and its influence on Hegel and others, it must be said that his use of the term development is vague and uncritical : and this is apparent from his failure to draw any clear distinction between natural and spiritual evolution.

Hegel's grasp of the notion is of course more subtle and profound ; it was substantially a revival of the Aristotelian idea. Development for him meant the unfolding of what has already potential existence, and its course and end, alike in the regions of nature and of mental life, are determined. Nothing, strictly speaking, can arise *de novo*, and the process is only a bringing to manifestation of what already has being somehow. The same movement of thought takes place in all levels of existence, and Hegel has no hesitation in affirming that what is substantial in history is mind and the process of its development.[1] Thus we find him saying : "As the germ carries within itself the whole nature of the tree, the flavour and the form of the fruits, so the first vestiges of mind virtually contain the whole history."[2] The

[1] *Philosophie der Geschichte*, p. 21, ed. 1848.
[2] *Op. cit.*, p. 23.

essence of mind is freedom, and Hegel declares that freedom—the full and harmonious realisation of human capacities as Herder put it—is the goal and moving idea of history. But the universal Idea can only work itself out in the medium of particular human interests and passions : the two in their inseparable connexion constitute the warp and the woof of the growing web of man's history. The Particular stands in the foreground and enters into oppositions and is involved in conflicts : the Idea stands in the background, and through the shocks and jars of time calmly and inflexibly brings forth the predetermined end.[1] It is here that Hegel shows that there is a difference between natural and historic development ; for in the former the process goes on in an immediate and unhindered way, while in the latter progress is through antagonism. And this because in the sphere of history the passage of the Idea into realisation is mediated by human consciousness and will.[2] It is no part of our purpose here to consider how Hegel treats history as the realisation of freedom with reference to the historic nations. But there is a point in Hegel's conception of historic development on which he himself lays stress and which deserves notice. It is most important, he says, for the understanding of history, to grasp the conception of change, the process of transition.[3] The fact is borne home to us by the thought of ruined cities and vanished empires. Yet as life dissolves in death, so out of death arises new life. There comes a point, Hegel thinks, in the history of a people as of an individual, where that opposition between the latent ideal and the actual, which is the spring of progress, is overcome : it has now realised the function which it had in it

[1] *Philosophie der Geschichte*, p. 41.
[2] *Op. cit.*, p. 68. [3] *Op. cit.*, p. 90 ff.

to fulfil. The nation's historic office is discharged ; the fruit it brought forth goes to thrive elsewhere ; and it can only linger on in the life of custom. In the true sense there is no dislocation of the process, for the spirit which has wrought a relative completeness, by its negative movement transcends the given stage in order to find an ampler fulfilment. The strict continuity of the movement is asserted by Hegel when he declares that the stages which, from one point of view, are a succession in the past are really eternally present in the inner depths of the Universal Spirit.[1] The different national spirits are only the moments by which the Idea rises to a self-inclusive totality and comes to its goal. Contingency is excluded, and each element has its determinate meaning and function in the movement of the spirit.

Here we have the most profound and thorough application to history of that idea of development originally outlined by Aristotle. The difficulties it raises need not now be discussed ; they will to some extent be dealt with when we consider the general applicability of the idea of development to history. Meanwhile it may be well to refer to the less speculative use of the principle in the sphere of history by men like Spencer, Comte, and J. S. Mill. Here the thing insisted on is the presence of causal connexion between the parts and the evidence of the reign of uniformity in the region of historical phenomena. Mill, to whose statements we confine ourselves, thinks that "that which is only probable when asserted of individual human beings indiscriminately selected, [is] certain when affirmed of the character and collective conduct of masses."[2] At the same time he admits that as regards the succession of historical pheno-

[1] So also what we construe as future is already realised in the Absolute.

[2] *Logic*, sixth ed., vol. ii., p. 428.

mena our inference can at the most amount only to an empirical law, not to a law of nature. Yet this is not because the uniformity is less strict, but is due to our imperfect knowledge of the conditions. Historical science, like meteorology, is not certain in its deductions, but in either case law reigns. The aim of social dynamics would be achieved, "if every one of the leading general circumstances of each generation were traced back to its causes in the generation immediately preceding."[1] Progress, in so far as it exists, Mill agrees with Buckle in attributing mainly to increase of intelligence. The important feature in the views of Mill and those who follow him is, that they recognise no qualitative difference between historical and natural laws. They do not seek to interpret human progress through final instead of mechanical causes. Historical movements are explained rather by what has been than by what is to be ; the cry is to establish continuity with the past rather than to recognise the appeal and indwelling power of the end or ideal.

In Hegel and Mill, then, we see two well-defined types of historical philosophy which have points both of contact and of difference. Both agree in fully maintaining the sway of the principle of continuity : neither would admit the emergence of elements *de novo* in the historic process. But while for Mill the succession of historical phenomena is to be explained by an extended application of the principle of causal connexion, for Hegel it is to be interpreted through the idea of development. Here the end dominates the means, and for the deeper understanding of what is we must not simply consider what has been but what is to be. Whether either method is satisfactory is doubtful, but the only way to reach a decision on the

[1] *Op. cit.*, p. 519.

subject is by a closer examination of the idea of development itself.

If we regard the principle as it is illustrated by the growth of organisms, we find presuppositions involved. There is first of all a determinate basis called the germ, then a continuous process within the germ in virtue of which it assumes successive phases, then an end which is set over against the beginning and contrasted with each intermediate stage. The further assumption is made that the end is that for which the beginning was, and controls the movement throughout. In other words, organic development in its specifications depends primarily on internal character, and only in a secondary degree on external environment. The urgency of the teleological concept is partly due to the felt inadequacy of the ordinary causal view. For when we think out what the common idea of cause implies, we are inevitably led to the notion of the interaction of elements within a whole ; and this whole conditions the interaction of the particular parts, which interaction regarded in abstraction from the rest is termed cause and effect. And when we identify the relation of parts and whole with that of means and end, there is truth in Kant's contention that end is the complementary notion to that of cause and one involves the other. Obviously, however, this conception as it stands does not meet the case of development which requires progress in time, and where, in order to secure the operation of the final whole throughout, we postulate its potential or implicit existence in the earlier stages. Here the idea of cause is not merely completed, it is transformed by the idea of end ; and the question lies to hand, Can we justify the notion of an end implicitly operative ? It has been objected that by teleology we simply give the semblance of explanation by repeating as ground what we find as consequent.[1] But this criticism, it seems to me, depends for its validity on a particular application of the idea of ground. If it is taken to mean that the developed consequent really exists in miniature form in the germ from which it exercises a definite propulsive energy, then this no doubt is a sheer assumption, not a justifiable hypothesis. The problem raised by development is in no way furthered by denying the validity of the idea of final cause. It has been truly pointed out that our subjective experience has given content to the notion of end. Our sense of voluntary effort or effective causality embodies itself in our representation of end as something to be achieved, and our feeling-consciousness invests the realised object with a value as contrasted with the means. Nor do we deny that without the feeling and volitional aspects of our nature we should not evolve the teleological view. At the same time it is necessary to remember that it was experience itself out of which this idea grew and was generalised ; and so it must be *bene fundatum* ; there must be something in the constitution of experience of which it seeks to be the expression. And this would hold even if it could be shown, as has not been done, that our idea ot end is an illegitimate construction from our experience. Moreover it may be urged that the notion of end coheres with the principle of continuity without which we could not make our experience rational. Indeed teleology is only a more highly specialised application of the principle of continuity. And the intellectual need under which we are placed of so thinking experience is justified by the practical success with which the ideas work.

[1] Adamson, *The Development of Modern Philosophy*, vol. ii., p. 187. Prof. Adamson's criticism is exceedingly acute, but also, it must be added, very unsatisfying.

In what way, then, do we hold that teleological process obtains in nature? Evidently we must postulate that the elements which constitute the beginning prefigure in their character and disposition the complete result, and yet not in the sense that by themselves they are the sufficient means to the result: elements from without are always necessary. Further, if the end does not operate throughout, the process is not intelligible. We speak of the process having a law of growth, which law determines that the elements in the process of differentiation stand in definite relations to one another and the whole. If we say that the end which finds working expression in the law is only a subjective point of view, we simply make development a mystery. It is more profitable to ask what meaning the term law can have in this connexion. Obviously it cannot connote an ideal principle which rules the elements from without, and invests their actings with a necessity to which they would not otherwise be subject. Law is a name for the way of acting of the elements which are supposed to illustrate it, and expressed as a generalised formula is useful for purposes of description but not of explanation. A law of nature is essentially abstract; it expresses only a particular aspect of the behaviour of things, and its necessity is hypothetical; and the more concrete the experience the less adequate will be the attempt to express it in terms of mechanical law. Accordingly the explanation of organic growth must lie in the character of the elements themselves, which by their interaction make such growth possible. These elements are "compossible"; each is qualified by relation to the rest, and so all are subject to the limitation implied in mutual determination. The question is, then, What do we mean when we say that the given whole has a disposition to work out a particular line of development? If a mechanical propulsive power, a *vis a tergo*, is excluded, we seem compelled to postulate something in the connected elements which corresponds to awareness of the end to be produced, and conative impulse towards it. That is to say we have here something which, on a higher grade, appears as instinct, and finally as conscious volition. In other words the ultimate essence of the developing object is related to the psychical life, and so operates under the principle of end or final cause. The existence of a real continuity between the rational will in man and the conative life of a lower organism is our ultimate justification for interpreting living process through the idea of end, an idea whose psychological origin is in our own volitional experience. If this statement is accepted, it follows that the mechanical interpretation of experience can at no point in the scale of being be true, but it is less untrue in the lower than in the higher ranges of psychical existence. You can use the mechanical conception with good results in the case of a planetary system, while it is notoriously inadequate if applied to a social whole. But the temptation to transfer methods which are useful in a lower sphere to a higher is great; and the language of natural science has been applied to society with misleading results. Phrases like "social statics" and "social dynamics" introduce a false simplicity at the outset, and conduce to defective theories in consequence.

On the theory we have so far advanced we have now to ask, whether we can interpret historic progress as an organic development. Ere we try to come to a decision on this point, let us note certain differences between the conditions which obtain in the two spheres. And, in the first place, the elements which enter into organic development, if in their essence psychical, are nevertheless not self-conscious. There must be a difference in the reactions of a factor which stands on the level of conation merely and those of another which stands on the level of self-conscious will. For man plays a conscious part in his own development and a plant does not. We cannot suppose that antecedents are taken up into the focus of self-consciousness, whence they issue as consequents, and that the self exercises no efficient causality in the process. In the case of a psychical whole whose reactions are instinctive, the end may operate in the part with a uniformity which has the semblance of being mechanical. But with the self-conscious individual the relation of his conduct to the end will depend on the way he takes the end up into his conscious purpose. Hence in the historic life, which consists in the interrelated actings of a multitude of self-conscious individuals, the principle of teleology finds an altogether fuller and higher expression. A feature which emphasises the distinction between organic and spiritual or historic development is the presence in the latter of the momentous contrast of what *is* and what *ought* to be. As Prof. Ward has said, in history purpose carries with it the notion of good or worth, and the great difference between nature and history is that between what *is* and what *ought* to be.[1] Science and history set out from the same world of experience, but the one proceeds outwards, the other inwards : so the one deals with connected facts, the other with related values. To the historian progress means the realisation of value, and he appreciates events and characters by their relation to some value conceived as end. It may be objected that the contrast of fact and value is drawn too sharply, and it may be argued that the difference between what is and what ought to be is represented in the development of an organism. The "ought" is just the fulfilled idea, the completed process of growth, and each partial phase of evolution has to be transcended

[1] *Vid. Hibbert Journal*, Oct., 1905.

that the end may be achieved. But we have only to compare this conception with spiritual process to see that it does not rightly apply to it. The elements of an organic body have no meaning for themselves; in a social whole each unit has a unique self-meaning. In the one case we say the end *has* to be, in the other it *ought* to be, and the difference in the terms expresses a significant difference in the processes. Moreover, in organic growth each phase has a positive function and value as a step to the end: on the other hand, in spiritual development we find within the process itself elements which impede the realisation of the end and which ought not to exist. By no fair interpretation of the facts can we identify natural imperfection with moral evil. Hence historic development has a new complexity and depth of meaning as compared with natural growth, and this because of the unique individuality of the elements which go to constitute it.

There is a further consideration which should make us careful about trying to construe historical development after the analogy of organic growth. In all organic growth the process starts from a definite basis, which as beginning we contrast with the end. And the question lies to hand, Is it always possible to specify such a determinate basis in the case of historic development? Here we might take up the question discussed by Dr. McTaggart, whether society is justly entitled to be called an organism. And it is plain that if we accept Dr. McTaggart's definition of organism as that which is the 'end of its own parts,' society cannot be fairly regarded as the final end of the individuals who compose it.[1] On the other hand, it

[1] *Studies in Hegelian Cosmology*, p. 185 ff. One may doubt whether Hegel, in view of his treatment of the state as the objective Will and the realisation of Freedom, would have accepted Dr. McTaggart's statement as an adequate interpretation of his own doctrine. On this point, see the instructive remarks of Prof. Bosanquet, MIND, N.S., No. 25. But I have no claim to speak with

might be said that, though society is not a perfect organism, still it reveals some of the essential features of organic development; and especially that the historic process is the unfolding of an immanent idea operative from the first. Here the difficulty already mentioned confronts us, the difficulty, namely, of assigning a determinate basis on which the process begins and a well-defined whole persisting through change within which the idea works. Shall we take the nation as the unit within which historic development manifests itself? then we find it impossible to apply the rule that the whole moves altogether, if it moves at all. Within the whole we encounter very various degrees of spiritual culture, and while certain elements are progressive and make history, others are so fettered by prejudice and custom that instead of co-operating in a forward movement they are a positive obstacle to advance. Moreover, among the progressive parties there is commonly divergence of spirit and tendency, which issues in antagonism and conflict over the course to be pursued. Nor is it an unusual thing for the reactionary elements in society to triumph, for a time at least. These facts, if they do not disprove development, at all events show that the phenomena are too varied and complex to be satisfactorily interpreted on the analogy of organic growth. And, if further argument were needed, one might point out that, while in the physical organism the inward principle is of primary importance, and the environment, if essential, is still of secondary importance, the same cannot be said of any social whole which you choose to regard as the basis of historic development. For here interaction with other social wholes—tribes,

authority on the subject, and after all the point is not of importance for our present purpose. Dr. McTaggart may quite well be right in the view he advocates, but wrong in supposing that Hegel would have endorsed it.

nations, or races—is as important for the progress of the given social whole as its own internal character. To put it concretely, the historic development of a nation cannot be deduced from any assumed fundamental character of that nation, taken in abstraction from the influence of other nations.

Still more difficult is it to justify the application of the term 'organic development' to the history of particular phases of culture within a society. Phrases like the 'development of art' and the 'development of religion' occur very frequently, and convey a sufficiently definite meaning for practical purposes. But when you push your analysis a little deeper, you may find the phrase is made to cover unjustifiable assumption. For the language used often suggests that the particular type of culture has a vital principle within it, and unfolds its meaning by some inherent power of its own. It is needless to say that in speaking thus people personify an abstraction and treat it as having being and energy for itself. In truth a particular phase of culture only exists as an element in the self-conscious life of individual persons. To recognise this, however, is to recognise that the spring of progress is not in the given phase of culture by itself, but in the self-conscious minds of which it is an aspect. Accordingly it seems to me false to say that religion, for example, has a constitutive idea which can explain all the characteristic features of its evolution in a race. For religion as a state of the subject interacts with the other contents of self-conscious experience, and if it helps to mould these, it is likewise moulded by them. That is to say, the evolution of a people's religion can never be explained by isolating some particular feature of it and calling that its constitutive idea. It has developed as part of a larger interaction of elements, among which we reckon the political, the artistic, and the scientific consciousness.

The drift of the foregoing argument has been to show that the key to the meaning of historic development is not to be found in a generalised conception of the process as a whole but in the psychical life of individual selves. For the constitutive forces which make for progress, whatever be their ultimate explanation, have their living centre in the self-conscious minds which, by their interaction, produce development. Psychical events in men are the real kernel of history, as Sigwart justly remarks.[1] Any profitable discussion of the larger question must, therefore, base itself on the cardinal features of psychical development. What are these features? Here I make no pretence of saying anything new, but am content to state the results to which the best recent psychology points. Mental development is throughout teleological: it is so in its lowest as well as its highest phases. In mental process the equivalence of cause and effect which we attribute to natural process is not found; and no analysis of sensation-elements, for example, will explain how they come to be represented by a sense-perception. So instead of interpreting psychical development causally, we must read it as a purposive process which takes form in a continuous "acquisition of meanings." The point of view is inward, and the end functions in the conative unity of the subject. Hence we regard mental development, with Prof. Stout, as the study of conscious endeavour as a factor in its own fulfilment. We reach no satisfying insight into the process, if we treat it from the outside and try to establish a causal connexion between the elements.

In harmony with this inward reading of mental

[1] *Logic*, vol. ii., p. 441, Eng. Trans.

development, we find that its facts are more than facts: they are values, and each value stands for a unique experience. Mental contents in the individuals A and B, which we treat as the same, never mean exactly the same to each: there is a qualitative difference between them which is bound up with the unique self-feeling of the two percipients. And it may be pointed out that the ultimate justification for maintaining the unique character of historical succession, lies in the fact that history is a complex amplification of the psychical process in the individual.

Some further observations may be made in this connexion. On any level of psychical life purpose is practically operative, though the end is not the object of conscious reflexion. But the end always forms part of the content of will in the higher spiritual and artistic creations, and at each stage it is in some degree the object of self-conscious endeavour. On the other hand, it is true that the ends which ordinarily move us are proximate not final ends. And as a matter of common experience, the more distant objects of desire seem to define themselves and take on practical importance largely from the way in which we achieve our more immediate purposes. Still it may be said that the remote end actually moves us even in the region of common experience, and the final purpose is really latent in the proximate purpose which is its means. On this view the latent purpose would be an aspect of the reflective purpose, an aspect which is always coming into clear consciousness. Now it is true that a man seeks more than he can clearly define at any one point of his history, and as he ages he learns much. But the facts do not warrant us in trying to press the view before us into the service of a determinist theory of mental development. Both in the personal and collective history ideals are subject to growth, modification and decay; and to say that an ideal which prevails must have been implicitly present from the first is to beg the question. Here the matter is settled not on the evidence but by an *a priori* assumption, and the assumption is not indispensable that the process may have meaning. The way is open for us to hold that ends which have become objects of conscious endeavour to an individual or a society in the later stages of growth need not be latent in the earlier. None the less these remarks must not be taken as suggesting that remoter ends do not play a part in personal and historic development. For some who deny this come in the result to a non-rational view of all human progress. This opinion is held by one or two writers in our own country, and it has been forcibly advocated by Prof. Villa in his recent volume, *L'Idealismo Moderno*. Villa's psychology is based on that of Wundt, and he lays the greatest stress on the constitutive function of proximate ends in development. From this he is led to deny that more distant ends are really operative, and to affirm that the cogency of the proximate end is entirely a matter of the feeling-consciousness. So man impelled by certain value-feelings strives after nearer objects, but he neither knows nor concerns himself with the remoter issues of his choice.[1] In harmony with this, Villa expressly declares that history is the very antithesis of logic. It may be argued in support of this doctrine, how little of conscious purpose there seems to be in the evolution of a nation, how little clearness and concord as to ultimate aims among different classes of the people. I venture to think, however, that this is a theory which, starting from a sound psychological principle, overstrains it, and in the result

[1] *L'Idealismo Moderno*, 1905, pp. 205–209.

seriously misconceives the teleological aspect of history. While the nearer ends are of most pressing moment, the more distant ends are also kept in view, for man is a being "of large discourse" who looks "before and after." If immediate feeling is the constitutive force of history, it is hard to see how there can be progress; for feeling unqualified by a purpose which extends beyond the present resembles instinct in its working, and instinct, though it serves to perpetuate the species, does not minister to progress. But Villa's assertion that the immediate ends to which feeling prompts express values would seem to carry us further than the realm of feeling. For that which has value must have meaning and be distinguishable from other values. And since we exercise selection on our proximate ends, assigning to some more and to others less importance, it is obvious that we do so because we have introduced a certain coherence into our value-ideas by connecting them with some standard of value. That human conduct has a measure of order and consistency in it is only possible because the variety of approximate ends is appraised and co-ordinated by reference to a general end or higher good. This good, although not to be realised as an immediate end, operates in our choice of such ends, as is amply shown by the way in which man controls an immediate desire in the interests of his larger well-being. And the same holds true in the history of a society or a people. The policy of a nation is never determined simply by the proximate ends to be achieved. In selecting among such ends it will be found that the past history and the aspirations of the people work as influential factors, and that the nation not only considers what will serve the purpose on hand but owns the duty of bringing the policy of the day into accord with the national ideals:—

> Tu regere imperio populos, Romane, memento ;
> Hae tibi erunt artes, pacisque imponere morem,
> Parcere subjectis, et debellare superbos.

Probably it is not necessary to labour the point further. But what we have said leads naturally up to the question in what sense and in what degree the principle of continuity obtains in historical development. Already we have come to the conclusion, that the form of evolution which is the constant unfolding of an idea potential in the beginning and strictly fixed in all its stages cannot be shown on the evidence to apply to historical development. Still it is plain that, though there be not a rigidly determined continuity in the historic process, continuity of some kind there must be ; otherwise there could be no field for the historian who shows how the past prepared the way for the present and how the present is "great with the future." Neither in the case of individual nor people can we satisfactorily understand the conduct of to-day in isolation from the actings of bygone days. At this point in the argument it is necessary to distinguish between the general or universal element in the historic process and the individual element. The existence of both elements is indisputable, and the important thing is to relate them rightly to each other. The interaction of mind with mind within a social order goes to build up fixed dispositions and tendencies which have a collective value and perpetuate themselves. Although these general functions are only actualised through individuals, we do not find their explanation and source in the individual. Such social products as speech, custom, and belief, while they pervade society like an atmosphere and vitally affect the individual, are not the creation of private initiative and invention, but the outcome of social wants. Consequently they do not reflect the fluctuations of individual desire, but reveal the uniformity and constancy which fit them to function as the instrument of the continuous life of the collective whole. These universal, social creations go to constitute the mind of the individual, and they form the general background of his thought and action. What is personal in the individual's character must be developed upon this common ground and cannot be distinctive apart from it. Accordingly the attempt is sometimes made to bring the individual element in culture under the dominion of the universal, and to regard men of light and leading simply as the embodiment of tendencies potentially or actually at work in society. So J. S. Mill, while he thinks it wrong to attribute only a trifling influence to great men, yet lays the stress on that aspect of human evolution which can be "reduced to uniformity and law." In harmony with this we find him saying that the influence of great men operates rather in determining the *celerity* than the *direction* of movement.[1] Even more distinctly does Hegel make the individual factor in history depend on the universal. The great man is only great because the universal is immanent in his ends: his function is to bring the general unconscious inwardness to consciousness.[2] Nor indeed is any other result possible for those who hold that historic development is a strictly determined movement. The view, again, which lays stress on the individual element in development is sometimes called the "Great-Man-Theory," but it has not won the same amount of support as the other. A prominent advocate of this view was Carlyle, whose enthusiasm for dominant and heroic personalities led him to term history "the essence of innumerable biographies." On the same side

[1] *Logic*, sixth ed., vol. ii., pp. 535-537.
[2] *Phil. d. Geschichte*, pp. 37-39.

Prof. W. James has spoken some trenchant words: "The causes of the production of great men lie in a sphere wholly inaccessible to the social philosopher."[1] In contrast to Mill he traces the mutations of societies mainly to the examples of individuals, and thinks that the accidental presence of men of genius is the ferment which decides in what way society shall evolve.[2] In his own words, James emphasises the importance of "individual variations," not the "dead average"; but he sees that the indeterminism is not absolute; "not every man fits every hour." And one can sympathise with his outspoken declaration: "It is folly to speak of 'laws of history' as of something inevitable."[3] It is important nevertheless that we should not so exalt the individual aspect of historic development as to lose sight of the universal aspect, for in that case it would hardly be possible to speak of development at all. If we resolve the historic movement into centres of personal influence, we ignore the essential fact that it is only through their interaction within a whole that the process can have meaning and value. It is indeed true that psychical events in men are the kernel of history, but these psychical events are not intelligible apart from the social and spiritual environment which supports them. The action of well-known personalities can only show against that relatively stable background which embraces law, morality, and religion. These change; but they change slowly, and the effect of any isolated individual upon them is necessarily small. The pioneer of progress can only bring about progress by making the many experience the force of his appeal: as Lotze has said, "Any personal power requires for its efficiency the receptivity of the masses."[4] And to realise

[1] *Will to Believe*, pp. 225–226. [2] *Op. cit.*, pp. 227–229. [3] *Op. cit.*, p. 244.
[4] *Microcosmus*, vol. ii., p. 192, Eng. Trans.

this is to realise that a continuity will always be maintained between the present and the future.

The course of the discussion has brought us now to the point where we must try to give a definite answer to the question, how far the historic process is continuous. Put briefly the thesis we wish to uphold is this : the degree of continuity in development which satisfies our logical and ethical demands is not a continuity which binds progress down to one particular line. That is to say, within limits alternatives are possible : the previous development does not determine that only one of these alternatives can become actual. And here we must dissociate ourselves from the Kantian view, that successive events can only be taken up into the content of the one self-consciousness in so far as they are connected by the self in accordance with the principle of cause and effect. This is a proposition of which Kant never offered any satisfactory proof ; and if we may trust our own experience on this matter, we certainly can have knowledge of a succession without also qualifying it by the causal predicate. And this is still more obviously true in the region of psychical events, where we cannot say that *a* is the cause of *b*, *b* of *c*, and *c* of *d* ; for, while there is connexion, the connexion is teleological, resting not on the structure of the elements of the series but on the conative unity, the active interest of the self. Or, to put it otherwise, the connexion is not in the facts but in the active self of which they are the expression. So likewise in the case of moral action you cannot postulate character as a fact in time which, in virtue of its inherent causality, brings about a determinate succession of temporal acts. For it is a mere assumption that a man's character can be regarded as a complete and determinate whole, so that each act in time is related to it as effect,

Here again the fallacy seems to lie in taking the elements as if they had a connexion for themselves, while in reality it is the inward self which relates them to each other. Viewed from without character, as a whole of habits, dispositions and tendencies, is identified with the self. But here it must be remembered that we are qualifying the self by predicates which to some extent are discrepant. And so long as the self does not will as the completely unified character, diverse tendencies within character make it possible that a man's act should always be related to some aspect of his character, and yet that there should be an element of indeterminism in his self-development. In the psychological problem we postulate the apperceptive activity and selective interest of the self as giving coherence to mental events : in the ethical problem we postulate the self as will which expresses in choice, some aspect of character, and which is the ultimate ground why, when there is conflict of motives, one aspect of character is expressed in action rather than another. The question turns on the reality of possibilities, and our theory of moral freedom seems on the whole to square best with the facts of moral experience. It may be well to repeat also that it is necessary to distinguish the judgment of the spectator who interprets from that of the person who acts, and I venture to think that personal experience lends some countenance to the view here put forward.[1]

The interpretation we give to the freedom of the individual cannot but materially influence our way of regarding historical development. A strictly deterministic theory of personal character must have as its correlate the purely necessarian conception of collective evolution. What seems contingent in the historic process only wears

[1] That it does so has been conceded by so careful and unbiassed a critic as the late Prof. Sidgwick. *Vid. Methods of Ethics*, sixth ed., pp. 65–66.

the appearance owing to our imperfect knowledge; to a more comprehensive insight it would appear as a necessary factor in the general movement. To us, on the contrary, historical development in virtue of its individual aspect will always have a contingent element whose operation is real if subordinate. That it must be subordinate is apparent when we consider that what is distinctively new, even in the most gifted individual, must be relatively small in comparison with what he derives from the culture of the past and his social environment. And even the reformer who is in keen antagonism to an existing social order has his significance in virtue of his positive relation to the system against which he reacts. If the reforms he introduces are not susceptible of an organic relation to the existing structure of society, they must perish for lack of life. But to affirm this does not preclude the view that there are points in history where alternative courses were possible: we may assert this and still give a legitimate scope to the principle of continuity. For it must be remembered that these diverging possibilities are not introduced *ab extra* by great personalities, but are prepared for and presented by the prior development. To take a rude illustration. At a particular point it might be possible to divert a stream in one direction rather than in another, but the possibility is given by the previous course of the stream itself. With a different direction, or a different degree of fall, perhaps no such diversion could take place at that point. The alternatives which are open to those who "make history" are the alternatives developed by history itself; and therefore the process cannot suffer dislocation though either course is chosen, but the issue will be different. As the outcome of the historic drama, Luther was confronted with the alternative of defying the Pope or submitting to him. It is conceivable he might have submitted, in which case the religion and political evolution of the European peoples would have been materially affected. And yet can anyone doubt that the consequent development could have been made as coherent and intelligible to reflective thought as the actual development has been? In the light of the result the historian would have simply put another valuation on the spiritual forces at work, and if he were a determinist would have shown to his own satisfaction that the issue could not have been otherwise. Our conclusion in short is, that the process of historic development has within it a certain flexibility, but this flexibility is within the limits prescribed by the principle of continuity. In the case of personal development those alternatives only are possible which are presented by a man's character: in historic development they must be such as are presented by history itself. Hence at whatever point we examine the historic process, we shall never find it absolutely broken and disconnected. The most original genius must speak the language and use the forms of thought of his time, and no leader, however daring, can initiate a movement which will persist, unless the stream of the historic life has made the movement a possible one. It is given to a few individuals in each generation to find an answer to the problems of progress: the problems themselves have been set by the historic life of humanity.[1]

But while there is continuity in history, we cannot say that the movement is continuous in one direction, the direction of progress. A Philosophy of History, however optimistic its tone, has to find a place somehow for such facts as the decadence and final disintegration of a nation's life. Indeed the stream of culture seldom runs smoothly

[1] *Cf.* Lotze, *Microcosmus*, vol. ii., p. 188, Eng. Trans.

for a long space: it breaks into eddies in its course, and at points the current seems to move backward rather than forward. The ordinary spectator would hardly question the view that history presents at many points the spectacle of a loss, not an increase, in value. To this the reply from those who profess to look deeper will be that the loss is apparent rather than real, since it is compensated for somewhere and somehow. So it might be urged that the loss implied in the decadence of the intellectual and æsthetic gifts of the Greek, and of the Roman genius for law and civic order, has been more than counterbalanced by the contributions these peoples have made to the wider culture of the Western world. Yet it would hardly be possible to show by any broad inductive treatment of history that the principle of compensation always holds, and that there never is a good really lost. The conviction that "all things work together for good" can never verify itself to us as a simple generalisation from the facts: it is a postulate which rests on other grounds. The problem pressed on us here is one which we must deal with if we are to reach a satisfactory conclusion on the main point of our inquiry, which is the applicability of the idea of development to history. For development in the proper sense is more than continuity of process; it means that through the process an increase of value is brought about, and that the end is better than the beginning. When we put the problem in this way, we see that the answer is by no means a simple one and raises some perplexing issues.

The first question is: How are we to decide whether development is present in history or not? For it sometimes happens that the movement which one person terms progress another pronounces to be on the downward way, and the phase of culture which is rated highly in one epoch finds only a slender appreciation in another. Plainly this is because the ideas of value which form the basis of the judgments are not the same. And we can only come to some agreement as to the degrees of value revealed in the stages of the historic movement, if we agree on the standard by which we are to judge. If, for example, the theory of Eastern and Western Pessimism is correct, history is an evolution which spells deterioration; for it is a lapse from the unconscious which is best. Hence the paradox that the process of history brings about an increase of value by itself running out to a close. Such a theory of the good precludes the idea of a development in time, and is best refuted by the personal instincts and practical tendencies of mankind. History itself does not speak a clear word on the matter at issue, for history, as has been said, is the "battle-field of values," and the ideal takes new forms with the changing life of humanity. Yet we cannot remain enclosed in the sphere of relativity, and merely try to judge one type of culture by reference to another. For in the end we must either declare some type to be of primary worth, or relate the different types to an ideal as of ultimate value. Now we may agree that the ultimately valuable must be some form of "desirable consciousness," but to fill in the content of this consciousness is exceedingly difficult.[1] There is, however, a certain amount of agreement over the direction in which we are to look for the ultimate Good. For instance, few thinkers of importance at present would argue that the Absolute Value is to be construed in terms of pleasure, though pleasure may be an element in it. The trend of thought

[1] Prof. Mackenzie (*Social Philosophy*, first ed., p. 270) speaks of the ultimately valuable as what belongs to the consciousness of the world as "a systematic and harmonious totality." This is vague. Nor is it clear why the consciousness of the world as a harmonious system must be the most valuable form of consciousness.

is to find the Supreme End or Value in a heightened form of the personal life, in the full and harmonious realisation of personal capacities and powers.[1] For it must be through existing values, and more especially through the values realised in the ethical life, that we try to define for ourselves the general norm of our valuations. The ethical end from a formal point of view is adequately described by the term "self-realisation," taken to mean the making real by the will in the given personal life of the projected idea of a higher self. And the end of society would be to minister to the fullest, most varied and harmonious expression of the powers of human nature, in short, to subserve the development of personalities. Hence we can accept the test put forward by Höffding, here giving a fresh turn to Kant's thought, that perfection in a society is the degree in which each personal being is so placed and treated, that he is not only a means but also at the same time an end.[2] To those who object that such a test of social value is only formal, the thing to say in answer is that no other answer to the problem is possible. The traveller cannot describe in detail the country which as yet he only beholds afar off. The degree in which we have already realised value in our own lives is the only clue we have by which imaginatively to give content to the Ultimate Value.

That the Ultimate Value must be conceived in terms of persons can scarcely be doubted when one remembers that only in the personal life is value actualised. Every judgment of worth has reference to a self-conscious subject, and a society has neither mind nor will apart from the individual persons who compose it. We talk loosely of

[1] One may see tokens of this tendency even in such definitions of the ethical end as "self-conservation" and "increase of life."

[2] *Philos. Probleme*, p. 89.

the value which pertains to a definite type of historical culture, but in the last resort we must think that value as present in the spiritual subjects who, by their thought and will, give actuality to the form of culture in question.[1] Taking, then, this personal view of what is ultimately valuable, and bringing this standard to bear on the process of history, we ask : Is it possible to describe that process as a development in the sense of a movement from less to greater value ? The vagueness which attaches to the content of the ideal must militate against a confident dogmatism on this point. We may indeed reject the pessimistic theory of history with some firmness of conviction in virtue of the unjustifiable assumptions which it makes at the outset. And there is surely some warrant for the belief that the growing significance of personality, which is observable in the course of civilisation, is the sign of an advance in inner value. No doubt, as we have already seen, a calm survey of history does not entitle us to infer a uniform or consistent progress. At points the stream becomes stagnant, and sometimes the current moves backward. The state in one aspect is a means towards the development of the personality of its citizens, but the state may decline ; and corresponding to this the personal values of life will become poorer, as, for example, was the case with civic life under the later Empire of Rome contrasted with that in the palmy days of the Republic. But if we take a broad view of the historic movement, we seem justified in concluding that our Western civilisation at all events shows a real increase in the virtues of humanity, justice, and freedom. And if there have been losses of value in particular directions, we may fairly argue that these are balanced by a wider

[1] *Vid.* Grotenfelt, *Geschichtliche Wertmassstäbe in der Geschichtsphilosophie*, p. 165.

diffusion of good and a better opportunity of realising capacity. With some degree of assurance, accordingly, we hold that, on the average and over a wide area, the evolution of culture represents an increase in the value of personal lives. And our right to apply the notion of development would briefly be this: the process, if plastic and susceptible of modification from within, is still continuous. If there are losses in value there are also compensations. And in the light of the Ultimate Value, so far as we are able to define it, we judge with some confidence if not with certainty, that the movement of history discloses an increase of value in the line of the end or final Good.

We have reached a result, somewhat qualified indeed, yet so far definite. But our difficulties are not over, and if our argument is to be profitable these difficulties must be met. The objection will be urged that no value which is in process can in the nature of the case be final; while if the Absolute Value is conceived as a final state, the idea seems to lose what in our eyes is an essential quality. For to us the ethical values are ever associated with personal endeavour and the progressive realisation of the good. When we try to conceive the movement of history coming to its goal in a social order, the constituents of which are perfect persons, we cannot help feeling that such a life without spiritual ideal is something less than the highest. The life of growing goodness has an intrinsic quality which makes it preferable to that of stationary perfection; and a mundane society where upward endeavour and progress are impossible does not seem to us, as we are constituted, desirable. An attempt may be made to find a way out of this perplexity by discarding the idea of the Supreme Value as a fixed state, and asserting that what is ultimately valuable lies in the process of development itself. The final Good is just the continuous evolution of values. But here the old problem of a valid norm is thrust upon us again. For how is the standard to be defined where all is process? Clearly, as Siebeck has argued, we should have to define the Absolute Value in terms of the stages in which it is realised, and these in turn could only be appreciated by reference to the Absolute Value.[1] Besides involving ourselves in this awkward circle, we should have to meet the objection that moral evil with all the antagonisms it provokes is a constituent element of the Supreme Value, and thus sin in all its forms is unreal or merely good in the making. The argument followed out in either direction seems to lead to an *impasse*, for neither the idea of a perfect final state in time nor that of endless progress in time satisfies the demands of a consistent theory.

The truth is that, if we try to think out coherently the implications of the notion of development as applied to history, we are led into the region of Metaphysics. The final presuppositions of history as of ethics are speculative, not scientific. And however some people dislike the domain of Metaphysics—the scene, as they think, of incessant warfare where no victory is conclusive—our only chance of escape from the dilemma which faces us is by making an incursion into it. Now the crucial point of our difficulty in the present instance arises in connexion with the time-idea: neither a perfect final state in time nor an endless process in time is satisfactory. Shall we then say with Kant that time has no ultimate reality, but is only a valid form of perception for the phenomenal world? There are serious objections against the Kantian

[2] *Vid.* his *Religionsphilosophie*, section on "Die Bestimmung des Menschen"; also his *Rektorats-Rede*, *Ueber die Lehre vom genetischen Fortschritte der Menschheit*, 1892, republished in his brochure, *Zur Religionsphilosophie*, 1907.

treatment of time which it is not possible to discuss at present; but it must be pointed out how hopeless it is for any philosophy which makes time purely phenomenal to deal with history. For the historic process, with its gradual evolution of values, must lose its meaning and worth if time is declared to be fundamentally unreal; it becomes an idle show, a "tale of little meaning." Neither the interpretation of time as absolutely real nor absolutely unreal seems philosophically tenable, and neither view sheds light on the problems of historic development. For, to adopt one side of the alternative empties history of value, and to adopt the other precludes any consistent way of relating the process to its goal. In dealing with this formidable question the most hopeful method appears to be that which proceeds on the principle of Herbart: *Wieviel Schein, soviel Hindeutung auf's Sein.* An appearance cannot float unsupported in the void; it must have reference to the real, and it must be the appearance of something. Whether you say that time appears, or is a form in which things appear, at all events it is an experience and as such must qualify the real in some fashion. And if we reject, as we are warranted in doing, the Kantian figment of a pure form of intuition read into the matter of sense, we cannot avoid the inference, that there must be that in the constitution of experience itself which imposes on individual subjects the obligation to construe their experience in terms of time. Such a necessity cannot have its ground in what is accidental: the question here is one of epistemological validity. This question must be carefully distinguished from that of the temporal genesis and growth of our ideas of time. The problem in this case is psychological, and the way we answer it cannot be held to decide the validity or degree of reality in the time-idea itself. Yet the psychological aspect of the matter is certainly interesting and important. The highly developed and generalised conception of time which the modern civilised man possesses is very different from that of the primitive savage, who had no chronology and had not a generalised notion of time apart from the events which take place in it. Then in the stage of life-development represented by the higher animals, we find spatial and temporal percepts as yet undistinguished; for both are fused together in the fact of movement, a fact of the greatest importance in ensuring the conservation and maintenance of life. This varying practical attitude of living beings to time may suggest to us how the psychological significance of the idea must vary with the living interests which are bound up with it. We ought not to assume that our present time-idea, elaborated by intersubjective intercourse, is an absolute standard: a being higher or lower than man would have a different "time-span."

On the other hand, the valid element in the time-idea must lie in the fact that it has to be developed as a form of order out of the actual content of reality, and cannot exist as an empty form by itself. Aristotle has said that time is the measure of change, and we may agree with Lotze that the time-form could not possibly give rise to the real process of change. If this be so,—and I assume Lotze's argument to be justified—then, while the meaning of a series of events would not in all respects be the same to two beings with different conceptually developed ideas of time, still the view of either would be more than subjective, because grounded on the process of the real. On this theory history represents a real process of change, which we construe through our developed ideas of time, dividing it into the past, present and future. A Being for whom "a thousand years are as one day" would see farther and deeper into history than we do, but this would not make our view illusory. The speculative examination of the time-idea does not take away our right to predicate development of history, though it suggests that limitations attach to our use of the principle.

Yet the conclusion at which we have arrived, though it delivers us from the scepticism of treating such progress as we can see in the race as mere appearance, hardly serves to solve the problem we have on hand. The fact is borne in upon us that our present time-ideas are not adequate to the representation of the goal of history. A perfect society in this mundane time-order we found to be for us a contradictory conception ; nor, as we saw reason to conclude, is there any immanent law in history constantly working to bring about such a result. Indeed the evolution of the physical universe might preclude this.[1] Finally, even granting that such an Absolute Value were to be reached in time, how are we to relate it to the personal values of the historic process? Are all earlier forms of personal good only to have their meaning as a stage to the distant goal? If so, the means and the end seem utterly disproportionate to one another, and the many are sacrificed to the few. Here we have the same moral anomaly which is involved in the interpretation of history as an "education of the human race." The great multitude of human beings are reduced to a mere means of bringing about an end in which they can have no share. For practical purposes no doubt it is often legitimate to treat individuals as a means to the increase of the good of the social system. But our justification for

[1] Huxley, in the Prolegomena to his Romanes lecture on "Evolution and Ethics," anticipates such an issue. He thinks man's struggle to maintain the State of Art in opposition to the State of Nature will go on "until the evolution of our globe shall have entered so far upon its downward course that the cosmic process resumes its sway ; and, once more, the State of Nature prevails over the surface of our planet" (*Works*, vol. ix., pp. 44-45).

so doing is that the good of the whole is reflected in the life of the members ; in other words it is expressed by an increase in personal values. And in the last resort we must stand by the truth of the Kantian principle, that persons are ends in themselves.

The outcome of the argument is that, while our reading of history in terms of our time-idea is not illusory, yet when we try to give a satisfying meaning and end to the process in terms of this idea the statement is manifestly inadequate. We seem driven to the conclusion that the goal and meaning of history are not to be found in this temporal order of things at all. The facts themselves appear to necessitate the acceptance of some form of transcendency.[1] I am quite aware that this may seem the invocation of a *deus ex machina* to cut the knot ; still I venture to think that it is not a fair reading of the situation. The point, we repeat, is that we are not able to find a meaning in history, viewed as a mundane process in time, which will satisfy the reason and do justice to the moral values involved. That the process is not meaningless we are bound to assume. Accordingly we make the postulate that the ultimate meaning of history must lie in a sphere which transcends the present temporal order : and the postulate will justify itself in the degree in which it meets the demands of our moral and intellectual life. It will not do so if the possibility of continuity between the temporal and the transcendent values is excluded. This is a point which, as it seems to me, has sometimes received too little consideration from competent thinkers. Rickert, for instance, finds the timeless necessary to give meaning to the temporal process, and only timeless Reality, he says, can be the support of timeless values.[2]

[1] This conclusion is accepted by Siebeck, Rickert, Eucken, and Grotenfelt.

[2] See his article on the Philosophy of History in the *Festschrift* for Kuno Fischer, entitled *Die Philosophie im Beginn des XXten Jahrhunderts*, 1904.

Yet he holds that the temporal process must be real if there is to be a philosophy of history and a significance in moral endeavour. Nevertheless in Kantian fashion he regards the dialectic of ideas as evidence that we have reached the limit of our knowledge, and that the solution of the contradictions lies in the transcendent sphere. The difficulty here is that no way is left open of relating the mundane to the supramundane values, so that the latter might be regarded as the fulfilment of the former.[1] And if there be no continuity between the temporal and the eternal values, the elements of a solution are not present and the postulate fails to justify itself.

If our postulate is to work, the transition from the temporal to the eternal must be accomplished within the personal life, and cannot come merely as the result of historic progress. For it is persons who make history and embody the worth of the historic life; and, as we have seen, we involve ourselves in contradictions if we treat them as a pure means to a hypothetical development of the race in the future. By insisting on the inner relation of each personal life to the Eternal, it seems possible to do justice to personal values and likewise to maintain that the meaning of history is being realised at each stage of the temporal process. The crucial point is whether we can so conceive the relation of the temporal to the eternal in the personal life that a continuity between them is possible. That we can coherently think out the connexion between the two is not in the least likely, and the attempt to do so would involve the importation into the higher sphere of ideas and images which properly belong to the lower. We may suggest, however, that the Eternal must not be conceived as indifferent to, or taking no

[1] Eucken's position in this regard is also unsatisfactory, for he hardly discusses the relation of time to the suprahistorical and eternal life.

notice of, the distinctions which are implied in the time-process. If it be true, as we have contended, that our present time-idea grows out of the content of the real which changes, then it may well be that what we term an eternal state of being means simply the deliverance from the limitations of our present time-span, and is not incompatible with change and activity. In the case of God we are led on speculative and moral grounds to postulate that he is above the limitations of our time-idea, but also that he is active and comprehends the distinctions of our temporal history. And if it be true that the human spirit has its ground in the Divine Spirit, we may infer that the more fully man develops his essential personality in this eventful earthly history, the more completely is he being transformed into harmony with the Divine Nature. The faith that the deepening spiritual life reaches beyond the present time-order, is a legitimate faith that the values which give meaning to this life are not subject to decay and destruction because they are of God.

The reader who has accompanied us to this point may complain that we have travelled somewhat far from our original theme. Yet on reflexion he will perceive, perhaps, that we have been trying to follow the lead of the argument. He will remember that we saw reason to deny that history could be regarded as the necessary evolution of an immanent principle. Taking a broad survey of history we seemed to see evidence of progress actually achieved, but no evidence of a law of progress whose persistence was assured. Here the question emerged whether the meaning of the historic process did not depend on the assumption that it was a movement towards some perfect goal. Yet the discussion of the assumption appeared to yield the conclusion that it would not solve the problems at issue. And this led us to show that the more satisfying interpretation of history was to be found in a direct relation of the personal values to a higher order in harmony with the Eternal. On this view the meaning of history is continuously being realised, and does not depend on the mundane process coming to a perfect close.

"Do you then," it may be asked, "discard the idea of development in history? It would surely be a narrow gospel to tell men that the value of the efforts of those who 'spend and are spent' for city and country has reference to themselves alone. Those who toil patiently to bring in a better day are inspired by larger motives!" In reply we might point out how fully we have recognised the interdependence of the personal and the social values: in a real fashion a man saves his life by losing it in a wider service. The increase of the common good is reflected in the heightened value of the personal life; and the deepest good of the self cannot be gained apart from others. We go farther and urge that, in virtue of the solidarity of personal and social good, man must strive to promote the development of society even as he strives to develop himself. Moral and spiritual progress is a vocation for the race just as it is for the individual.[1] In neither case can the process work itself out by impersonal means. The development of the race is a task which lies before the men of each successive generation, and in the degree in which they fulfil this task will history reveal a growing good. As with the individual so with humanity, the exercise of freedom precludes us from characterising development by any rigid formula. In both cases we find fulfilment and failure to fulfil the higher vocation: the single soul instead of struggling upward to the light

[1] Here I agree with Siebeck, *op. cit.*

sometimes sinks back into the darkness, and in a society, and even through a whole epoch of history, we may see the tokens of retrogression, not of progress.

Development, historical and personal, is gravely hampered by the antagonistic forces of evil, and, though these are defeated, Proteus-like they assume fresh forms and return to renew the conflict on a later day. Yet those who are on 'the side of the angels' can find tokens which bid them hope. Humanity always holds within it regenerative powers, and if the potentates of evil win a victory and establish their rule, a reaction comes which breaks their sway and the tyranny is overpast. Looking backward we certainly seem to see evidence of development, though the development has not been constant nor uniform in its movement. That the upward movement will prevail, that mankind which has tasted the good things of the spirit will not relapse into barbarism and ignorance—this may well be our faith, though neither reason nor faith requires us to expect the advent of a perfect kingdom of God among men. The historic process has an ever present goal, when personal lives can through it so grow and deepen that they find their completion in a Good which is Eternal.

CHAPTER II

THE DEVELOPMENT OF RELIGION

An adequate interpretation of religious development involves an examination and valuation of the psychological factors of the religious consciousness. But my aim in the present chapter is not to unfold a complete theory of the development of religion, but to indicate broadly the nature of the facts and to make some general remarks upon them. Religious development is a phase of the development of culture in general, and the conclusions we came to in the preceding chapter have a close bearing on the present subject. For the particular sphere must participate in the features of the movement of the larger whole, though at the same time it possesses special characteristics of its own. The broad principles of historic development must therefore apply to religion. Hence we are prepared to find in the history of religion a continuity, each stage of religion maintaining a connexion with that which went before and that which came after. Yet the continuity will not always mean progress, and there will be instances of decadence as well as of growth. And as we found we could not construe history as a rigidly determined process, where the end was immanent in the beginning and operative in every detail throughout, we cannot expect such a law to hold in the evolution of religion. We may gather evidence that mankind has made progress in the spiritual consciousness, but we cannot hope to discover any indwelling spiritual law which will infallibly bring about this result. For here, too, progress is the spiritual vocation of humanity: it is a task which it sets to itself, not an inherent necessity of its constitution. The religious, like the ethical ideal, is freely pursued, and what ought to be is never that which perforce must be.

Turning now to our subject proper, we state a few facts in regard to the History of Religion on which most competent investigators are agreed. At the outset, then, we note that the history of religion in its broad features shows a gradual advance from the sensuous to the spiritual. In its lower stages piety is governed by material considerations: afterwards it is purified and elevated by ethical elements. Good illustrations of this process are to be found in the ancient religions of Persia, Greece and Israel, in all of which we can trace clearly how the advance in moral conceptions brought about a purification of the naturalistic elements in the earlier faith. But, on the other hand, the process is by no means visible everywhere, nor when it does obtain is it always effective in its working. There may be counteracting forces coming from without, or resisting factors acting within the religion itself. The latter is likely to be the case where the religion has developed a complex ritual, for here the inner side of piety is overlaid and depressed by the practices of the cult. Nevertheless there is, as we have said, a general tendency in religion to advance from the sensuous to the spiritual, and this corresponds to and is the reflexion of man's social evolution. As men gradually organise themselves in higher forms of society, there ensues a growth in the personal life which takes form in higher needs and an enlarged outlook on the world. And this social development demands as its counterpart a development of religion. Accordingly there is a movement towards the organisation and articulation of religious beliefs which shall correspond to the needs of the new and larger order of society. With Tiele we may describe this process as one both of differentiation and integration : of differentiation, because religious beliefs in the primitive stage are vague and ill-defined and have a general sameness throughout : of integration, for the movement is towards a graduated order and some degree of system in religious ideas. These processes are never entirely separated the one from the other, but differentiation is more a feature of the earlier and integration of the later stages of religious development. The nature of this movement will become clearer if we consider the steps in the social order out of which it arises. These are briefly the tribal, the national, and the universal. The tribe is the rudimentary form of social union, and it coincides generally with human history in its primitive and barbarous stage. Here the pressure of material needs is predominant, and the impulses which move men proceed chiefly from their physical wants and fears. Reflective consciousness is undeveloped ; law is represented by the custom of the tribe ; and the individual is simply a unit in the social whole with no independent value over against it. The tie which binds together the members of the clan or tribe is a physical one—that of blood, and the religious beliefs of the individual are as a matter of course just those of the group to which he belongs. Anything like individual criticism and selection of beliefs is absent, and change is in the main a slow and an unconscious process. One of the foremost anthropologists of a former generation has suggestively described the religion of the savage. "The religion of savage man is a sombre belief in spirits and ghosts, without inner connexion, a condition far removed from every unprejudiced contemplation of natural objects, and where under far-reaching superstition the heart is plunged from one unrest into another."[1] The haunting fear and anxiety which mark primitive religion are impressively conveyed by these lines of Virgil (*Aen.* viii. 349—52):

> "Jam tum religio pavidos terrebat agrestes
> Dira loci; jam tum silvam saxumque tremebant.
> Hoc nemus, hunc, inquit, frondoso vertice collem—
> Quis deus, incertum est—habitat deus."

The common characteristic of tribal religion is Spiritism, which is the outgrowth of the animistic view of the world common to all primitive races. That this phase of belief was once universal is apparent from the fact that the vestiges of it may still be traced behind all later developments of religion. Nevertheless competent students of primitive culture such as Chantepie de la Saussaye and Pfleiderer incline to the opinion that the earliest worship was not restricted to objects conceived as the abode of a spirit, but was also directed to the personified forces of nature. The flowing stream, for example, was sometimes reverenced as a living being apart from any idea of a spirit inhabiting it. This is probable. But the distinction between Animism and Spiritism is by no means sharply defined, and the one passes by invisible degrees into the other. If among the multitude of personified natural phenomena which encompassed primeval man certain were selected as objects of worship, this could only have been because

[1] Waitz, *Anthropologie der Naturvölker*, vol. i, p. 363.

they were conceived by him to possess power to help or hurt. And between this and the spiritist interpretation of the object there is no hard and fast line, while the transition from the one to the other is psychologically intelligible. If this be so, then we need not suppose, with Réville, that the greater nature-worship was developed out of the minor.[1] For phenomena like sun and moon, wind and cloud might be naturally personified and reverenced at a very early date; and there is no proof that man had to people stocks and stones, springs and trees with spirits, ere he began to extend this process to the greater phenomena of the world around him in order to make them objects of worship.

The question has been raised whether there is not such a thing as a pre-animistic religion, and it has been suggested that there was a more rudimentary stage out of which Spiritism grew. "The root idea in this Pre-animism is that of power everywhere, power vaguely apprehended, but immanent, and as yet unclothed with personal or supernatural attributes."[2] Now if Animism be taken in the sense of Spiritism, we admit the probability of a pre-animistic stage where the natural object itself was worshipped. But you cannot call a vague awe of power everywhere religion, though it describes the feeling-tone associated with the birth of religion. That the religious consciousness may become actual there must be an object before it possessing power, and capable of relation to the subject. Power apart from its concrete embodiments could mean nothing for primitive man; and an act of selection by which the subject, who is conscious of need, relates himself to the

[1] A. Réville, *Religions des Peuples non Civilisés*, vol. ii, p. 225.

[2] Mr. E. Clodd in a paper published in the *Transactions of the Third International Congress for the History of Religions*, 1908, vol. i, p. 34.

object, which has power to satisfy the need, is the essential step that brings religion into being. But it has been argued that it is just the attribution of this "power," as something magical or quasi-"supernatural," which is the distinctive mark of religion and supplies its "minimum definition."[1] That the notion of a "supernatural" power dwelling in certain objects, and capable of being exploited by man, is closely interwoven with primitive culture must be granted. But I do not see that its mere presence in an object can safely be taken as a test of a religious attitude to the object. For the relation to it may be purely magical; its value for man may lie merely in the fact that its virtue can be controlled by his will and made to serve his purposes. And though such notions have constantly intruded themselves into religion, they do not belong to its essence which postulates dependence, not self-assertion.

The relation of Magic to Religion deserves a few further words. Some writers have regarded the former as a degenerate product of the latter, but this is improbable. And there is even a tendency at present to derive religion from magic, Dr. J. G. Frazer, for example, holding that it was the failure of magic which drove men to religion. Mr. Lang and others have shown good reasons for rejecting this theory, and the present writer has noted some of the objections which can be urged against it in a former volume.[2] At the same time I confess that magic is not simply to be disposed of as "a lower outgrowth of the religious consciousness"; and for this reason, that the psychological motives which led to magic may have begun to operate as soon as and

[1] By Mr. R. R. Marett, in an able paper on *Mana*. *Op. cit.*, vol. i, p. 56. The paper is republished in his volume *The Threshold of Religion*, 1909.

[2] *Studies in the Philosophy of Religion*, 1904, pp. 120–122.

alongside of those which led to religion. Magical ideas enter into the life and habits of the most primitive peoples; and they may even produce an exuberant crop of superstitious practices at a higher level of development, as in ancient Babylonia. Magic is a natural development from primitive man's outlook on the world—an outlook into which causality in the modern sense of the term does not enter. The mere fact that anything may be the cause of anything gives a free scope for bringing about desired results by imitation or sympathetic magic. Magical ceremonies would easily link themselves with religious practices, and they could naturally be regarded by the worshippers as a form of co-operation or communion with the spirits. And once admitted to the cult, they would tend to be preserved even after their original significance had been lost. A progressive religion will of course strive to purge itself from these lower elements, though how difficult this is we may see in the case of a large part of the Christian Church at the present day. On the other hand, when the spiritual content of a religion deteriorates, this may prove the opportunity for magic to assert its claims at the expense of religion. An interesting example of the tendency of magic to intertwine itself with a fading religion is seen in the case of the Todas of Madras. Apropos of this Dr. Rivers remarks, "It is possible that we have here evidence that during the process of degeneration of a religion, religion and magic may approach one another—an approach which recalls their common origin from those low beliefs and ideas of the savage to which the name neither of magic nor religion should perhaps be properly applied."[1]

The term Spiritism cannot be made to cover all the features of tribal belief, for these include special

[1] *The Todas*, Macmillan & Co., 1906, p. 460.

phenomena like Fetishism, Totemism, and Ancestor-worship. But it has been suggested, that the worship of spirits in nature and the worship of the spirits of ancestors are the two independent sources of religion. Tylor and Tiele have, I think, shown that Fetishism is not an original phenomenon of religion, but marks the degradation of a pre-existing Spiritism. Between Totemism and Ancestor-worship there is some bond of connexion : the totem may be worshipped as an ancestor, and both totem and ancestor are objects of reverence because they are in some way the source of the life of the clan or tribe. We have to ask, then, if worship of spirits in nature and worship of ancestors are primitive as well as independent religious phenomena, or if it is possible to indicate a development from the one to the other. The question cannot be settled on historical evidence ; it is largely a matter of psychological probability, and it is hardly possible to avoid the "psychologist's fallacy" when we try to reconstruct the psychical states of primitive men. We can indeed say with some confidence that Animism and Spiritism seem to be universal in the lower culture, while Ancestor-worship is not. And even where tribes are familiar with the idea of spirit-ancestors, it does not always follow that they make them objects of worship. Thus the natives of central Australia everywhere believe in the reincarnation of the spirits of ancestors and the possession by these spirits of superhuman powers. But if we are to accept the statement of such impartial and careful authorities as Spencer and Gillen, they do not think of propitiating them or of seeking their help.[1] The truth appears to be that Totemism and Ancestor-worship are widely-spread phenomena in primitive culture, but there is no proof that they are universal. On the

[1] *The Northern Tribes of Central Australia*, pp. 490–491.

other hand, some awe of the spirits of the departed is found everywhere among savages, and it seems to run back as far, or nearly as far, as the beginnings of religion itself. But Animism is certainly not to be explained, as Herbert Spencer supposed, by an extended application of the belief in ghosts, for the motives which led to Animism were everywhere and independently operative. And, on the other side, it may be argued that the idea of a ghost shows some elevation of the spirit above the material object with which it is connected, and is therefore a development of the animistic principle. Moreover, the conception of Ancestor-worship postulates some advance in social feeling. It is a reasonable hypothesis, that mankind advanced from nature-worship and Spiritism to the specialised Spiritism which took form in the cult of the souls of the dead and reverence for the ancestors of the family and the tribe. The remains of palæolithic culture are no doubt scanty; but we may perhaps support our conclusion by pointing out that the cult of souls, as attested by funeral customs, has left its traces on neolithic and not on palæolithic culture.[1]

Without attempting to discuss further the different aspects of tribal religion in their relations to one another, we go on to characterise briefly the general features of religion at this stage. Corresponding to the meagre development of personal life, the character of the gods or spirits is dim and ill defined. One is very much like another, and they are distinguished chiefly by the place and manner of their operation. All are conceived to wield power, and as this power may be employed for the weal or woe of men, the obligation is imposed on men of

[1] Since writing the above I am glad to be able to cite the opinion of Zeller, who thinks the idea of soul and its endurance after death too remote from sensuous perception to be attributed to the earliest culture. *Vid.* his *Vorträge und Abhandlungen*, vol. ii., p. 53.

establishing a right relation with them. To be true to the bond which connects the individual with the tribe and the gods of the tribe is piety, and piety expresses itself in the due performance of the relevant ceremonies and practices of the cult. On this low level men are engaged in a constant struggle to secure the necessities of life and to protect themselves against the forces of nature or the attacks of enemies, and primitive religion is the reflexion of these material wants and fears, hopes and desires. The spirits to whom man appeals are the counterpart of his own shallow and fitful inward life, acknowledging the sway of the same selfish motives and capable of being moved by the same external offerings. The god exacts his *quid pro quo*, and the worshipper acts on the motto *do ut des*. How was the transition to a higher form of religion brought about? Not by a process of reflexion pure and simple; for man's reflective powers were still undeveloped, and could work only slender changes within the traditional circle of beliefs. Savage tribes up to the present time continue on a low level of spiritual culture, and occasionally show features which indicate religious decadence rather than progress. Now the transition to Polytheism from a vague Spiritism means, as Tiele has said, that the spirits acquire definite names, fixed functions, and a specific character.[1] The enhanced powers of reflexion that were necessary to carry out this movement were mediated by social changes. For it is now generally agreed that the movement towards a higher stage of religion did not have its origin in a conscious and deliberate criticism of traditional beliefs, but arose out of the practical needs which accompanied a

[1] *Elements of the Science of Religion*, vol. i., p. 89. Usener's theory is that gods at the lower level were merely designated adjectively. *Vid.* his *Götternamen*.

fresh advance in social organisation. It was the emergence of new wants and the rise of larger ideas, through the blending of tribes in the greater social whole of the nation, which became the ground of a further development of the spiritual consciousness. How the formation of the nation was accomplished we have no clear historic evidence, though we may infer it with some degree of certainty. War was a natural feature of primitive culture, and there is no probability that any nation was formed by a peaceful fusion of elements. One tribe more powerful than the rest established a rule over the others, and the process may have been precipitated and the union cemented by the pressure from without of common enemies. By such a union of tribes in a greater whole nations like the old Egyptian, the Persian, and the Roman opened out for themselves a rich future development. Only we must remember that, as the result was achieved by forcible means in the first instance, time for fusion was necessary, and the growth of a national consciousness was gradual. And, as has been pointed out, the conservative instincts of tribes which had been merged in a larger unity still persisted, and that more especially in the sphere of religion.[1] Thus, for instance, behind the cult of the Olympic deities in Greece, or of Amon-Râ in Egypt, there was a religion of the folk, older and less developed but still possessing a tenacious life—a religion which had its roots in tribal culture. The same phenomenon is visible in India to-day. "The peasant knows little of the greater gods of the faith. He will, it is true, bow at their shrines, and he has their names sometimes on his lips. But he trusts more to the host of godlings who inhabit the pile of stones under the sacred tree which forms the village shrine."[2]

[1] *Vid.* Prof. Menzies's *History of Religion*, pp. 76, 426.

[2] W. Crooke, *The North Western Provinces of India*, 1897, pp. 244-245.

The new religious development, then, is to be understood through the new needs which have emerged. The old local gods and spirits dear to the tribe are inadequate to the wants of the larger and more complex society, and a national god must have a more determinate character and a more extended sphere of operations. The tribal gods who were connected with the greater phenomena of nature could best be made to meet these demands. Hence in the polytheistic systems of the national religions it is very common to find deities who were originally personifications of the greater powers of nature, such as Zeus, Jupiter, Indra, Râ, and Marduk. Sometimes however a national god may originate in the cult, as Brahma, or may represent a mythical ancestor or hero of a dominant clan or tribe. Some deities again signalise a fresh step in culture. Hephaistos, Vesta and Hestia point to the discovery and use of fire, while Dionysus and Bacchus connect themselves with the cultivation of the vine. The important point to note is, that the gods now assume a more definite character with special attributes. They become the representatives and the protectors of particular departments of the nation's life and of particular activities of the people. At this stage of the religious consciousness imagination, not conceptual thinking, prevails ; and imagination works fruitfully in giving form and content to the gods on the basis of the given social order. The imaginative qualities of a race are reflected in the degree in which it gives definite outline and specific character to its departmental deities. In this connexion the contrast between the Greek and Roman gods is striking and suggestive. Specially significant is it when, through the development of social morality, the gods become the guardians of the moral order among men, and their old natural character is transformed into an ethical one. Ahura

Mazda, Varuna, Zeus, Osiris and Odin are illustrations of gods who have in this way acquired a moral meaning. Then the unity and graduated organisation of earthly society act as a stimulus on thought to bring about a corresponding system in the celestial sphere. The simplest method of achieving this is through the monarchian idea. Zeus is described as "the Father of gods and men," and Jahveh is "high above all gods."[1] But the movement towards unification is also seen in what, after Max Müller, it has been customary to call Henotheism. Here, though many gods exist, worship is reserved for the one. And it is but an easy step to suppose that the one is somehow in the many.[2] Or, as the counterpart of the law on earth, a law may be conceived to which even heaven is subject. Thus in India we find the principle of Rita, in China that of Tao, and in Greece μοῖρα and τὸ θεῖον. Where the speculative interest is strong and the sense of moral personality weak, unity may be reached by the pantheistic reduction of all the deities to phases or appearances of a single underlying substance. This was the line taken in India and among the priesthood of ancient Egypt and the later philosophers of Greece. On the other hand where the ethical interest is dominant, as in Israel, Monarchianism and Henotheism issue in Monotheism.

The growth of ethical character in the gods and the development of the idea of a higher law that binds men to them—a law to which individual caprice must be subject—these, if in one aspect they are the result of an advance in man's inner life, in another react on that life and help to deepen the personal side of religion. "So develop the notions of *fas* and *nefas*, of *pietas*, of ὁσιότης

[1] *Vid.* Iliad viii., 1–35, Ps. 97, 99.

[2] So in the Rig Veda: "O Agni, thou are born Varuna, thou becomest Mitra, all the gods are in thee."

and εὐσέβεια, and real religion can now take its roots in the inner spirit of man."[1]

It is through an advance in the ethical and spiritual life that the further step is made possible by which religion passes from the national to the universal stage. The more inward and personal religion becomes, the more universal is its appeal, the more insistent its demand for those moral qualities which know no limits of place or time. This living development of the personal religious consciousness it is which breaks down the barriers set by a national religion, and utters its message to the world. Here is the point at which the prophet and inspired teacher step upon the scene, proclaiming the worth of the inner life, and declaring its superiority to external rites and ceremonies. The beginnings of this movement are illustrated by the pre-exilic prophets of Israel, who preached the law of God written on the heart, and beheld all peoples flowing to Zion to share in the one true worship. Ritualism and nationalism in the end triumphed over the spiritual universalism of the prophets, and Hebrew religion hardened into a legalism narrower in tone and outlook. We have to come to the gospel of Christ ere we find a truly universal religion developing on Jewish soil. Centuries before this, in India the other great universal faith had been ushered into the world—the religion of the Buddha who declared, "My redemption is a redemption for all men." Christianity and Buddhism are diverse in their ideals, but they are one in this, that they appeal to man as man; and, as against all distinctions of caste and class, they lay the stress on the inward qualities of the soul. The conception of Nirvana is negative and poor compared with the rich content of the Christian idea of perfection, but still the goal to which

[1] Usener, *Vorträge und Aufsätze*, 1907, p. 50.

both religions point is for universal humanity. The redemption they preach is for the whole world, in the one case for the world stricken by suffering, and in the other for the world lying in sin.[1] Finally, if we take Christianity as the most perfect expression of the religious idea, then, corresponding to tribal, national, and universal religion, we have the phases of religious belief broadly represented by Spiritism, Polytheism, and Monotheism.[2]

So far we have tried to state those leading features of the evolution of religion which are agreed on by most intelligent students of the subject. The question we have now to discuss is, how far the History of Religion shows us a development, or true progress, in the idea of religion itself. To return an answer we require to satisfy ourselves about the nature of religion and the religious relationship; for we must have some criterion by which to judge how far the ideal is fulfilled at one point as compared with another. Here of course, if we are to follow a scientific method, we cannot simply solve the problem by identifying the ideal with a particular religion at the outset. We must rather try to show if possible what is normal, what is characteristic and persistent in the religious consciousness. In other words we have to inquire what is constitutive and essential in religion, and the inquiry cannot proceed otherwise than on psychological lines. In religion as elsewhere it is only from the pheno-

[1] Or, as Eucken puts it (*Hauptprobleme der Religionsphilosophie der Gegenwart*, 1907, p. 83), Christianity as compared with Buddhism does not save the world but a particular aspect of it.

[2] Instead of the division into national and universal religions, Siebeck (*Religionsphilosophie*, 1893) adopts that of Morality-Religions and Redemptive-Religions. The distinction, though suggestive, is not so clear and simple as the one here given; and it depends to some extent on a particular theory of the nature of religion. With Siebeck's division it is interesting to compare the phases of the religious consciousness distinguished by Eucken as Universal and Characteristic Religion. *Wahrheitsgehalt der Religion*, p. 155 ff. and 339 ff.

menology, the existence of the thing in time, that we can try to rise to the conception of its nature. An insight into psychological principles rests, therefore, on wide and accurate historical knowledge. And here, let it be granted, it is hard to avoid allowing a personal preference to determine our selection of materials and our interpretation of evidence.[1] Our safest method in an investigation of the kind is to keep an open eye to the facts, and to try not to permit any prejudices of our own to distort our view of them. In this connexion I may remark that A. Dorner, in his work on the Philosophy of Religion, inverts the true order when he puts the Metaphysics of the religious relation in the forefront, and treats the Psychology as complementary to it.[2] For the Phenomenology and Psychology of Religion represent the body of religious experience, which a speculative theory of religion must try to understand and explain. To begin with Metaphysics and end with Psychology is surely to court the danger of construing our facts to suit our theory.

But even on the psychological level it is plain that, in order to judge whether particular stages of religion are to be read as development or not, we must have some ideal of religion as our standard; we must have some notion of the essential elements it ought to contain, the presence or absence of which goes to determine our appreciation. Yet a really adequate definition of religion, if it were possible to give one, ought not to precede, but to be reached through an exhaustive study of the facts; and even then there is a danger that, in the effort to embrace everything, our definition should become unwieldy or colourless and abstract. Still, a strict definition

[1] The difficulty is exemplified by the divergence in results between two such competent thinkers as Siebeck and Höffding. The former finds the essence of religion to be *Weltverneinung* and the latter *Erhaltung des Wertes*.

[2] *Grundriss der Religionsphilosophie*, 1903, p. 199 ff., 249 ff.

is not indispensable ; and for our purpose it is sufficient if we can show the essential factors, or constitutive elements of the religious consciousness, and can understand the demands they make.[1]

Here we must ask the reader to take it as sufficiently verified, that in all religion we have a subject, an object, and a bond of relationship between them. On the subjective side the consciousness of this relation is piety, and it appears as worship, reverence and adoration. In the individual himself there is always a sense of need, a feeling of defect of some kind, which impels him to go beyond himself. Then, on the other side, the object worshipped is always the embodiment of a value which distinguishes it from other things, and it is believed to be able to do for the worshipper what he could not do for himself. And through the fulfilment of the religious relation man wins an inner satisfaction, a harmony with himself and his environment, which lies beyond his own powers. Hence we find truth in Pfleiderer's description of the essence of religion as "that reference of a man's life to a world-governing Power which seeks to grow into a living union with it." A religion will stand higher or lower as it does justice to all the elements involved, and brings about a rich and enduring harmony of the personal life.

Still it may be objected that the inner harmony and satisfaction of the soul is a formal principle only, and it cannot be safely applied as a norm of religious valuation. If the stress is laid on the subjective feeling, it would be hard to prove that the experienced satisfaction of the totem- or fetish-worshipper is not as strong as that of the

[1] If one wanted to reach a definition of religion, the only methodical way, it seems to me, would be to follow Plato and begin with a provisional definition, afterwards modifying and supplementing it by a continued and searching examination of the facts.

adherent of an ethical religion. Yet we do not hesitate to place the satisfaction of the one far below that of the other. In truth the idea of inward harmony, in so far as it is purely formal, is not sufficient as a standard of value: it would not work in practice, and we must look to the spiritual content as well. Not merely the degree but the kind of satisfaction counts in our judgments of value, and we cannot help setting the ethical above the natural and the spiritual above the sensuous. Nor do I see that we can go on to assign and amplify reasons for this without presupposing the conclusions we wish to establish. To say that the spiritual life is a fuller and higher kind of harmony, or that it works more effectively, is just to say that it is better. There is a self-evidencing character about the good which makes it futile to go beyond it: and we judge, and are compelled to judge, that the life of the spirit is intrinsically better than the life of sense. Accordingly in our valuation of religion we have to combine form and content, and look to the spiritual and ethical character of the harmony that is realised.

If we apply this standard of appreciation to the historic movements of religion, we find tokens both of growth and of decline. In some religions the process of development goes on, while in others it is arrested at a certain point, and they gradually decay and become effete. The law of continuity is not broken, and we can study the causes which have sapped the vitality of a faith once vigorous; but development in the true sense of the word has ceased. And where this happens we shall generally find that the harmony of the elements in the religious relation has been sacrificed; that the religious consciousness has gone astray by ignoring or perverting some essential element, or by the exaggeration of one element at the expense of the rest, and so deterioration has ensued. For example, when Animism and Spiritism pass into pronounced Fetishism, as among the West African Negroes, we understand the nature of the process but read it as a retrogression. Here the felt need of help in the religious subject has undermined the sense of dependence on the divine object and degraded it to be the mere instrument of its own desires. Or again, when we see the Polytheism of the Vedas turning into Pantheism, we recognise an advance towards unity, but not an advance in the line of the religious ideal; for the mind's demand for unity has sacrificed essential elements of the religious relationship. But in the organisation of the Olympic pantheon in Greece, in the rise of the religion of Zarathustra, and in the appearance of Hebrew prophetism we discern progress, because we note a higher statement of what the religious bond implies. Still it is very plain that in the history of religions we never meet with constant and continuous progress. Religions have their exuberant spring-time and their decaying autumn season. A period of great inner vitality and spiritual interest takes form in a large expansive movement: and then the spiritual forces seem to fail, and an epoch of stagnation follows. But the life is not fled; it is only lying dormant for a while, and at a later day under favouring influences it blossoms forth in a new development. Or, the time of growth once passed, a time of decay ensues and goes on more or less steadily till extinction is reached, as in the religion of ancient Rome. In harmony with this a religion often presents different features at different periods of its history, and the earliest and latest phases may be very unlike each other. Contrast, for instance, modern Hinduism with the primitive nature worship of the Vedas, or the Catholic creed and worship of the later Middle Ages with the simple gospel of Jesus.

In these circumstances it is not likely that we shall be able to explain the evolution of any religion by some dominating idea which existed in germinal form in the beginning. We must remember that the history of every religion is marked by a complex interaction of elements, and not all these were present from the first. Thus the blending of tribal worships in a national religion, and the influence of the new and higher social system which has mediated the change, make it impossible to discern all the features of the national faith in any one tribal cult. Moreover we have to consider the influence of nations one on another, and we have also to bear in mind the development of science and philosophy at the riper stages of culture, both of which powerfully affect and modify the general religious consciousness. When these facts are kept in view, it becomes plain to us that no typical idea passing from germ to completion can explain the actual course of any religion. The complex interaction of elements coming into play at a later stage introduces features which could not have been prefigured in the primitive stage. None the less it cannot be denied that we do sometimes observe a characteristic idea or ideas maintained throughout the history of a religion. This is notably the case where, in the formative period, there has been little interaction with other phases of belief. The spiritism in which Roman religion had its roots was reflected to the last in the crowd of "little gods" who had a place in the worship of the State: the cult of ancestors has been an outstanding and persisting note of religion in China. But this phenomenon is more evident in the case of the prophetic religions. Here the spiritual genius and attitude towards life of personal founders, even though they do not explain the whole evolution, yet give abiding features to a religion. Zarathustra and Buddha, Confucius and Mohammed are examples. And this is most distinctly so where the person of the founder is identified with the ideal of religion itself; for then the ideal receives a concreteness of presentation, and is invested with a force of appeal, which give it a central position and a power to assimilate or reject other elements. This imparts to the religion a deeper coherency and a greater continuity of character. It is well to add, however, that it is just these prophetic figures who give a new impetus to spiritual progress, whom we cannot entirely "explain" through the circumstances of their age and environment. If the inspired religious teacher steps forth on the scene in "the fulness of the time," we can never show that he does no more than bring "the general unconscious inwardness" to explicit consciousness. No doubt there is a continuity between the new and the old, otherwise the new could not live and prosper. The life and message of Buddha, for instance, are not intelligible apart from Brahmanism. And yet in such cases no study of the existing factors of the situation yields the sufficient reason of the fresh development.[1] And in general we may say, that the power of the personal element in religious history makes it impossible to hold that the evolution of the higher ethical religions was implicitly contained in the lower forms with which they have a connexion. "The condemnation which a great man lays on the world is to force it to explain him," so it has been said. But if this means that we must try to make the past explain him, our effort is foredoomed to failure. For the past which influences him is not the dead past of average humanity, but the past as illuminated and vivified by his own spiritual genius.

Keeping to the psychological point of view, I think we

[1] A still more striking illustration is furnished by the origin of Christianity.

are led to the conclusion that the evolution of religion and religions is teleological, for they reflect the character of human experience which is purposive throughout. The substantial identity of human nature is mirrored in the universal needs out of which religion arises, and at each stage a religion represents the demands of the human spirit for satisfaction. But, it need hardly be said, not every demand is religious ; in order to be so it must conform to the character of religion and be related to the constitutive elements of religion. And these elements are, individual subjects conscious of needs and the idea of a divine Power, or powers, conceived as in some way related to the life of man and capable of satisfying these needs. In the exercise of religion men seek to maintain such a communion with the divine that their own lives may be harmonised and completed. And the evolution of religion is teleological, because at every stage it reveals an endeavour of the spirit to work out the fulfilment of this principle. But while the formal ideal of religion remains the same throughout, the content of the ideal changes with the changing life of men, on the whole becoming richer, yet sometimes growing poorer as the result of social degeneration and decay. Religion therefore develops, not in obedience to some impersonal idea but as the outcome of man's striving after an ampler self-fulfilment. Here we have no rigid dialectic, bringing what must be infallibly to pass, but a teleological movement which is rooted in human freedom. The process from one point of view expresses an effort towards a deeper self-consciousness, a fuller personality. And as every personal life has its ground in the social life, and wins spiritual content through the same, so both the individual and the collective elements are involved in religious evolution and act and react on one another.

Consequently with the growth of culture the personal consciousness becomes complex : it has its scientific, ethical and emotional aspects, which are never perfectly harmonised. But as religion is an aspiration after what man conceives to be his final end, the other elements should be consistent with and find a meaning and value in the central purpose. It is just when a one-sidedness or discord among the elements is prominent, that the felt need of new movement becomes insistent. Thus, at a certain stage, the awakened sense of political unity throws into relief the divisions of religious belief and incites to religious unification. At a later date the deepening of the ethical spirit calls for reform of religious practice, and gives fresh content to religious ideas. Similarly advances in scientific knowledge demand modification and reconstruction of religious ideas, so that spiritual belief and practice may not jar with developed thought. On the other hand, when one of the elements secures a decisive preponderance—a cultus, for example, grown stereotyped but strengthened by the resources of emotion and sentiment —readjustment through development may be impossible and decadence ensue. In which case a religion may sink into a mere embodiment of superstition, incapable of ministering to higher wants. Then we can say of it what Hegel said of nations that had run their course, its historic office is gone, and it will only linger on in the life of custom. Spiritual deliverance can only come to the people through a new and higher faith ; so it was that the old Roman religion, grown effete, was supplanted by Christianity.

The kind of teleology we have found to obtain in the History of Religion, the teleology which springs from the universal demands of the personal, spiritual life, suggests to us an interpretation of a religion's decay and disintegration. The immediate explanation of its dissolution is, that it is incapable of inner development in harmony with the developing life of mankind. It has become hard and mechanical, most probably through the influence of ritual and cultus, and resists the inner reconstruction which would bring it into harmony with the growing needs of the race. So religions die because they have ceased to satisfy, and the spirit and life of a people have moved beyond them. Still it does not follow that the elements of good in the culture, of which that faded religion was an aspect, are lost to the spiritual development of humanity —and this though we cannot directly show their influence on the future. Greek thought and the Roman sentiment for law and order went to broaden and enrich the life of Christianity: and elsewhere many a religion no doubt conserves within it the result of some quickening impulse, some fertile idea, derived from contact with a form of faith which has long passed away. It is just in this receptivity to influences from its environment, and in its power to select those of value and mould them to its use, that the developmental capacity of a religion consists. There is indeed no virtue in the mere ability to borrow, and a religion cannot prosper by syncretism. But a vital religion is able to transmute what it appropriates and so to preserve its essential character, while at the same time enriching its inner life. On this fruitful process of interaction depends the power of a religion to grow with the growing life of men and to prolong its youth by the process of self-renewal. And of the historic religions there can be no doubt that in Christianity we find the best fulfilment of this ideal.

The spectator who tries to gain a full and comprehensive view of man's religious development finds that obstacles lie in the way of a complete vision. Standing as he does in the middle of the process, he can neither see its beginning nor its end. The former must be more or less a matter of conjecture, while the latter can only be a matter of faith. But faith is not the clear sight which can give definite form and body to the distant future. Consequently after gathering up the facts about man's religious development, and giving them the best arrangement he can, the enquirer has to remember that he has only seen part of the field and not the whole. But though he cannot penetrate the dim past or the far future, he may hope from the study of the accessible facts to know something of the elements and principles that are at work in the process, and he may legitimately conclude that these have worked and will work at periods where the possibility of authentic record is excluded. For there is a spiritual identity in the nature of man which is not lost amid all the diversities of environment and culture.

The result of this preliminary study justifies us in saying that the development of religion, as we have traced it broadly, means a deepened self-consciousness and a growth into richer and more harmonious personality. The whole evolution of culture is a gradual evolution of higher needs which imply corresponding spiritual satisfactions. But what the religious spirit seeks it finds through a living relation to a divine object, not within itself. And an index of the level of a religion is seen in its conception of this object. The growth of the religious mind brings more and more clearly to light the inadequacy of a deity who is merely a part of the material and temporal system : and the rising spiritual life makes demands which are not to be satisfied by the anthropomorphisms of older faiths. As man becomes increasingly spiritual his devotion is directed to a spiritual God whose worship must be in spirit and in truth.

It may be well to add a word on the office of the
sychologist in regard to the facts of religious develop-
nent as arranged by the scientific student of religion.
Iis task is that of an interpreter, and he tries to read the
rocess on its inner side. We speak, and can hardly help
peaking, of social "forces" and "ideas" bringing about
eligious changes, and perhaps we even go so far as to
alk of climatic and geographical conditions generating a
articular type of religion. Yet it only needs reflexion
o remind us that social "forces" and "ideas" are
bstractions apart from living minds; and it is not the
nvironment but the reaction of the mind upon it which
enerates a religious belief. The psychologist then stands
or the inner point of view. If the question is to elicit
he significance of the transition from a lower to a higher
orm of belief, he tries to interpret it through the inner
nature of man and the psychical principles which work
there. In this way he strives to keep in touch with the
process itself, with religion in the making. Our next step
is to acquaint ourselves with these principles.

CHAPTER III

THE PSYCHOLOGICAL BASIS OF RELIGION

A STRIKING feature of the recent development o philosophical study is the growing attention which i being paid to Psychology. While the relation of th psychical elements to their physiological basis is bein made the subject of special investigation and experiment the psychologist is also passing further afield and is open- ing out new spheres of enterprise. Not only are w taught the value of psychological knowledge in th domain of education and art, but a rewarding line o work is set before us in Comparative Psychology— a discipline which embraces the study of menta phenomena in lower races as well as in the higher anima forms. Psychology, in short, bids fair to be recognise as an independent study, to some extent at least yielding results which are beyond the cavil and dispute of riva schools. It is matter for congratulation, indeed, that i has broken away from its old dependence on Metaphysics for the method of reaching the analysis of consciousnes through a general theory of reality, even though it ha the support of names like Herbart and Lotze, has serious disadvantages. It is not desirable that we should approach Psychology in the light of a preconceived metaphysical theory, a theory which at the best must be of a provisional character. We are likely to fare better if we advance through the relatively firm ground of Psychology, ere we adventure ourselves in the high and difficult region of Metaphysics.

While Psychology has thus been progressing in different directions, it was to be expected that it would bring the realm of religion within the scope of its operations. The field to be explored in this instance was a rich one, for prejudices, both metaphysical and theological, had stood in the way of scientific and dispassionate enquiry. But our age has witnessed the decay of many prejudices; and few who are competent to judge will now maintain that any phase of human experience is better to be shielded from the light of reason. Recently a good deal of attention has been devoted to the Psychology of Religion in Europe and especially in America. As the study is a comparatively new one, the work done as yet has been of a preparatory character—the spade-work which is the indispensable preliminary to larger results. The labours of men like Starbuck and James have produced a considerable mass of testimony bearing on the phenomena exhibited in various phases of religious experience, though much still remains to be accomplished in collecting, comparing, and sifting evidence before the task of construction can be satisfactorily carried out. As it is, the value of the materials to a student engaged on the Psychology of Religion is somewhat unequal. For clearly the psychologist must try to see his subject on its inner side, and to this end he has to draw largely on the spiritual experiences of others. Now it is often by no means plain how far the individuals who report their spiritual experiences do so accurately, and are not confusing facts with inferences. And, on the other hand, one has to face the question in what degree some of these experiences are pathological, and so not a witness to the normal activity of the religious mind. It would certainly be injudicious, to take an extreme case, to find in the reports of a particular revival movement a guide to the universal working of the religious emotions. And while the great spiritual autobiographies have a high value, for example those of Augustine and St. Teresa, Bunyan and Wesley, we cannot straightway assume that they are typical of universal religious experience.

The problem therefore faces us at the outset, how we are to recognise and interpret what is essential and normal in the religious consciousness. Plainly the point from which we must start is the existing religious consciousness, or religion as we experience it in ourselves and observe its working in those around us. No doubt this, at the best, is only a small section of the great and wide field of religious experience ; still it furnishes the only key at our disposal by which to understand and sympathetically appreciate types of spiritual life which are often very different from our own. The utterances of religious faith in a bygone age or in an alien culture may be in marked contrast to the dominant religious spirit of our time and place, but they only become significant to us when they awaken some response within, when they appeal to some element in our spiritual nature. And as a matter of fact we do find that there is a continuity as well as a community in the manifestations of the religious consciousness, and in the very vagaries of religion we discern the working of some element in human nature which has its counterpart within ourselves. Even the pathological in religion is not due to the presence of non-religious factors, but is the result of the exaggeration or the degeneration of some genuine and abiding feature of spiritual experience. The raptures of the mystic or the sufferings of the ascetic are not due to the intrusion of a foreign factor, but are simply the expression of a one-sided development of a normal religious motive. For the normal, though it is seldom realised in practice, is a well-balanced spiritual life.

While we must interpret religious experience through our own experience, our own experience as it stands cannot be made the norm or standard. A particular period or a particular culture may present an excess of one element or another of the religious spirit, which renders it unfit to serve as a standard for judgments of value: and normality, as we remarked, must mean the proper balance and harmony of the elements which go to constitute religion. The psychologist, in trying to bring to light what is essential and universal in religion, must endeavour imaginatively to supplement his own particular experience by a study of the historic religions. And as the fruit of this study he must seek to show the permanent factors that enter into the making of religion, however they may vary in their strength and in their relations one to another in particular instances. The larger logic of history must help us to correct the one-sidedness that clings to a given phase of culture or stage of development. The pressure of those needs which bring about a new growth of religion helps to guide the discerning student to a knowledge of what is essential to the spiritual man; and even the paths which have led to failure and disappointment afford an indication of the better way. It may be we shall come to the conclusion that normality is not to be identified with any rigidly defined type; yet even though this be so, the knowledge of the formal elements involved, and of the claims they make, will enable us to distinguish broadly what is genuinely religious from those phenomena of religion which tend to become untrue by becoming extreme. Everywhere in religion the personal and the social factors are in closest relation to each other. And just as the general religious consciousness in a given social system furnishes the ordinary test of abnormality in a particular individual, so the student of religion will discern in the large working of the universal religious consciousness, as it develops in time, a guide to what is permanent and essential in man's relation to the divine.

Keeping in view, then, that we must ultimately interpret different phases of religion through our own self-consciousness, we find, as is natural, our greatest difficulties in the beginnings of religion. It is hard to revive the image of an epoch a few centuries distant from our own, and it is only in the hands of a man of genius that the picture is convincing. But it is far harder for the modern man, the product of an age-long development, to recreate the mind of the primitive savage. Of the psychical reactions of primitive man, as Prof. Ladd has remarked, we know little or nothing certainly : and though we may learn something from the study of contemporary savages, it would not be justifiable to take them as samples of what is truly primitive. For they, too, have a long past behind them ; and we cannot assume that barbarism, if relatively immobile, is absolutely so. In truth there is evidence to the contrary, and the ages which lie behind the savage life of to-day must have brought with them changes, changes in habits, mental character and social organisation. If carefully used the records of contemporary anthropology will prove helpful and suggestive in an enquiry into the origins of religion, but we must guard ourselves against the inclination to gather from them certain testimony to what is really primitive in culture. An attempt to reconstruct the earliest human religion must, in the first instance, depend on inferences from the religious rites and practices which are found in the oldest forms of culture of which there is a record. The investigator finds there traces of a common body of belief which is the heritage of a past still more remote; and from this he may draw inferences more or less plausible as to the dim beginnings of religion among mankind. At the best the hypothesis he frames will be of the nature of a rough sketch where many details cannot be filled in. But what, again, were the psychical states that found expression in the acts of the primitive worshipper is a matter of further inference—an inference that in this case must take the form of a hypothesis which there is no adequate means of verifying. And what justification we have in trying to reconstruct hypothetically man's primitive religious consciousness is based, as we have said, on a real continuity in man's mental development, a continuity which we know to exist in the growth of the individual, and which we are entitled to postulate in the case of the race. The psychical life of mankind has one fundamental character, however it may differ in its degree of organisation and functional development; and it is only on this ground that the far-reaching similarities of human custom and belief are intelligible.

The fact that men everywhere and always have developed religion—for there is no evidence that any tribe or race has existed without it—points to the truth that religion must have its roots in human nature. No accident of environment or tenacity of tradition can account for what is constant and persistent: that which is universal in experience must be a genuine expression of man's inner life. What element or elements, then, are there in the nature of man which constitute him a religious being? In former days when the departmental conception of human nature prevailed, and the faculty psychology was in vogue, it was usual to trace religion to a particular faculty or sentiment. Religion was a specific aspect of culture, and so it was referred to some specific feature of the human consciousness, call it conscience, the religious sentiment, or some other name. And even those who did not postulate a definitely religious faculty supposed that religion was due to the working of some single element in the mind. Thus Hume, repeating the thought of Epicurus and Lucretius, traced the religious attitude to the emotion of fear: the gods were the shadowy projection of the dread which filled the human soul in presence of the mysterious powers of nature. Schleiermacher likewise found the springs of religion in feeling, but for him the feeling was not fear but that of absolute dependence. Kant, on the other hand, sought to eliminate the feeling element and connected religion intimately with the will; the religious man was he who interpreted the duties prescribed by the legislative will as divine commands. Some, again, have referred religion for its source to the thinking faculty, and have argued that man became religious just because he was a being who could think. In this class Hegel and some of his followers might not unfairly be reckoned.[1] It is not, it seems to me, necessary to enter into a criticism of these views, for they can hardly be said to express the mind of any large and influential body of thinkers at the present day. Recent advances in Psychology have all been in the direction of emphasising the unity of the mind, and have shown the difficulty of supposing any one aspect to be operative in abstraction from other aspects. Neither

[1] An interesting summary of theories on this subject is given in Flint's *Theism*, pp. 343-348.

pure feeling nor pure thought is to be met with in experience. As a matter of fact the theories we have mentioned are right in what they affirm, and only wrong in what they deny: it is true that fear and the feeling of dependence, that will and thought, are involved in the making of religion, but it is not true that any one of them by itself will explain its origin.

While there is not so much risk now that a merely abstract and one-sided theory of the psychological origin of religion will obtain a favourable hearing, there is still danger of an exaggerated importance being attached to one element. And there is a tendency at present to give to feeling such a preponderating influence that thought assumes an altogether subsidiary rôle, perhaps only the office of passively recording the verdicts of its superior. One of our foremost psychologists, Prof. W. James, has given a lead in this direction, and he has been followed by others. But what is characteristic and suggestive about James's position is, that he sees in feeling the doorway which connects the individual mind with a subliminal and subconscious region. It is from this deeper level that spiritual experiences well up into consciousness, and thought only toils to find reasons for what is essentially independent of reason. "The unreasoned and immediate assurance is the deep thing in us, the reasoned argument is only a surface exhibition."[1] And one of his followers tells us, "It must be recognised that many of our most important impulses and desires spring, so far as we can see, from a region which is not conscious at all:" and he feels himself called upon to insist "upon the unique and vital importance of our instinctive life as manifested in the feeling background

[1] *Vid. Varieties of Religious Experience*, pp. 73-74. Cf. 431-432, 510-512, and *passim*.

and as seen particularly in the religious consciousness."[1] Now we may agree that the higher mental life emerges out of the non-rational and impulsive, and this in turn goes back to an undifferentiated whole of feeling. Nor will any psychologist dispute the existence of a subliminal consciousness, for he finds himself driven to postulate it in order to explain phenomena which fall within the focus of consciousness. And we may admit that there are features in the experience of mystics, and in those occasionally occurring outbursts of collective religious feeling, which seem at least to be partially due to subconscious influences. But we demur when we are asked to conclude that it is through the dim feeling background, shading off into the unconscious, that what is essential and distinctive in religious experience comes to birth. There is a danger of falling into a false abstraction when you trace conscious experiences to subconscious processes ; and as a fact the unconscious derives its meaning and value from its relation to consciousness. The latter is the completion and goal of the former ; and if, as Aristotle might have said, conscious process follows unconscious in the order of time (γενέσει), it precedes it in the order of reality (φύσει or οὐσίᾳ).[2] The subliminal consciousness can no more be made an adequate explanation of religion, as a phase of conscious experience, than an abstract aspect can explain the working of the concrete whole to which it belongs. Or, to take another illustration, it would be as impossible to explain perception by regarding only the brain changes which are its material basis. And when we reflect on the ordinary features of the religious consciousness, as seen at different stages of its growth, there seems

[1] Pratt, *The Psychology of Religious Belief*, pp. 26–28.

[2] *Cf. Meta.* M. 1077^{a}, 19. τὸ ἀτελὲς μέγεθος γενέσει μὲν πρότερόν ἐστι, τῇ οὐσίᾳ δ' ὕστερον, οἷον ἄψυχον ἐμψύχου.

no reason for calling this principle in question. For religion means a practical attitude which rises above the domain of fluctuating feelings, and finds expression in ideas that can be communicated and in ends that can be made the object of common endeavour. If ideational activity did not go to the making of religion, one cannot see how religion could be diffused through a society or maintain itself in a living tradition from generation to generation. Moreover, it is apparent how often feeling in religion, taking the form of religious emotions and sentiments, gathers round ideas and receives its direction and meaning from them. In short, if you are serious with the notion of progress in religion, you will find it impossible to deny the importance of the thinking aspect of the religious consciousness, for ideas are the great instruments of progress. And, to sum up, I do not see that it is possible to come to any other conclusion than that, though the feeling and subliminal consciousness may cast light on certain facts of religious experience, it is not the chief source and explanation of that experience.[1]

The basis of religion, then, is not to be found in any one faculty or region of the mind, but in the mind as a whole. For a man brings his whole self to his religion, and an extended study of religious phenomena goes to show that no aspect of consciousness can be discarded as non-essential to the result. Any partial view of the spiritual self leaves phases of spiritual experience without psychological explanation. The distinctive ground of religious experience is not to be reached by elimination, but by showing how in this experience the elements of consciousness are related to one another and to the object. It is

[1] Varieties of religious experience like the rapturous absorption of the mystic, or the wild emotionalism and psychical infection of the revival, may be better understood if the subliminal consciousness is taken into account.

in the manner of the internal relationship, and in the way in which the self as a concrete whole refers to its object, that what is psychologically specific in religion, in contrast to science and art, will reveal itself. And with man's psychological development there goes a corresponding development in that relation of the subject to the object which all religion involves. To put the matter generally, religious development is an aspect of psychological development, and the characteristic features of the latter will be reflected in the former.

The question of the fundamental elements of the psychical life is not free from difficulty. From the Greek thinkers down to the time of Kant, it was customary to give a twofold division; but Kant vindicated the claim of feeling to a place, and the division into feeling, thought, and will has been familiar since his day. At present there is a disposition in some quarters to return to a twofold classification. As a reason for this it is urged by some that will, being in its nature more fundamental, cannot be fairly co-ordinated with the other two aspects. Or, it is argued that conation is so much more closely allied to feeling than to thought, that the two may be treated either as will or feeling in contrast to intellection.[1] As regards conation and feeling it is not to be denied that each stands nearer to the other than to thinking process. In feeling-attitude a potential conation is always involved, and conation reports itself to consciousness in terms of feeling. But this does not justify a sheer identification of one element with the other, and the degree of feeling consciousness is not in constant proportion to conation. In point of fact if you are to identify

[1] So Paulsen (*Einleitung in die Philosophie*) adopts the former alternative, and Pratt, in the work cited, the latter. Prof. Stout (*Groundwork of Psychology*) treats conation and feeling-attitude together under the head of interest.

them, you must expand the meaning of one of the terms so as to include the other. It is of more importance for our present purpose to consider the objection, that will cannot be co-ordinated with the other psychical elements and treated as a factor in the mental life. Now there need be no question that the developed will is not a datum of which we are immediately conscious, for our knowledge of it involves a process of inference and ideal construction. We trace the development of volition back through conation to activity; and we do not apprehend activity as such directly, although it is implied in all subjective process.[1] In other words, it is not activity itself of which we are immediately aware, but the sensation or feeling which is associated, though not to be identified, with it. Activity, as has been said, is always the content of an experience which involves comparison.[2] And the question has been raised whether this conception may not be eliminated from Psychology, just as some physicists have eliminated the conception of force or energy in their treatment of nature. To this the answer seems clear that, if Psychology is to be a purely descriptive science, it is possible to dispense with the idea; but when it becomes explanatory this is no longer practicable. For the synthetic connexion through which a fact of conscious process has meaning postulates the reality of activity. Moreover, to say that an object of knowledge is a mental construction is not to discredit it, provided we are driven to make this construction and it is not shown to be illegitimate. Nor am I able to see how those

[1] The difficulty of treating will as a specific element, and its tendency to spread itself over the whole field of mental process, appear to have been felt by Aristotle. εἰ δὲ τρία ἡ ψυχή, ἐν ἑκάστῳ ἔσται ὄρεξις, for, as he notes, ἔν τε τῷ λογιστικῷ γὰρ ἡ βούλησις γίνεται, καὶ ἐν τῷ ἀλόγῳ ἡ ἐπιθυμία καὶ ὁ θυμός. *De Anima* III., 9, 432b.

[2] Adamson, *Development of Modern Philosophy*, vol. ii., p. 216.

who desire to do away with the notion of activity can meet the argument of Prof. Ward against the Presentationist Psychology, that, if the ego is not active, it ought to be free from the *illusion* of activity. The idea is involved in any attempt to introduce coherence into mental phenomena, for all consciousness implies a synthesis of elements; and if you deny that the self is active, you must surreptitiously introduce the qualification into conscious states in order to explain their connexion. What one must guard against is the inclination to posit will, in the narrower sense of volition, as a primitive aspect of consciousness. For volition can only emerge as the result of a conceptual differentiation of the subject from the object, in virtue of which the impulse as subjective feeling is contrasted with the change produced as objective result. With this proviso I do not see that the fact that our consciousness of activity, or will in the wider sense, is mediated need debar us from treating it as an aspect of psychical life: especially so when we cannot regard it as an illusory inference, and when we find it plays a characteristic part in conscious development. I may add that the psychologist of religion would cut himself off from a highly important means of explanation, if he refused to regard the will as an essential feature of self-conscious experience. The facts and phases of religious experience can only be understood when we postulate the interaction of thought, feeling and will. In dealing, then, with the psychological basis of religion, we shall not hesitate to follow the familiar distinction of subjective process into these three aspects: and it will be of advantage now to consider how these elements function in mental development.

It will be generally agreed that, whatever differences of opinion may be admissible as to the nature of mental development, it cannot in any case be regarded as the appearance of entirely new functions, which are somehow superimposed on a pre-existing basis. Mind can only be intelligible if there be a continuity in its evolution, for the sudden emergence of powers which have no contact with what already is turns development into mystery. The more highly organised faculties must be prepared for by forms simpler and less definitely organised. Reflective will, for instance, leads back through the stages of impulse and of non-voluntary movement to that conative unity which is involved in reflex action, and is even presupposed in vague feeling. The further back we trace consciousness, the nearer does it approach a general *continuum*, or feeling whole, in which the qualitative differences are latent which subsequently become explicit. The primitive *continuum*, though it seem qualitatively simple, must already contain the preparation for those differentiated functions which are not added on to it but grow out of it. So mental development is teleological: it is the process in time by which mind realises its idea or nature, and it is by reference to this idea that each step in its unfolding has a definite meaning. The end is not an external norm or pattern, but is contained in the conative activity which is revealed on every level of experience or life. With the notion of conscious activity that of interest is inseparably connected, and interest implies the exercise of purposive selection. This purposive activity is the inner note of all subjective experience, and it is by means of it that the rudimentary mind slowly brings its latent resources to birth. But the conative unity, though continuously maintained, could not *per se* ensure the typical character of mental development, unless it had reference to, and were the expression of, the completed structure of conscious life.

The primacy of the will might seem, then, to be the

corollary of the profoundly teleological character of menta evolution, for this character is most intimately related t the conative or active side of experience. And it is doctrine which has won much support recently. It i advocated by thinkers like Wundt, Paulsen, and Höffding and our present day Pragmatists are forward in insistin on it. Nor, if kept within its limits as a psychologica principle which works well in its own sphere, is ther any need to object to it. We only feel called on t protest when we are asked to believe that will is th metaphysical first principle, that thought is a secondar product of will, and that in religion, as in other matters our final criterion of truth must be that an idea "works, that it satisfies the will. To this we reply tha Psychology gives us no warrant for treating will as th source and explanation of ideation. No derivation of th latter from the former can be made even plausible ; an if ideation appears later in time than feeling and will i does not follow that it is inferior in function and valu To say, for instance, that impeded will develops idea as a means to its end implies that the will is alread qualified by an ideal element which at this stage be comes more explicit. The truth is, that if one aspec of experience is made the source of other aspects, the it must receive inward enrichment to fit it for th office.

We go on to consider in fuller details the stages c mental development. In the order of evolution feelin comes first, and the most simple and rudimentary form c consciousness is, as already noted, a mere *continuum* c feeling in which differences are submerged. Some time ag it was not unusual to speak of the ultimate elements c feeling as a "manifold of sensation" and a synthetic activit of the *ego* was invoked to bring connexion and coherenc nto this manifold.[1] The so-called "manifold," however, ıas turned out an abstraction of the philosopher which psychological analysis discredits. There is no need to call on thought to join together what has never been asunder, and the thinkers who waged so vigorous a war against the atomistic view of experience were unconsciously influenced by it in their own assumptions. Psychical experience, at whatever point you take it, is always a connected whole, and the difference between its higher and lower levels is that of the degree of differentiation within the whole. This feeling *continuum* stands for a mere awareness, and it ies below the level at which the rudimentary distinction of self and not-self begins to appear. In this feeling-mass, however, conation is potentially involved, and it is only hrough conative activity that differentiation of feelings and their reference to a common centre are made possible. n other words, the emergence of distinctions of feeling within the organism depends on changes which proceed rom the reactive activity of the organism. The will, in leveloping out of the feeling-whole in which it has its oots, appears as conation, which first takes form in specific eactions on stimulus. And it is on the basis of reactions which are involuntary, even though they imply selection, hat impulse develops.[2] Here the beginning of an nvoluntary action is felt with an idea of the end to which t leads. It may be as Höffding has suggested, that mpulse was at first simply sanguine expectation.[3] Development would lie in the ideal element differentiating itself over against the non-voluntary movement with which it vas originally bound up ; and we cannot doubt that

[1] Students of philosophy need hardly be reminded how large a part the manifold" played in the writings of T. H. Green.

[2] So low down as the amoeba reflex action is selective in the sense that it is rected towards life-preservation.

[3] *Psychology*, Eng. Trans., p. 236.

impulses to begin with were only directed outwards. Th development of reflective will out of impulse presuppose the growth of cognitive process in virtue of which sensa tion, as coming from without, is distinguished from feelin as belonging to the subject ; and so, in contrast to th subjective side, the idea of the result to be produce could be defined as falling on the side of the object. I fact, just as feeling to evolve depends on conative activity so the latter in turn calls for ideational process in order t attain the form of reflective volition which utters itself i deliberate choice. A great development of the ideationa function is implied in the progress from movement following straightway on stimulus, to the reflecting wi which carries into act a consciously selected idea.

The importance of ideation in the higher animals, an especially in man, is attested by a significant brai development. I refer to the evolution of the cerebra hemispheres and the cortex which, by supplying a basi for association and retention, give new possibilities o ideational advance. In the lower reaches of psychical lif the familiar distinction of impression and idea is no evolved, and no representative element differentiates itsel from the act of sense-experience. Representation at firs appears simply as a function of the sensory impressio and is bound up with it. The phrase "tied idea" ha been used by Ward after Höffding in this connexion, an the latter symbolises the conception thus, $(\overset{a}{A})$, $(\overset{b}{B})$, th large letter denoting the impression and the small th "tied idea." The crucial point is the acquisition o independence on the part of ideas originally tied by whic they were able to function as free. The liberation o ideas, however it was brought about, was of high import ance, for it is only on the level of free ideas that the tru memory-image and mediate recognition are possible; and these form the indispensable basis of that associational process by which the higher mental development is achieved. Though many of the higher animals appear to possess free ideas, it is only in the sphere of human consciousness that the ideational process, under the lead of interest, works itself out in a continuous acquisition of meanings and values. And the acquisition of meaning, as Dr. Stout has said, is the indispensable minimum necessary to intelligent learning by experience.[1] The process by which ideas are associated—not indeed as isolated and independent ideas but as mental contents—is the significant feature in the development and enrichment of mind. But it is important to remember that these contents, which act and react on one another, only do so because the self is implicitly present as the unity that holds them together. The *ego* is not to be explained by a sort of mental chemistry. That is to say, you can never explain the construction of the self out of an interplay of associated or presented elements: for that constant centre of reference is already implied as a connecting principle in the growth of relations and distinctions. The conception of identity is of the greatest importance in the evolution of mind, and it is just because the mind recognises an identity in the self which maintains itself through differences, that it is able to recognise an identity in experienced objects. In further development the self plays an increasingly valuable part, becoming the centre through which the given mental whole, or apperceptive unity, interacts with each new experience, both determining it and itself receiving further determination through it.

At this point it is necessary to call to mind the value of speech for man's psychological development. The use

[1] *Manual of Psychology*, 1898, p. 87.

of language opens out a very wide field for association and by greatly extending the bounds of possible retentio it supplies a basis for new mental progress. Think for example, of the vast stimulus to thought given by intersubjective intercourse, and reflect what a poten instrument is the generalised concept embodied in the word. "Without speech we could have had no reason and without reason no religion, and without these three essential components of our nature neither intelligence nor the bond of society."[1] It would be difficult to overestimate the value of conceptual thinking, which is made possible by language, to human progress. Develope self-consciousness is a conceptual product, because the differentiation of the subject from the object, by which the self is contrasted with an objective world, rests o inferential processes and the use of generalised ideas Then the definite content included in our notion of sel depends on intersubjective intercourse and on interactio with other selves in a social whole. The concept, in short is a most efficient tool by which the socialised individua grasps, communicates, and works with experience in practical and theoretical regard. Without this living interchange of ideas personality could not be formed And there seems to be a substantial amount of truth i Prof. Royce's contention, that we must get our *socia* consciousness ere we attain the full consciousness of a *objective* world.[2] The growth of the thinking facult which language renders possible reacts on the will b giving a great development to the ideal side of impulse and in virtue of this the self as will gradually acquire control over the appetites and impulses and assumes th

[1] Hamann, quoted by Ratzel, *Hist. of Mankind*, vol. i., p. 20.
The relation of the religious consciousness to language is important an deserves more thorough investigation.

[2] *Vid. The World and the Individual.* Second Series, cap. iv.

function of deliberating on ends and selecting between motives. This growing preponderance of the ideal element breaks the tyranny of impulse and progressively brings the impulsive life under the dominion of reason. And the reflective will goes on to organise conduct in relation to higher ends which are finally connected with ethical and spiritual ideals.

As it is with the will, so it is with feeling: the development of ideation reacts on it and gives it a fresh range and meaning. The articulation of mental life, and its organisation into subjective and objective aspects, make possible that higher phase of the feeling life which we term the emotions and sentiments. Emotion distinguishes itself from diffused feeling where differences are lost to view, by the fact that it is recognised to be a subjective attitude which has reference to an object. Thus joy or anger is *my* feeling in regard to some *thing* or *person*. Emotion as such has always a meaning and value which can never belong to mere feeling; it expresses a significant attitude of the self. In their primary form, at all events, emotions are relatively simple states, and are closely related to the conative and impulsive life. Sentiments, again, while they develop out of the conations and emotions are more loosely related to them, and are qualified in a greater degree by the ideal element in experience. They do not as a rule have the intensity of the emotions; they are, so to speak, spread over a wider space and have more the character of permanent dispositions. Consequently, they belong to a later period in personal development when reflexion has given the individual an enlarged outlook. I will only add here that ideational activity furnishes important objects and rallying points to the emotional and sentimental life, while the latter in turn reacts on and stimulates the train of ideas. The significance of this for the Psychology of Religion is obvious.

We have dealt at some length with the subject of psychical development, for the foundations of a Psychology of Religion must be securely laid in general Psychology. And the evolution of the religious consciousness must, in the first instance, be connected with and interpreted through the growth of the psychical powers. Experience, to use a suggestive phrase of Prof. Ward's, shows "the plasticity of a growing structure," where the higher functions are always continuous with the lower: and the development of religious experience reveals in a large way the same traits.

It has been usual in recent biological works to emphasise the analogy between evolution in the individual and in the race; the ontogenetic growth repeats, we are told, the phylogenetic. In other words, the highly-evolved individual conserves and repeats in the evolution of its own structure the characteristic features of the racial evolution which lies behind it. The general truth of the statement will not, I suppose, be impugned, and what holds of biological development may be fairly supposed to apply to psychological. There is certainly an analogy between the psychical growth of the individual man from infancy to maturity and the psychical development of the race from primitive barbarism to full civilisation. There is the same orderly growth of functions, the simple appearing first, the more highly differentiated coming later in time. In both cases the feeling and impulsive life are dominant in the early stages, while the reflective powers emerge afterwards. On the other hand, we are certain to go astray if we assume that what at best is a helpful analogy can be regarded as a strict identity. For a race is not an individual, and cannot be logically treated as if it were actually one. So we cannot conclusively argue from some known feature in the individual's growth to a precise counterpart in the development of the race. For example, the remark is often made that primitive tribes are just great children; and in point of fact they do reveal many of the traits of childhood. But they are also grown men and possess qualities to which the child has not attained. It would be a hazardous procedure to frame hypotheses about the psychological development of our primitive ancestors from what we know of the development of the child-mind to-day. Suppose we were more sure than we are of the psychological attitude of the child to its environment, we could not certainly infer that this is the pattern of what obtained in the childhood of the race. The analogy will prove useful in giving concrete form and direction to our thoughts; but it is not a perfectly accurate analogy, and we shall fall into error if we take it to be so.

I go on to fill in the outline of mental development already drawn by discussing some of the psychical characteristics which distinguish the races of the higher from those of the lower culture. The bearing of this on the development of the religious consciousness is evident, and I will deal with the point more directly before bringing the chapter to a close.

The psychology of lower races has only recently become a serious subject of study, and the difficulty which attaches to the interpretation of evidence in this sphere is likely to make progress slow. But the importance of the enquiry is great if we would realise the nature of the need to which religion ministers, and the way in which that need expands with the expansion of human culture. Regarded from without the life of primitive peoples is more simple, much less highly organised, than the life of civilised peoples, and the latter has a stability that does not belong to the former.[1] As opposed to the civilised man the senses of the savage are more keenly developed, for he has to depend far more upon them for his maintenance, and he excels in the receptive rather than in the productive qualities. His psychical life lacks balance and regularity, and, as a consequence of this, he is to a far greater extent under the dominion of external impressions. The savage is especially deficient in that coherency of mind which renders continuous acquisition possible on the basis of what has already been acquired. "We find in low stages a poverty of tradition which allows these races neither to maintain a consciousness of their earlier fortunes for any appreciable period, nor to fortify and increase their stock of intelligence either through the acquisitions of individual prominent minds or through the adoption or fostering of any stimulus."[2] The link which binds a primitive society to its earlier stages is custom, and custom, at this period the only rule of right, is obeyed instinctively rather than intelligently. But though custom, in so far as it implies a form of conduct to which the individual must conform, acts as an instrument of good, yet it also works as a repressive factor; by steadily resisting change it makes progress hard.

Looking to the different aspects of the psychical life, we note the predominance of the affective side in primitive races. They show an emotional instability which is manifested in rapid transition from one mood to another. The negroes and American Indians, for instance, constantly pass from fits of apathy and dulness to out-

[1] For some hints in what follows I am indebted to the suggestive book of A. Vierkandt, *Naturvölker und Kulturvölker*, 1896.

[2] Ratzel, *The History of Mankind*, vol. i., p. 22.

bursts of strong emotion. And the wide-spread inclination to idleness on the part of the savage, joined to a keen love of the excitement of war and the chase, is an evidence of this psychological trait. The emotional tendency finds scope in the feasts and dances which are so frequent on the lower level of culture, and act as an outlet for the feelings. In the affective life of primitive man there is a great preponderance of the strong but transitory feelings in contrast to those which are weaker but more permanent: the emotions prevail over the sentiments. This liability to sudden discharges of feeling has been noted among races which ordinarily seem phlegmatic. Closely connected with this emotional character is the extreme impressibility of primitive man; and emotion working through suggestion exercises a controlling power over him. The fact is well-known to anthropologists that frenzy, illness, and even death can be induced by playing on the imagination of the savage. Here lies the secret of the strange power of the sorcerer and medicine man. The greater mental coherency of the civilised man enables him to criticise the impressions that come to him. This relative incapacity on the part of primitive man to control and correct the suggestions occasioned by his environment has its bearing on the rise of religion. Again, on the conative side of experience, we find, as we might expect, that the impulsive will plays a far larger part than in civilised society, where it is governed in a much greater degree by reflexion. The savage has not the developed and rational will that works deliberately, and inhibits the impulses which clash with the central purpose. His tenacity in pursuing an end proceeds from emotion and passion rather than from calculating insight. And the poverty of the inner life makes him very dependent on circumstances, and, lacking inner stability, he is very easily moved by influences coming from without. The want of self-control among low races has often been remarked, and this fact, probably as much as anything, has led to their being described as "great children." This weakness of the reflective will, and the strength of the proximate motive over the savage, render distasteful to him the methods of developed civilisation where the deliberate organisation of means, in order to realise remote ends, plays a great part. He is not a being "of large discourse" who "looks before and after"; and this radical distinction of means and ends hardly appeals to one who shrinks from making the unpleasant a way to the pleasant.[1] Indeed the complex organisation of conduct through a system of means and ends requires powers of abstraction which races on the lowest level of culture do not possess. This feebleness in the capacity to abstract and generalise is one of the outstanding differences between the civilised and the uncivilised mind; and it helps us to understand the contracted vision of the one and the large outlook of the other. Linked to this defect there is the unrestrained tendency to personify on the part of the savage. Where life is an immediate struggle for existence that differentiation of thought from feeling and will, which is conspicuous in developed civilisation, cannot freely work itself out. This absence of reflective power of course implies a defective control over the course of ideas. The primitive man can neither govern his thoughts nor his acts so well as we can, and this incoherency of his own inner life he projects into the world which environs him. Anything may be the cause of anything, and associations in place and time take the place of rational connexions. *Post hoc ergo propter hoc* is a widely applied principle in

[1] *Cf.* Vierkandt, *op. cit.*, p. 260 ff.

the logic of the savage, and his belief in sympathetic magic shows his idea that a result can be brought about by imitating it. Injury done to the wax image of a man will do hurt to the man himself! Closely allied, and showing the same inability to grasp the notion of causal connexion, is the wide-spread belief that the part of an object has all the properties of the whole and may be substituted for it. Hence the care of the savage that neither his hair-clippings nor his nail-parings should come into alien hands! The mental development by which a degree of coherency is introduced into given experience forms a basis for assimilating fresh experience and learning from it; and the thinking capacity by which to amass, interpret and develop experiences is the main feature of civilisation. There is at least a real element of truth in the saying, "In man there is nothing great but mind."

These features of primitive psychical life are of course reflected in primitive religion.[1] Thus, corresponding to the dominance of the feelings in the psychology of early peoples, we expect, and as a fact find, that the feelings are very prominent in the beginnings of religion. Over the earliest phase of religion which is known to us there hangs the sombre shadow of anxiety and fear. Encircled by invisible beings, man felt they were powerful for weal or woe without understanding how. Emotion made him tremble before the spirits and filled him with thoughts of impending harm, while hope in turn suggested to him ideas of help and deliverance. A vague terror of the souls of the dead runs as far back as we can follow human culture; but it is a warning to us how impossible

[1] It may be well to say that, though we have taken the features of savage life as it exists up to the present to be a clue to what is relatively primitive, we do not mean to do so in the absolute sense. As already remarked, the psychical reactions of the earliest men are a matter of conjecture.

it is to trace the evolution of religion to a single emotion, when we find social feeling qualifying this fear in the worship of the spirits of ancestors. For thus early men felt religion was not only a shield from harm but a link which, in binding them to the forefathers of the clan, also bound them to one another. Emotional suggestion, arising out of special experiences, would seem to be the means which served to distinguish and define the objects of his worship to the primitive animist. Moreover the later stage at which intellection differentiates itself from feeling and will is suggested by the fact that the principle of explanation is hardly present in the most ancient strata of religion. In saying this I do not mean to deny that curiosity and wonder are early traits of the human mind as distinguished from the animal. But at the primitive stage it is the emotional not the intellectual aspect of these states that prevails ; and they belong to a lower level of mental development than the feeling of wonder to which Plato traced the origin of philosophy.[1] The crude and incoherent spiritism of the earliest religions was the fruit of man's instinctive projection of his own experiences into nature : it was not designed to serve as an explanation of facts, for the need of explanation was as yet hardly felt. The spirits were altogether conceived in terms of "working value," to use a modern expression : in other words, their meaning lay in their relation to human needs and ends. After the gods become better defined and acquire a name, they are made the object of myth ; and in mythology we witness the dawn of the desire to explain. This tendency becomes explicit at the stage when cosmogonies arise.

In psychical development, while ideation assumes its

[1] Μάλα γὰρ φιλοσόφου τοῦτο τὸ πάθος, τὸ θαυμάζειν. οὐ γὰρ ἄλλη ἀρχὴ φιλοσοφίας ἢ αὕτη.—*Theat.*, 155 D.

distinctive character at a relatively advanced stage, the will is bound up with the feeling-consciousness from the first, though not of course in the form of reflective will. In keeping with this, religious feeling from the beginning takes a practical aspect: it utters itself in definite acts and observances. The expression of this practical attitude is worship, the means by which the clan or tribe strives to establish and maintain a favourable relation with its gods. At this level we are indeed very far from the idea that practical religion means "a way of life," a settled course of conduct: such breadth of outlook is alien to the savage. The beginnings of the cult probably lay in the impulsive acts, under stress of emotion, by which man sought to avert a harm or gain a favour from the spirits. And as the social bond was operative even in the origins of religion, these acts straightway came under the dominion of custom, and the road was barred to individual fancy and caprice. In the rude life of primitive man the dominant impulse was self-conservation, both in its individual and its social aspects: the tribe and its members were alike impelled to maintain their existence against the dangers which encompassed them. And religion is necessarily taken up as an element towards the furtherance of this egoistic and self-preserving will. The specific acts of religion are the serviceable means by which the invisible powers are made the partners of man in the attainment of his immediate ends. The impulsive will, reacting on the environment, suffers check, and man finds himself thwarted in his efforts and disappointed in his desires. Primitive worship expresses very clearly the means developed by the human will in order to reach its goal. The purification and elevation of the egoistic impulse which pervades early religion is gradual, and comes through the enlarged conception of the self which is the fruit of social growth and organisation.

At the risk of repetition a few words may be added on the teleological conception of religious development. Mental development is always purposive, and, as we have remarked more than once, the religious consciousness is one of its aspects. And hence the first problem for those who would understand the growth of religion is to see how it represents and reveals the expanding powers of the human mind. An enquiry of this kind is the necessary preparation for any profound and far-reaching synthesis. We have noted how the psychologist traces the growth of mind from the feeling *continuum*, by a gradual process of differentiation, to the fully articulated self which both unifies and distinguishes its elements. From another point of view the process is one that moves from instinctive to conscious and finally to self-conscious experience. Development is a process which the mind itself works out, so becoming a conscious factor in its own fulfilment: and what is evolved is always prepared for, never merely added on to what exists. Through the whole movement the will, following its selective interest, is realising its end; and the movement comes to its goal in self-conscious personality.

Society reflects in its own evolution the main features of psychical development. And so religion, when it begins to show as an element in primitive culture, is largely instinctive in its character. By this I do not mean unconscious, but mainly a product of the feeling and impulsive life. This appears in belief as a feature of primitive religion. There is no talk of certainty at this stage, nor is any distinction drawn between the real and the possible. The worlds of "solid reality," of dream, and of imagination melt into one another, and facts and inferences are not distinguished. Early man was as little accustomed to doubt, question and criticise his beliefs as the present-day child is; and if asked why he believed, the question would have seemed meaningless to him. The path from instinctive to conscious belief lay through many a hard experience—experience which taught man that everything is not to be taken at its face value, and that the real and the imagined are not one and the same. Of the child we can say that "as it grows it gathers much," and so with the race; mankind in learning to doubt learned also consciously to hold for true. But even in polytheism, where belief, though conscious, is divided in its objects, the subject cannot attain to spiritual certainty, for it cannot come to unity with itself. At the stage of self-conscious religion belief in the developed self has become faith, a permanent spiritual attitude which is the expression of the inner life. Here the *ego* has achieved the consciousness of its own riches, and utters its spiritual faith in the Supreme Value. "The conviction that a God or gods exist, which is conditioned by the earlier stages of the religious consciousness, passes over into the character of faith in God as the ground of the good."[1]

Then as to the other point, the continuity of development. This continuity, we hold, may exist without implying a deterministic theory of evolution: it is enough if the present and the future have living points of contact with the past. And the obligation man is under of maintaining the purposive continuity, and so the internal coherency, of his psychological growth is equally necessary in the religious life of a social whole. The great religions all have their roots in the historic life; in no case have they been sprung on the world as new

[1] Siebeck, *Religionsphilosophie*, 1893, p. 183.

creations. Philosophical religions, artificially superim posed on society, cannot enter into an organic relatior with its spiritual history, and perish speedily for lack o: nourishment. If a religion is to live it must supply a need, and that need must express some aspect of the purposive life of the past. And there will ever be a new development of religion when men realise that the olc forms and symbols demand change, if they are to revea through them the deepened consciousness of their spiritua end. To some looking backward this rise and fall o faiths suggests a drama, whose inevitable movement is only the image of man's changing environment reflected in the medium of futile hopes and fears.

> "Creeds pass, rites change, no altar standeth whole."

A more generous eye regards the old as yielding up its life to the new, and sees man advancing through changing forms of faith to the clearer consciousness of his spiritual destiny and the fuller realisation of his persona life.

CHAPTER IV

THE FEELING ELEMENT IN RELIGION

In the present chapter my aim is not to classify the various emotions and sentiments in which the affective element in religion takes form, nor to appreciate their relative function and value. However interesting and necessary this might be in a work devoted to the Psychology of Religion, it goes beyond my purpose in the present instance. What I will try to do is to characterise broadly the office of feeling in the religious consciousness, and to examine in some detail the part it plays in the development of religion. That part, if not simple and uniform, is, as we shall see, both interesting and important, and must be carefully considered by anyone who would understand the process.

In the feeling-life the *ego* does not go beyond itself and expend itself on the object, as in the case of intellection and will. Thought and volition carry with them an objective reference which is not essential to the feeling consciousness, where the subjective reference is emphasised. There is something personal and private in feeling which we cannot communicate to others as we can our thought and practical activity, something which is closely inwrought with our consciousness of personality. This indefinable somewhat it is, which, interwoven with the self in the religious attitude, makes a man realise his religion as vital and individual. The objective and impersonal attitude, which is the ideal of thinking, cannot yield those value-feelings that are indispensable to the religious consciousness; and it is matter of common knowledge that, when feeling is dead, individual religion decays and becomes formal and ineffective. If we say that a man is personally interested in religion, we imply that his religious consciousness is suffused with a certain warmth of feeling.

In this connexion it is natural to put the question, Is feeling the essence of religion? In other words, is feeling that indispensable element which by its presence constitutes a state of mind as religious? It is at all events true that there is no religion without feeling, and a purely intellectual being, if such were possible, could never assume that frame of mind which men are agreed in calling religious. *Das Denken ist auch wahrer Gottesdienst* may sometimes be true; what is not true is that thinking is *ipso facto* a religious act. It is well known that the leaders of the Romantic movement in Germany, in the beginning of last century, claimed that feeling was the very essence of religion. Schleiermacher declares in his *Reden* that, if you except what is morbid and unhealthy, "there is no feeling which is not religious." And Novalis has said, "Religion arises whenever the heart comes to itself, when it makes itself into an ideal object: and all absolute feeling is religious." While we recognise a value in this as a protest against the dreary intellectualism of Deism and Rationalism, still we cannot fail to see how exaggerated was the claim here put forward for feeling, and how dangerous it might become in practice. Religious emotions have impelled people to strange extravagances.

And the apostles of the great Idealist Movement were doing religion a service when they subjected the demand made on behalf of feeling to a drastic criticism. They at least made it clear to all who had the will to understand the lesson, that feeling, apart from the universalising and controlling activity of reason, is a perilous guide, and cannot be trusted to lead those who follow it to the land of light. The pity was that the champions of Speculative Idealism, in their zeal for reason, forgot that feeling really has a claim to serious treatment.

The present attitude of writers on the Philosophy of Religion on this point is usually broader and more discriminating. As an example of this I take the statements of two such well known writers as Pfleiderer and Höffding. The former finds the essence of religion to be a direction of the will corresponding to the idea of Deity. But he is far from saying that feeling is only a subordinate element which must be transcended by the higher spiritual consciousness : if not the essence, feeling, he holds, is a note of the actual presence of religion.[1] Höffding, on the other hand, says that religious experience is essentially feeling, a feeling on his theory determined by the destiny of values in the struggle for existence.[2] The significance of religious ideas is, that they express the mood, the striving, and the desires of man in this struggle. Here the feeling and conative interest is central, but thought is recognised as necessary to express the relation of values to existence. While I cannot follow Höffding in making the essential reference of religious ideas lie in the subjective sphere, I confess to a difficulty in agreeing with Pfleiderer that feeling is not of the essence of religion although its constant concomitant. I doubt whether if man's

[1] *Religionsphilosophie*, third ed., 1896, p. 327.

[2] *Religionsphilosophie*, 1901, p. 96. *Cf. Phil. Probleme*, pp. 97–98.

practical attitude to a God or gods were not suffused with a feeling tone, if it did not embody an emotional response, it would be recognised by us as a religious attitude at all. For feeling seems to be essential to the life and inwardness of religion. The truth appears to be that all the psychical elements are involved in the essence of religion, and it cannot maintain its character in the absence of any one of them. At the same time, if we are to distinguish, in my judgment feeling lies nearer the centre of religion than intellection ; and the affective life is more directly expressed in piety than the thinking activity. Philosophy may live in the dry light of reason, but religion has never flourished apart from an atmosphere of feeling. Piety somehow does not thrive in an age which glorifies the understanding and seeks to bring all experience before the bar of clear and distinct ideas. It is feeling which redeems the object of religious belief from externality and gives inwardness to the religious relationship.

The important part played by the feelings in the beginnings of religion is not disputed by any well-informed student of primitive culture, and in the previous chapter we have made some reference to the subject. The emotions were prominent as exciting causes in bringing about religion in the earliest peoples, though they were by no means its ultimate explanation.[1] We have remarked on the great susceptibility to impressions among races in the lowest culture, and on their inability to control and criticise these impressions. And one cannot doubt that emotional reactions caused by the phenomena of nature were the stimuli which elicited from savage man the rudimentary expressions of religious consciousness. These manifestations of emotion depended on a general feeling-attitude by which man was already differentiated

[1] *Vid.* Tiele, *Elements of the Science of Religion*, vol. ii., p. 15.

from the animal world where religion has never developed. This disposition of the affective life corresponded, one may conjecture, on a lower level to what we experience as a blending of awe and wonder; and it was on the basis of this feeling-mood that specific emotional reactions took place on stimulus. But as the object was ill defined, so were the emotions shifting and inconstant, "lightly raised and lightly laid again." Along with this feeling-attitude to his environment, by which man was distinguished from the animal creation, there went a deep-rooted impulse which had its ground in the animal and instinctive life. I mean the self-conserving impulse. It was through the operation of this deep-seated instinct that primitive man's feeling attitude to the things around him was so frequently concentrated in the emotion of fear. The general awe of the mysterious beings who encompassed him, quickened by incitement from without and suggestion from within, became fear and even terror of their power to hurt or destroy him. Hence in the beginnings of culture the frequency with which man strove to propitiate the evil spirits who might do him harm.[1] Here the stimulus was a strong emotion setting in movement the self-regarding instincts of human nature. The naïve confession of present-day devil-worshippers, that it is needless to worship the good spirits for they will not hurt them, represents a point of view which was familiar to our barbarous ancestors. The cult of hostile spirits is often met with in savage tribes in modern times: for instance among the Tschi peoples of the West African coast, among the Algonquins and Dacotah tribes of North America and the Dravidian tribes in India. Dread of malignant spirits oppresses the native Australians, and, as Réville has noted, it is well marked among the wild races

[1] *Cf.* Waitz, *Anthropologie*, vol. i., p. 362.

of South America, who fear to stir abroad at night on that account. In this connexion what Messrs. Hyades and Deniker, two modern anthropologists, report of the Yahgans, a low tribe of Tierra del Fuego, is interesting.[1] They believe in phantasms and ghosts, and, it seems, have frequent panics due to terror of the man-devouring demons. It would perhaps be rash to conclude that such a terror of malignant beings was universal in the earliest stages of religion ; but dread of unseen powers was probably widespread, and acted as a stimulus urging man to give utterance in visible ways to his pre-existing disposition towards religion. The stress of feeling drove him in self-defence to the performance of religious acts.

But if one were tempted to take the familiar saying *primus in orbe timor fecit deos* as a complete key to the origin of religion, a fair consideration of the psychological facts would show that this is inadmissible. The single emotion of fear is far too meagre to beget the complex result. And while this is more apparent in the higher stages of the religious consciousness with its revelations of love and sacrifice, even at the outset it is necessary to postulate other motives and emotions. The being who could fear must also have been able in some rude way to hope and trust ; and if nature often terrified the savage, she had also her benignant and gracious moods. The self-regarding instinct which inspired the fear of evil powers would also prompt man to turn for help to friendly spirits. That such spirits existed, gratitude for deliverance and joy in good things gained would surely suggest. Man, either savage or civilised, cannot live on negations ; when repelled in one quarter he must seek help in another. And no fruitful growth of religion can take place when the positive feelings of trust and hope, of gratitude and

[1] As quoted by L. T. Hobhouse, *Morals in Evolution*, vol. i., p. 46.

kinship, do not find scope and utterance. Where terror of ghosts and evil spirits ousts or suppresses reliance on powers possibly friendly, as it sometimes does in the lowest culture, then religious development is arrested; and to the casual observer savage tribes whose only creed seems to be a vague fear of malignant beings may appear to be destitute of religion altogether. The truth is that we have here cases of religious decadence, or examples of incipient religion which, owing to adverse conditions, inward and outward, has not advanced from the dim borderland of animism to the region of clear and settled belief.[1]

In the normal course of things, however, the negative element is counterbalanced by the positive; and if man is driven by fear to religion, religion on its part offers to him objects of hope and trust by which he is able to quench his fear, or secure some respite from its haunting presence. Auguste Sabatier has termed religion the *salto mortale* of faith—the upward spring by which the soul seeks to win deliverance and life. And the movement is something more than a blind leap for safety: behind the act lies the emotional assurance that deliverance and help are to be found in the unseen world. Even in the rude beginnings of religion, trust is the antidote to fear. The Babylonian Epic of Gilgames, though not itself primitive, illustrates this well:—

> "I came to a glen at night,
> Lions I saw and was afraid,
> I raised my head and prayed to Sin."

The very pressure of dread drives the spirit to an act of trust in a being who is able to save. The twofold

[1] In the case of the Yahgans the wretchedness and insecurity of their life, a constant struggle against the forces of an inhospitable nature, seem to be reflected in their meagre and sombre religious beliefs. *Vid.* Ratzel, *op. cit.*, vol. ii., pp. 87-91.

working of emotional feeling in early religion is thus clear to us. As fear in its various degrees, it impels man to religion as a refuge and defence. On the other hand, emotion gathers round the attitude of trust and the sense of kinship, and lends intensity and vitality to the religious consciousness. This latter aspect is, of course, the more important, for it belongs to the substance of religion and grows with its growth. And if not so prominent in the earliest stages of religious activity, it is nevertheless present and contains within it the promise and potency of progress. Specially noteworthy is it that, even in the beginnings of culture, social feeling appeared as qualifying the religious relationship. The bond which linked the members of the clan or tribe one to another also linked them to the god, and sacrifice could be conceived as a meal in which men and gods alike shared. The feeling of kinship is strong in primitive society: in virtue of it the members of the clan or family act as one, and the injury done to a single individual is resented by all the rest.[1] And this sentiment of kinship, resting on the idea of community of life or blood, is very definitely marked when the totem, or ancestor of the clan, is worshipped as a god. It was natural for the savage to suppose that the obligation of mutual help within the social group also extended to the god who was bound up with the life of the group. This idea of kinship with the gods, at root resting on a physical conception, would be reinforced by the human desire to be on friendly relations with beings who had it in their power to help man to the good things that he desires. On the lower levels of culture the emotional aspect of this relationship is but slenderly developed, and material considerations are

[1] The blood-feud is widespread in primitive society. *Vid.* Westermarck, *The Origin and Development of the Moral Ideas*, 1906, vol. i., chap. xx.

ɔpermost. Yet here we have, in crude and rudimentary
rm no doubt, the notion of a bond between the human
ıd the divine which, at the highest stages of spiritual
ılture, is the source of the loftiest and purest emotion.
arly man's feeling of being drawn to his gods is the
im foreshadowing of an emotion which, purified and
ınobled in the course of ages, becomes the ethical love
f God.

On the whole we may conclude that the feelings
ıvolved in primitive religion are of a simple and element-
ry type, with a marked physical basis. The brute
ruggle for existence and the needs of the body are
eflected in the way the savage deals with the spirits and
ı his feelings towards them. Neither man himself
or the object of his worship has assumed that personal
orm, with well-defined attributes, which gives scope to
he higher emotions and to sustained feeling-attitudes.
eeling figures rather as an impulsive source of religious
cts than as an abiding quality of the religious relationship
tself. The relationship had to take a higher form ere
he latter was possible.

The path towards a development and an organisation
ɔf religious feelings was supplied by the cultus, the
stated forms of worship by which man sought to maintain
ıimself and his tribe in right relations with the powers on
which he conceived their well-being to depend. It formed
he rallying point around which the different emotions
ıssociated with religion could gather and find common
and recognised modes of expression. The violent fits of
excitement to which the savage is subject here gained an
appropriate outlet, and were invested with a religious
significance. The war dances of the American Indians
and the witch dances of the African negroes, the elaborate
initiation ceremonies of the Australians, the sacrificial

feasts found in the lower culture of the New and Old Worlds, as well as the varied rites by which uncivilised tribes seek to ensure success in war or avert the ravages of disease,—all these illustrate the way in which primitive religion gives scope for the emotions. The excitement usually generated by these performances has a religious value for the savage, and intoxication and frenzy are construed by him as possession by the spirits. Ecstasy has been called the "central mystical experience" of the older and ruder religions, and was held to mean that the patient shared in a divine mode of life and being. How widely spread this phenomenon was among the lower races the anthropologist is well aware. We find it among the Angekoks of the Esquimaux and the Shamans of the Mongols, the Medicine-men of the American Indians and the Witch-doctors of the Negroes. The savage soon learned how the state of transport might be induced by artificial means. Nor was the excitement confined to the "possessed": the thrill of awe and fear went through the onlookers as they beheld the workings of the spirit. A classical instance of the impression produced by divine possession is that of the Sybil in the Sixth *Aeneid* :—

> "*Gelidus Teucris per dura cucurrit*
> *Ossa tremor, funditque preces rex pectore ab imo.*
>
> . . . . .
>
> *At Phoebi nondum patiens immanis in antro*
> *Bacchatur vates, magnum si pectore possit*
> *Excussisse deum : tanto magis ille fatigat*
> *Os rabidum, fera corda domans, fingitque premendo.*"

Let us now try to put down in a succinct form the part we conceive the feelings to play on the level of the nature-religions.

(A) In the first place the emotions stimulated the magination and vivified the religious beliefs of primitive nan. We cannot indeed say that the crude beliefs of the avage are a pure product of emotion, for they have their oots in the instinctive life ; and an emotion, say of fear, lready implies the presence of belief of some kind. But n giving intensity, and therefore practical efficiency, to udimentary belief the feelings played a highly important part. We know in the case of civilised man how the emotions can work on the imagination, and induce beliefs which have no foundation in fact. And when this happens where the individual has some conception of logical consistency, much more easily could it occur where this criterion did not exist. The wonder or dread of the savage at some object or phenomenon of nature had the reflex effect of making more vivid and intense his idea of the mysterious powers associated with it. And thereby the impulsive force of the belief was increased and bore fruit in religious acts. The primitive animist did not worship every spirit, he selected from among them ; and we may suppose the selection was connected with the emotional experiences which led him to attach a greater practical value to some spirits than to others.

(B) The second function of the feeling-consciousness in early religion is that of acting as a support and defence to religious practice. It is very clear that emotion, in the lower culture, did not figure as an incentive to changes in religion. On the contrary, it invested the rites and ceremonies of the cultus with a sanctity which made them strong to resist change. I have already referred to the cultus as forming a centre and rallying point for the feelings connected with religion, and at present I will only add a few remarks, reserving a fuller discussion for a later stage. Worship being the central religious act, the

feelings converged towards it, and were provided throug
it with definite modes of expression. And to primitiv
man, devoid of the idea of inward piety, the scrupulou
performance of the rite was that which mattere
Hence his feeling was enlisted in the service of the cu
from the first, and to perform the ceremonies of religio
in the manner handed down from the fathers became a
object of most anxious care. To nothing do uncivilise
men cling so tenaciously as to custom. This tenacit
they themselves cannot explain, but its secret is the dept
of feeling-life which supports the custom. Grave evils, i
is believed, would follow its violation ; and no doubt the
sometimes do follow as the result of imagination. Eve
in the lower culture feeling is the defender of what i
established, and already it has entered on the rôle, whic
it plays so successfully throughout, of upholdin
religious tradition and maintaining the continuity o
religious practice.

Development, we have seen, is mediated by socia
changes begetting new needs ; and at this period though
begins to play a conscious part, both in the way o
imaginative construction and by its endeavours afte
unification. Feeling lags in the rear while these change
are being accomplished, but by and by it enters into the
larger sphere and finds scope for a richer exercise.[1] This
larger scope is made possible by the increased definition
and the fresh content which the object of the religious
consciousness now receives. Corresponding to man's
personal development and enhanced social activities, we
have polytheism with its personal gods presiding over
departments of life and possessing distinct attributes of

[1] This statement must be qualified by the admission that the feeling-consciousness among the less enlightened continues to cling to the ruder religion of the tribe, and often keeps it alive for long in a changed environment.

their own. The gods now form relatively stable centres round which the emotional life can gather, and so assume a more lasting character than was previously possible. The god is no longer a wayward spirit, but has an individual character that enables the worshipper to enter into a personal relationship with him—a relationship in which the old physical and magical basis is virtually transcended, though it can still work powerfully as superstition. This elevation of the religious relationship brings about a purification of the feelings which are associated with it. More room is given for fellowship and trust, and unreasoned fear of the spirits, so prominent in the lower barbarism, is transmuted into the dread of doing that which offends the god. A point to note is, that the religious emotions, necessarily incoherent and fluctuating on the previous level of culture, now tend to grow into fixed dispositions recognised as having a value of their own. These dispositions are stable compared with the shifting emotions and bursts of excitement which prevail in the crude nature-religions. In fact we have now come to the stage when the sentiments in contrast to the emotions fill a large place in religion, and give a constant tone to the religious mind. An emotion, as distinguished from a sentiment, is a simpler state, naturally more intense and limited to a particular time. A sentiment is more complex, drawing its character from several emotions, and is qualified in a greater degree by the thinking aspect of experience. The reader will find these features illustrated if he compares the emotion of fear in religion with the sentiment of reverence which appears at a later stage. It is important to note that religion, when it has reached the level on which permanent sentiments have developed, affords through the latter a fresh play for the emotions.

Mr. A. S. Shand has pointed out that the sentiments, being relatively stable complexes, function as substantives which the emotions in turn qualify as adjectives.[1] Thus the sentiments, developing out of the emotions, become themselves a source of various emotional reactions. The richness of the affective life in the ethical religions is made possible by this process, which affords a basis for many kinds and degrees of feeling-tone. Indeed we may safely say that in the highly organised religions the emotions are more often those which qualify sentiments. For instance, the emotion of joy or sorrow felt by the worshipper will frequently be found on analysis to link itself to a permanent sentiment or disposition, which has entered into the attitude of worship. It is not a simple and elementary state.

The expansive and pervasive character of the feeling-life in religion deserves notice. Worship is the central act in religion, and is the natural focus both of sentiment and emotion. But the affective life, when it attains to any degree of intensity, expands and overflows its original boundaries, and suffuses associated elements. It thus augments their feeling-value by bringing them within the feeling-life which encompasses the primary object. Hence the sanctity with which man has invested the persons and things which are more intimately connected with worship, though not themselves objects of worship. The temple where prayer and sacrifice are offered becomes consecrated and must be guarded from profanation. The altar and its utensils are sacred, and the instruments of sacrifice must retain their primitive simplicity. The ministering priest, not the member of a privileged caste in early religion, becomes a holy man whose services are indispensable and whose person is inviolable. The books in

[1] *Mind*, N.S., vol. v., pp. 217–218.

vhich the lives of spiritual teachers and their message are
vritten by and by acquire a mysterious sanctity, and are
ometimes made the objects of superstitious veneration.
Even the stated days of worship share in the holiness of
he purposes to which they are dedicated ; and holy times
nd places have figured largely in the history of religion.
The gradual growth of sentiment, intensifying sanctity, is
roved in such cases by the fact that in the early stages
of religion veneration was by no means so pronounced.
When religion casts its shield over a custom, or lends its
uthority to a social obligation, it intensifies the feeling
which makes for its performance and which strives to
prevent its infringement. Feeling here performs the
mportant function of binding together the parts of the
eligious life and solidifying its complex structure.
And by interfusing itself with the associated elements in
eligion, it enables religion to spread wide its roots in the
social life, and to defend itself with tenacity against the
forces which make for decay and disintegration. Even
he "creed outworn" reveals a strange persisting power ;
for, though reason is silent in its defence, it has the secret
support of the feelings.

In normal and healthy religion feeling functions as an
ntegral factor of the religious consciousness along with
ntellection and will. It ought to co-operate and harmonise with these, not to rule and dominate them. But
the balance and harmony of the powers are never perfectly
realised in the historic evolution, and one or other
element seeks to prevail over the rest. And so it is that
the emotional factor frequently strives to reassert its
claims to supremacy, alike on the level of national and
of universal religion. The reassertion may take different
forms, and these very diverse in their significance. When
the physical aspect is strongly accentuated, we have a

recrudescence of the frenzied and ecstatic conditions which are so common in the lower culture, but which at this stage wear an abnormal appearance. This movement breaking through the restraining influences of the social environment, shows how the capacity for "some wild trick of his ancestors" may persist in the civilised man. An illustration of it is the Dionysiac rites in Greece. The cult of Dionysus was not indigenous in Greece, and is in sharp contrast to the tone of Greek culture. It is Asiatic in its affinities, and its home was in Thrace whence it spread into Hellenic lands. Its ritual, so out of harmony with the Hellenic love of order and measure provided an outlet for the wild emotions and savage instincts which lurk beneath civilised and semi-civilised life. The rites associated with the ἐπιφάνεια, or return of the god, were picturesque in the extreme, but orgiastic in character, marked by boundless excitement and the phenomenon of Μανία, or possession. The celebrations took place at night on the lonely hills, under the glare of torches, accompanied by loud music, the clashing of cymbals, the beating of drums, and the shrill noise of flutes. The celebrants, largely composed of women, stirred to frenzy broke into wild circling dances, and finally in ungovernable fury precipitated themselves on the sacrificial animals, whose flesh they tore and devoured raw.[1] The savagery of the original cult was softened and humanised under Hellenic influence, but not without survivals which revealed the ecstatic character of the worship. The secret of its influence lay in the outlet it provided for those powerful emotions bound up with religion in its beginnings, which civilisation can subdue without being able altogether to eradicate. A like

[1] For a vivid description of these rites the reader may consult Rohde's *Psyche*, 1898, vol. ii., p. 9 ff.

phenomenon is exhibited in the Asiatic worships, introduced to the Roman world in the days of the Republic, which became so prominent under the Empire. Here again we encounter a religious movement which is in sharp contrast to the fundamental features of the spiritual life of the people among whom it appeared. For the main characteristics of Roman piety were order, sobriety, and a prevailing regard for expediency. The religion of the Roman state, neither imaginative nor enthusiastic, was pervaded by a respect for tradition, common sense, and utility; and it offered little or no outlet to passionate emotion. As Mommsen has said, there is a lack of awe and mystery about this religion, and the Roman fear of the gods was earthly, like that of a debtor before a powerful creditor.[1] Yet even among a people so formal in religious things the emotional life asserted its claims; and this explains how the Eastern cults when introduced prospered greatly. In the worship of Cybele, with its passionate mourning and rejoicing over Attis, the emotions had free play. The cult of Isis evoked the wonder of the masses by the pomp and display of its ritual, and it attracted many by the scope it offered for the outpouring of the feelings over the dead Osiris. One reason—not, of course, the only reason—for the success of these cults was the outlet they afforded for collective excitement and the discharge of the feelings, an emotional need not satisfied by what has been termed "a sober but uninspiring faith."

The claim of feeling to dominate the religious life—and feeling with a strong admixture of physical excitement—may be further illustrated from the history of the Christian religion. The rise of Montanism in the second century was, in one aspect, a recrudescence of the

[1] *History of Rome*, Eng. Trans., 1888, vol. i., p. 182.

emotional element in religion, and a protest against the supremacy of the intellectual factor. It revealed the features of spiritual possession and ecstatic prophecy, and fostered the excited expectation of the approaching end of the age. In the atmosphere of tense physical feeling which encircled Montanism, there is a falling away from the spiritual balance of higher religion towards a ruder and less disciplined religion. And this is also true, in some degree at least, of the "revivals" of modern times. Whatever moral benefits flow from these movements, no one can deny that they often degenerate into a wild excitement and an unrestrained emotionalism in which some, not without justice, discern a recrudescence of "primitive traits." The presence of a great crowd is itself a stimulus to excitement, and the emotion which breaks forth in one individual communicates itself to others, till the whole atmosphere is charged with feeling. Hysterical confessions, outbursts of weeping, frantic joy expressed in continuous song are well known incidents. The physical effects are sometimes remarkable, taking the form of collapse, convulsion, or trance. Wesley, in his *Journal*, has recorded a number of such instances at his gatherings. The following entries are suggestive. "About three in the morning, as we were continuing instant in prayer, the power of God came mightily upon us, insomuch that many cried out for exceeding joy and many fell to the ground." Again, preaching at Newgate, and insisting strongly on the text that "God willeth all men to be saved," he records, "Immediately one, and another, and another sunk to the earth; they dropped on every side as thunderstruck. One of them cried aloud." Once more, "I was interrupted almost as soon as I had begun to speak by the cries of one who was 'pricked at heart.' Another person dropped down. . . . A little boy near him was seized in the same manner. A young man who stood up behind fixed his eyes on him and sunk down himself as one dead; but soon began to roar out, and beat himself against the ground, so that six men could scarcely hold him."[1] Such incidents could be paralleled from more recent revivals, and one can hardly doubt the presence of subconscious influences and psychical infection. The danger of such emotional orgies within a highly developed religion is, that the spiritual equilibrium is upset and acts of excess may ensue. In any case such tense physical excitement cannot continue for long: a reaction must follow, which is fraught with spiritual peril. The remark is a very true one:—"Unless emotion is spiritualised by its association with large ideals, it degenerates into the merest beating of the air, as aimless as the gyrations of dervishes."[2]

So far I have dealt with the dominance of feeling in its pronounced emotional forms. This is not, however, the only way in which feeling puts forward a claim to govern the religious consciousness. Physical excitement may be associated with religion at any of its stages, and, as a matter of fact, is found in the highest as well as the lowest religions. But the movement to which I now refer only takes place at a relatively advanced point of development. For Mysticism always involves a certain degree of reaction against the pretensions of the understanding and the claims of discursive thought to lead man to the sanctuary of spiritual truth. It is only intelligible, in its spirit and purpose, when we assume that methods of divine knowledge already exist, while it opens out a higher and more excellent way. The mystic craves immediacy of religious experience,

[1] Wesley's *Journal* under dates January 1, April 26, and May 21, 1739.

[2] Granger, *The Soul of a Christian*, 1900, p. 169.

a direct fulness of divine communion; and, in the exalted emotional mood through which he enters into the possession of the divine life, no intrusion of the understanding can be tolerated. In his rapt communion with the Deity the mystic has transcended all divisions and differences: God becomes all in all, man is absorbed in divinity, and human personality dwindles to insignificance, or seems to vanish altogether. Hence the tendency of Mysticism to conceive God pantheistically, and to look on the soul as having in some mysterious way lapsed from him. That the mystic state has predisposing physiological and psychological conditions is true, and it can be promoted through ascetic practices. While the experience lasts the limitations of the body seem to fall away, and the soul appears to lose itself in the possession of the infinite object.[1]

The mystical movement has shown itself in various religions, and, though taking a colour from the spiritual and intellectual environment, the mystical state everywhere reveals common traits. Traces of Mysticism are found in Taoism among the Chinese: it is fully developed in India, where the Yogi by ascetic exercise enter into Samâdhi, a higher state of consciousness in which the individual achieves union with the divine.[2] "Not with words, not with the understanding, not with the eye can it be apprehended. Only by one who says 'it is' is it comprehensible." In Persia the Sufis are the guardians of a mystical pantheism strangely at variance with the Mohammedan creed. Mediæval Mysticism is

[1] St. Teresa says of the state of ecstasy: "I know not if in this condition there remains life enough in the soul to be able to breathe. If it breathes it has no knowledge of it at all."

[2] With the methods of the Yogi we may compare the self-inflicted martyrdom of some of the mediæval mystics, *e.g.*, Suso, in order to mortify the rebellious flesh.

too large a subject to discuss here, but it may be well to recall how its exponents urge the need of abandoning the understanding and will in order to find God in the region of mystical feeling. Thus Eckhart, "The emptier you are the more susceptible are you to the working of his influence." "God is nearer to me than I am to myself." Böhme, in his *Dialogues on the Supersensual Life*, says, "Cease from all thy thinking and willing, then thou shalt hear the unspeakable words of God." And in the *Theologica Germanica* we read: "Nothing is forbidden and nothing is contrary to God but one thing only, and that is self-will." "God is the being of all who are, the life of all who love, the wisdom of all who know." But mystical states, if essentially feeling-states, have what Prof. James has termed "noetic quality": they reveal truth, and in the moment of illumination the veil that guards the mysteries is lifted. The mystic, in his exalted mood, sees by intuition things withheld from the ordinary consciousness. So St. Teresa declares, "In mystical theology the understanding ceases from its acts, because God suspends it." She records that, "one day being in orison it was granted to me to perceive in one instant how all things are contained in God." And again, "Our Lord made me comprehend in what way one God can be in three Persons."[1] But what is here claimed to be immediate intuition really rests on an interpretation of experience.

Mysticism is valuable as a protest against the burial of a living faith beneath the barren waste of a scholastic theology, and it utters a timely word against the sober reign of understanding in spiritual things. In principle it opposes the tyranny of priestly mediation and the abuses of a sacrificial system, for it asserts the great truth

[1] *Vid.* James, *Varieties of Religious Experience*, p. 411.

of personal communion with God. But it has the defects of a one-sided development in which essential needs do not come to their due. Feeling, when it breaks away from thought, brings the religious consciousness to an *impasse* and makes progress impossible. And Mysticism, with its tendency to pantheistic absorption, becomes untrue to the idea of the religious relation, where the factors must be distinguished as well as united. Hence Mysticism contributes nothing to the strengthening of the soul through the forms of worship, nor does it offer any help in the problem of carrying the religious spirit into the conduct of life. Recognising, like Mysticism, the claims of feeling, but truer in the place and function it assigns to it, is Pietism, or what may be termed Evangelicalism in this country. Pietism appeals to the emotions, for it realises that only through these can religion gain the warmth and inwardness which make it personal and energetic. But it steers clear of pantheism, and for absorption in the divine substitutes anxiety for salvation. It is a religion of the heart ; and the heart, as Pascal said, "has its reasons which the reason knows nothing of." But, while Mysticism despises, Pietism treats too lightly the claims of thought, and it fails to consummate a union with the speculative mind.[1]

In the remainder of this chapter I shall try to make clear a twofold working of the feeling consciousness in the developed religions. This working may be termed *dynamic*, on the one hand, and *conservative* on the other. On the one side the feelings are enlisted in the cause of

[1] The following passage from Novalis shows largeness of vision. "The Moravians annihilate their reason, the Emotionalists annihilate their understanding, the Intellectualists annihilate their heart. No act is more common than the act of annihilation." *Hymns and Thoughts on Religion*, translated by Hastie, p. 98.

reform, and on the other in defence of what is established in religion: in the former case the emotions are chiefly involved, and in the latter the sentiments.

(I). Turning now to the first, or dynamic aspect, we distinguish two forms of its operation, the social and the individual.

(A). By the social aspect I mean those marked movements in the religious life of a people by which reform or renewal is brought about. Here the stimulus which leads to change is supplied by the emotions. In this instance there is no question of an exclusive supremacy of the feelings over the other elements: the emotions work in making *ideas* more vivid and in urging the will to carry them into action. And only when ideas can draw the emotional life into their service do they make victorious progress within a society. If we seek more closely for the explanation of such movements, we find they take place when religion has lagged behind the advance of the social and moral consciousness, and there is a discrepancy between the ethical spirit and religious practice and tradition. The emotional reaction will be specially strong when the vital spirit has ebbed from a religious system, and the system itself has become the shield of privileges and abuses. But the emotions, while they impart energy, cannot lead in the path of progress: they require the guidance of ideas and the control of the will, that their motive power may be turned to good account. And though the masses of a people feel dimly the discord which exists, they are not able collectively to evolve the ideas which define the road to reform and progress. Men of spiritual genius are needed whose feelings are more vividly touched, and who see further and more clearly than their fellows. These gifted prophets and teachers create the purified religious ideas of which the masses dumbly feel the lack, and by their sympathy and imagination they make them live in the minds of the people. By an appeal to reason alone they cannot inspire the masses with their gospel: they must make them feel as well as think with them. And only when the ideas which form the substance of the prophet's message evoke an emotional response in the popular heart does the movement gain the energy that leads to victory. Such a vocation demands great inward gifts, and by its capacity to produce these spiritual leaders the regenerative powers of a society will be measured. One or two illustrations may be given. Though Buddhism is now regarded as a continuation of rather than a reaction against Brahmanism, one cannot fail to see in it a new spiritual movement breaking away from the materialism and externality of current religious practice. Buddha discovered the secret of life not without, but within, and, beholding all the travail of the world, in accents of sympathetic tenderness he pointed his brethren to the way of unselfish service and inward peace. His religion expresses a revolt against mechanical observance and outward sacrifice, and an impassioned demand for a right spirit within. And the deep emotional response called forth by the teaching and example of the Buddha became an impelling force which made the new way a religion for multitudes. In the Buddhist movement the strength of the sympathetic feelings is most prominent: in the Prophetic movement in Israel the reaction of moral feeling is more pronounced. We see this in the prophets' strenuous insistence that Jahveh is a moral governor, and in their passionate protests against materialism of worship and gross selfishness of life. They plead in powerful words for the purification of religion, for the law "written on the heart," and for national righteousness; and they denounce with unsparing severity the breach between religion and morality. One cannot read the prophetic writings of the Old Testament without realising how strongly the emotions were stirred, and how vigorously the teaching on the need of spiritual reform and renewal was reinforced from the side of the feeling-life. Their work stands for a protest against formalism and outwardness in religion—a protest in which clear ideas were impressed on the people with the surpassing force given by intense emotion. Somewhat similar is the lesson taught us by the Protestant Reformation in the sixteenth century. Here is the old story of a religion once full of life but now decadent, the inner side of piety neglected, formalism and superstition rampant, and the whole system laden with abuses. And again we find the ideas which formed the message of the reformers made vivid and compelling by the tide of emotion which rallied in their favour. Luther not only saw clearly, he also felt intensely; and it was because the new thoughts on religion which were filling the minds of the spiritual leaders drew into their service the emotional fervour of the Teutonic races, that the spell of an age-long dominion was broken and the day of spiritual reformation dawned. Without attempting further illustration, our conclusion may be stated in a word. In the higher religions movements towards reform and progress are due to personal initiative in the first instance; but the power which carries the ideas to a victorious issue is inspired by the emotional response they evoke in the souls of the people.

(B) I now turn to the second, or individual form, in which feeling appears as a dynamic agency in religion. And here I have in view the well-known phenomenon of conversion, a matter to which psychologists have devoted attention recently, especially in America. The subject has been studied both in the experience of contemporaries and in the more important religious autobiographies. In this way a good deal of evidence, varying no doubt in value, has been collected within the last few years. Of course we can only touch this large question at a single point, and that is the significance of emotion in the conversion process. That the affective life plays a large part in the process no one who studies the facts will deny; but feeling is here linked to and works upon ideas, which the individual derives from the religious system within which he lives. These ideas give to the experience its specific meaning and distinguish it from related movements of the feeling-life. Under a different system of religious concepts the experience would differ in character. Christian conversion is essentially connected with the ideas of sin and salvation, ideas which become central and intensely vivid to the individual in the stress of the emotional process that works itself out in him. In this reference it is worth while noting that conversion usually takes place in youth or early manhood, when the affective life is very full and vigorous: conversions in mature years or in later life are comparatively rare. Starbuck, in his *Psychology of Religion*, points out that the process falls naturally into three stages: the beginning, the transition, and the end, each distinguished by its own feeling-tone. The preliminary stage, probably originating in the subconscious region, is marked by feelings of anxiety and distress, a sense of dissatisfaction and division in the self, with fluctuations of mood; and it is associated with a more or less pronounced consciousness of sin. A very graphic account of this phase has been given by John Bunyan. "O how gladly," he exclaims, "now would I have been anybody but myself! anything but a man, and in any condition but my own! for there was nothing did pass more frequently over my mind than that it was impossible for me to be forgiven my transgressions, and to be saved from the wrath to come." Again, "Oh! methought this sin was bigger than the sins of a county, of a kingdom, or of the whole world, no one pardonable, not all of them together was equal to mine; mine outwent them everyone."[1] This period of anxiety and wretchedness ripens to the crisis when relief comes. The decisive point seems to be the surrender of one's own will and the cessation of struggle: the individual now enters into a larger life and has the sense of sin forgiven and fellowship with God. The strain and tension within has gone; it is succeeded by a feeling of peace and newness, and even the world around wears an altered aspect. "Old things are passed away": henceforth life is organised round a new centre, and the emotions are harmonised and receive a fresh direction. The change is primarily one of feeling-tone and carries with it the sense of self-renewal, of being "born again." The notable feature after conversion is the inward power which the individual often has gained to overcome former sins and to live a better life. What the ultimate source of this power is does not belong to our present enquiry, and we do not suggest that a psychological explanation is final. But beyond doubt the new spiritual life works through the emotions, drawing from them strength and energy in carrying out its transforming task. The process does not so much involve new ideas, as the investment of old ideas with new significance and feeling-value. This reorganisation of the feelings round a fresh centre of interest gives a new feeling-tone to ideas: the converted man sees things in another light, and the harmonised emotions powerfully reinforce the will in the endeavour to make conduct

[1] *Grace abounding to the Chief of Sinners*, par. 149, 172.

cohere with the higher ideal. The dynamic part played by the feelings will be apparent, when we remember how often after conversion a man is able to conquer an evil habit from which argument aforetime had failed to turn him. It is not that the old is annihilated, but it has been driven from its ruling place by the "expulsive power of a new affection."

(II) We pass now to consider the second form in which feeling functions within the development of religion. This is the conservative aspect. And if the way in which feeling operates in this regard is not so striking as in the former instance, it is none the less most important. As dynamic the action of feeling is visible and dramatic, as conservative it is secret and continuous. We remarked how in this conservative aspect of feeling we have to do with the sentiments, the relatively fixed dispositions and feeling-attitudes which are evolved from the emotions. Sentiments gather round religious objects, customs, and ideas, forming a permanent spiritual atmosphere which acts as a protective covering. Their strength where religion is concerned is the main reason why innovations and reformations are so difficult to carry out. The growth of sentiment, silently enveloping the object, gives to old usage its sanctity, and, interfusing itself with the details of the cult, endows the ritual of religion with a tenacious life. Hence the ritual is always the most venerable element in the structure of a religion, and, to the trained and experienced eye, often yields information on bygone phases of belief and practice. The phenomenon of "survival" in religion is promoted by the guardian care of the feeling-dispositions, and is fostered by the facility with which a religious act can take on a new meaning while remaining to outward appearance the same. For example, the ritual details of sacrifice may survive, while the meaning of the rite passes slowly from a material gift to a propitiation for sin. The idea of a sacrament, as an act of ritual communion with deity, goes back to primitive culture and has its roots in early belief. In the Christian sacrament we see how a primeval rite can be inwardly purified and spiritually transformed. Very often, on the other hand, a religious observance persists when its original meaning has been forgotten, and it is out of harmony with existing beliefs. The funeral obsequies of Patroklos, described in the *Iliad* (XXIII, 192 ff.) were those of a prince in Homer's time. But certain features in the ritual can only be explained as a survival from a barbarous age, and must have been inspired by fear of the ghost rather than desire to do honour to the dead.[1] Modern students of anthropology widely recognise the fact, that the study of the ritual of a religion is the most promising path by which to attempt a reconstruction of its prehistoric traits. Much in the same way biologists endeavour from rudimentary organs in existing creatures to spell out their remote lineage.

The feeling-life, as already noted, inclines to extend itself to related elements, and the sentiment which gathers round the cult also rallies in support of the ideas and doctrines which hav grown out of it. But doctrine is not so stable a structure as ritual, for it cannot so easily accommodate itself to progress by becoming patient of new meanings; and it is easily transformed into a ground of dispute and conflict. Sometimes in the evolution of religion the sentiment which is linked to a doctrine receives such vigorous support from the emotions, that it is quickened into a passion and becomes intolerant of opposition. This is the mood which begets persecution. Nevertheless dogma is the point where religion comes

[1] *Vid.* Rohde, *op. cit.*, vol. i., p. 14 ff.

into close contact with science and philosophy, and against the strong pressure of the intellectual environment sentiment cannot endow doctrine with the comparative fixity of ritual. The reaction against advance in theology is no doubt often strong, and progress is necessarily slow; but the assailants may be armed with the same weapons as the defenders, and beat down resistance. In other words, the new ideas may win the emotions to their help and become inspired by a passion for the truth: and ideas supported and intensified by emotional interest succeed best in the warfare with tradition. That they should prevail from time to time is essential to the interests of religion itself, which cannot continue in health if in discord with its intellectual surroundings. Indeed, the conservative function of feeling in religion, valuable for securing continuity, in turn grows a source of danger to the spiritual life. Because if religion hardens down into a fixed and stereotyped system, intolerant of change, the life it once contained ebbs away and it becomes mechanised. Then we have the *opus operatum*, the virtue of the mere act apart from the piety which alone can vitalise it.[1] When a cult is thus mechanised, the office of religion has gone, although the outward form persists: men perform the outward acts as a tribute to expediency, but the desire of their hearts and the interest of their lives are elsewhere. And the feeling-life which has contributed so much to establish this fixity, in its turn falls a victim to its own success. The sentiment which has gathered round worship deteriorates, and ceases to be able to gather to itself any fresh flow of emotional life. But if religion, in its existing institutional forms, provides no outlet for the deeper

[1] The process of mechanising worship is seen when prayers are recited in an obsolete language, not understood by the people and sometimes not by the priests themselves.

feelings, these will expend themselves in some other direction. The artistic and æsthetic associations of religion in these circumstances may continue to evoke the emotion which at one time was felt for religion itself. "To one who has no more heart for the Messiah of the Gospels there always remains that of Handel, and he who no longer celebrates Good Friday still gladly enjoys the Passion Music of Bach."[1]

If we now try to gather up the fruits of the foregoing discussion, the result, I think, will be a full recognition of the importance of feeling in the religious consciousness. It makes for development in stimulating belief and lending dynamic energy to the will; but of itself it cannot mark out the line of progress nor control the movement. On the other hand, in the form of sentiment feeling plays a conservative part and lends its support to what is traditional. It resists the disintegrating activity of reflective thought. The spiritual health of the soul is attained when harmony prevails, that ideal δικαιοσύνη which, as Plato taught, means that each element comes to its due and all fruitfully co-operate in the interests of the whole. And the value of feeling in religion is at its highest when it coheres with the practical and intellectual functions, neither dominating the other elements nor being suppressed by them, but playing its own part in sympathy with the other parts of the human system. In harmoniously fulfilling its office feeling proves itself an indispensable factor in religion. Without it piety in the true sense is impossible, as the consciousness that religion is real, personal and inward, only comes through the feeling element. In the beginnings of religion feeling was present in the emotional impulses which prompted to worship: and at the highest stage which religion has

[1] Rauwenhoff, *Religionsphilosophie*, p. 119.

reached it blends with the human attitude to the infinit and eternal Being. The clear and distinct ideas by whic man manipulates and organises his temporal experienc are painfully insufficient when he strives to constru through them the Ground of all experience, and th highest category at his disposal cannot exhaust the depth and riches of the Absolute. The secular labour o thought has not dissipated the mystery which overshadow the world and human life ; and the dread with whic early man regarded the mysterious powers behind th moving spectacle of nature survives in the awe whic mingles in the attitude of his latest descendant to th Being he calls God.

CHAPTER V

THE FUNCTION OF THOUGHT IN RELIGION

The importance of the psychical function we term "thinking" in the organisation of experience is generally recognised. The activity which the psychologist terms "ideal construction" plays a large part in fashioning the world as we know it, and in this activity thinking is specially involved. And as we ascend to higher levels of experience the value of the intellectual process becomes increasingly clear. Moreover, though thinking is not by itself the sufficient reason of human progress, there can be no doubt of the prominent share it takes in the movement. If it does not supply the motive power, it at least controls and guides its exercise, as well as gives some assurance that the movement will be in the line of the good. In religious development the thinking function represents a tendency which is in the main contrasted with that of feeling. For the tide of feeling usually sets in the conservative direction, while thought on the whole works for change and advance, and seldom acquiesces long in the dominion of tradition. Thought, in its attitude to its object, is both critical and constructive, and it is always striving after a systematic coherency in the given content which it never fully attains. The idea of finality turns out an illusion, and reason only reaches the vantage ground towards which it has been struggling to find itself condemned to engage in a further ques The doom of thought is restless enterprise. And it is i religion as it is elsewhere: when thinking become conscious or reflective, it works for movement. But it sway is never undisputed either in the individual or i society, for it is subject to the counteracting influence c the other elements in the spiritual whole.

The tendency of recent philosophy and theology ha been to magnify the office of the feeling and volitiona factors of the religious consciousness, and to assign t thinking an altogether secondary rôle. Thinking moves o the surface, we are told, putting forward interpretations offering reasons and adjusting means to ends, but it doe not touch the vital substance, it does not belong to th essence of religion. I have remarked, in the previou chapter, that feeling lies nearer to the centre or essenc of the religious consciousness than thought; but to give to the latter a purely secondary function seems contra dictory and impracticable. For one thing, religion neve comes to birth except on those levels of psychical experi ence where there is a development of intellection, which would suggest that thinking has a constitutive function i this regard. Moreover, the religious subject alway relates itself to the object within a certain world-view which may be either naïve or reflective, but in either case appears indispensable to the meaning of the relationship To the development of this world-view thinking is neces sary, and it is implicit both in primitive belief and imaginative representation. And the developed religiou consciousness always makes the postulate that its *Weltanschauung* must satisfy thought as well as feeling and will If it turns out to be at discord with thought, then religion is compelled sooner or later to seek deliveranc rom the contradiction. To assert that the world-view s only an external appendage to the spiritual consciousness s, it seems to me, inadmissible, for it is implied in the neaning of that consciousness. The bare reference of he religious subject to the divine object would leave the elationship hardly intelligible. Nor can you say that aith, working only through the value-judgments of feeling, occupies a sphere apart and wields supreme jurisdiction in its own realm. In point of fact these judgments of value presuppose an activity of thought, and could not be what they are in isolation from that activity. To set hem over against thought, and to claim that they contain n abstraction from thought the whole essence of religion, s to ignore the obvious facts of the case. No doubt the excessive claims made for reason as pure thought have provoked a reaction in favour of the claims of feeling and will, a reaction which has been fruitful in many ways. It has become plain that to postulate for thinking a supreme and all-embracing function in religion is impossible. And against a morbid mysticism it is always well to insist on a healthy exercise of the understanding, if piety is not to become futile and incoherent. But to demand in this connexion some intellectual standard of validity is as impossible as it would be in art. Poetry and religious faith are akin in this, that they involve heights and depths of feeling which are not to be measured by a purely intellectual criterion. Indeed you cannot make intellectual consistency the norm of religious value without a withering effect on piety, as experience has clearly shown. The dry rationalism of the Socinian and Deistic movements, while it was fruitful in intellectual dispute, failed to quicken the flame of piety or to foster an active and energetic faith. Under the exclusive dominion of the intellect religion cannot thrive, and its spiritual inwardness and vitality suffer loss when men act on the assumption that clea and distinct ideas are the one sufficient test of religiou value.

In what follows I shall try to justify the view tha thought is an essential, though not the supreme, factor o the religious consciousness by tracing its genetic function in the development of religion. On every level o religious experience thinking is implied, although it is not present in the same degree in different phases o religion, nor is its work equally obvious. In the primitive period it is in bondage to the instinctive life, and is compelled to clothe itself in the garb of sense : man draws no conscious distinction between thinking and sense-perception. The weakness of thought in the rudimentary stage is a main reason of the comparatively unprogressive character of primitive religion ; for active thinking is incompatible with rigidity of form and the dominance of mere tradition. Thought by its very nature seeks connexion and coherency in experience, and so is driven to transcend what is given in its quest for unifying principles. The outcome of this generalising and connecting activity is a world-view which, as objective, corresponds at every level to the degree of subjective development. The outward evolves *pari passu* with the inward. Hence we find, accompanying and conditioning the expansion and organisation of experience, a growth in self-consciousness ; and the more fully man is self-conscious, the more fully articulated is the world in which he lives. If we try to characterise the broad features of this evolution, we may describe it as an upward movement from the instinctive, through the conscious, to the self-conscious stage. Or, to put it otherwise, it is a progress from purely naïve to deliberate thinking, and from this to the reflective thought which is fully conscious of itself as well as its object. It is not possible to draw hard and fast lines, and to give thoroughly accurate designations to the phases of a spiritual development: but I think it would be substantially true to say of these three stages, that instinct rules in the first, imagination in the second, and reflexion in the third. But the process is too gradual to admit of anyone saying where the one period ends and the other begins; and, moreover, there are always survivals of the lower in the higher, and sometimes anticipations of the higher in the lower. In tracing the development of the thinking process through these stages we note its continued growth towards independence and mastery over its materials. At the outset playing an unconscious part as the servant of the senses, it comes to recognise itself as a constructive spirit which sets its impress on the world of our experience. Looking now for the tokens of this movement of thought in the growth of religion, we trace its beginnings in the realm of instinctive beliefs. The animism of primitive culture is only man's involuntary projection of his life into things, and thought plays no conscious part in forming the belief which accompanies it. The imaginative spirit awakens to life in the formation of myths and cosmogonies, and finds later its congenial task in giving outline and character to the departmental deities of national religion. The dawn of the reflective era is signalised by the growth and articulation of religious doctrines, and these finally take form as a theology. The work of thought in religion ultimately finds expression in a philosophy which strives to read the deeper meaning of religious experience, and to appraise its value in the larger whole of life. In following out our task in detail we shall learn both how thought helps to mould the religious consciousness from within, and how it sometimes reacts on it from without : and in any case we shall see evidence of its important function.

In the primitive religious consciousness the dominant element is undoubtedly feeling, as we have already observed ; but of course we cannot isolate from feeling the activity of the will which reacts on the stimulus of the emotions. Primeval man, like the child, was susceptible to impressions and ready to respond to them, but he was no more capable than the child of deliberately thinking out the meaning of his experiences. Intellection in the race, as in the individual, was the aspect of psychical process that developed latest. We are guilty of the "psychologist's fallacy" if we suppose that explicit thinking played a part in the origins of culture and the first strivings of the religious spirit. It is an erroneous reconstruction of the remote past even to suppose that then the "function of Religion is to give satisfaction to the cravings of the mind to know the cause and origin of things."[1] And those who speak of religion as well as science having its sources in "intellectual curiosity," should certainly explain what meaning they suppose the phrase is to bear in the region of primeval culture.[2] For everything goes to show that, not "the desire to know," but "the will to live" is dominant at this stage ; and it was out of this practical need, taken in conjunction with the reactions of feeling, that religious beliefs emerged. The error of those who suppose that religion began with a demand to understand the whence and whither of things seems to be partly due to a false identification of

[1] Crozier, *Civilisation and Progress*, 1892, p. 255.

[2] Prof. Ladd, though well aware of the supremacy of feeling in primitive religion, still says: "Religion, as well as Science, has been found to have its sources in intellectual curiosity." (*Phil. of Religion*, vol. I., pp. 418–419.) "Source" must mean here psychological cause, and I cannot find any proof given for the statement.

existing or recent types of savage culture with the remote beginnings of the race. If it be true to say that religion always postulates a "theory of reality," it must be with the proviso that the "theory" which lies behind the dawn of the religious consciousness in mankind is instinctive, not consciously elaborated.[1]

The lowest stage, then, of religious development is that of instinctive belief: thinking is present only implicitly. As the indispensable minimum the religious relationship postulates an act of belief, a judgment on the part of the subject that an object, taken as real, is qualified by the predicate divine. Here is faith in its rudimentary form. A being that could not perform this act cannot be called religious in any justifiable sense of the term; the word would be as inapplicable as it is at present to the ape or the dog. That man had sub-human ancestors, who were incapable of such an operation, may indeed be presupposed in the light of evolution; but such a stage lies entirely outside an enquiry into the origins of religion. We begin therefore at the point where belief exists, and ask what this implies. Obviously "free ideas" are involved, but also something more: for the higher animals show signs of these without being capable of religion. Free ideas must have become wedded to sounds, and man must have already acquired some linguistic facility ere he could enter on the development of religious beliefs in the proper sense of the word. The bearing of the growth of language on our problem is intimate, but unfortunately it was long neglected owing to the artificial ideas which prevailed on the subject. Happily it is now possible to conjecture with some plausibility the steps in the evolution of speech. The beginning would be reflex

[1] The phrase, however, is misleading in this connexion, for a "theory" is the answer to questions consciously put.

cries; and Paul has suggested that there was a long period when sounds were chaotic, and man had not acquired the power of producing particular sounds at will.[1] The outlines of a significant order in speech slowly emerged through the need of mutual understanding among men, linked with the capacity for imitation. Behind the inflected forms of speech there lies an earlier and uninflected stage in which root forms were used, probably onomatopoetic in their origin, and certainly acquiring definiteness of reference through a liberal use of signs and gestures. On this level subject and predicate, if psychologically distinguished, were not verbally differentiated, and words were implicit propositions and stood for processes. Our cry of "fire," or "thief," to borrow an illustration, represents these primitive propositional ejaculations. The oldest words, philologists tell us, are verb-roots which express activities: this is psychologically intelligible and supports the view, in itself inherently probable, that primitive man's attention was specially devoted to what seemed active and living. The development of pronominal suffixes, and the use of one root form to qualify another, marked important steps of progress. Speech was now ripe for the explicit statement of the relation of predicate to subject. As the judgment unfolded itself it universally took the shape of a reference of attributes to substances, of activities to things. That it should be so cannot have its sufficient ground in the experienced content. The idea of identity and difference implied in this connexion of adjectives with a subject cannot be a generalisation from experience, but must

[1] "The original human being, who has as yet not spoken at all, is as incapable as a new-born babe to utter at will any sound of speech. He has to learn such sound first: in his case it is only gradually, owing to a manifold activity of the organ of language, that a motory sensation associated with a sound-formation can develop, which may serve as a regulator for his future speech." *Principien der Sprachgeschichte*, Eng. Trans., p. 187.

express the nature of mind itself in accordance with which it constructs its experience. In other words, the notion of identity is not abstracted from experience, but is a postulate involved in the simplest experience of the self. We see the rude expression of this principle in the representation of the thing as a persisting centre or source of its attributes and activities ; and this mental process gained facility and fixity of form through the instrumentality of speech. The essential feature, says Jerusalem, in the act of judgment is the forming of the content in representation, whereby the thing is conceived as a source of power in the process whence its activities and properties flow.[1] But of course it has to be remembered that no logical and linguistic evolution could in itself bring about the rudimentary idea of powers or activities ; for that is due to man's reading his own conscious experience into things.

This is the stage of primitive or instinctive animism, where things are conceived as the living possessors of powers or properties. At a lower level, where thought and language have not so far developed as to be able to express this belief in ways which can be communicated, nothing worthy of the name of religion, I venture to think, could exist. But when an object, or phenomenon of nature, conceived to be powerful, is in some manner a source of emotional reaction to human beings who can communicate their feelings, a rudimentary religious attitude can begin to develop. That attitude would be possible before man had come to distinguish at all an indwelling spirit from the natural phenomenon ; and the probability is that Spiritism gradually grew out of an earlier Nature-worship. But how did the natural phenomenon, conceived as divine, become an object of worship to a clan or tribe ? Had it a name ? Or, if not,

[1] *Die Urtheilsfunction*, Wien, 1895, pp. 82–85.

how was it defined so as to function as a god to a social group? The credit of raising this question of the bearing of language on primitive religion is due to the late Hermann Usener, and his views, though not free from difficulties, had the merit of directing attention to points which needed discussion. Usener can hardly be wrong in holding that the earliest gods were not addressed by proper names; their content was too meagre and ill defined for this, and even the use of generic terms implies a considerable progress in thinking. Hence Usener's theory that the appellatives were originally adjectival, more especially in the sense of *nomina agentis*, is plausible.[1] In other words, such definition as the object received would be given through that aspect of its activity which impressed the subject as divine. If such definition seem to us too slender, we must remember that the earliest worship was thoroughly sensuous and would be offered in the presence of the deified thing. On the other hand, when Usener goes on to say that this religious attitude must have been built up from a more primitive stage of individual experiences in which "gods of the moment" (*Augenblicksgötter*) were invoked—for example, the lightning flash, the thunderbolt, or any chance object deified in the stress of danger and need—I confess it is harder to follow him. We may grant that the fact that we cannot translate ourselves into the mood which produced "gods of the moment" is not in itself an objection; but it is a difficulty if we cannot find the transition from one stage to the other psychologically intelligible. The idea of a religious relationship, instead of being formed by

[1] *Die Götternamen*, p. 4 and *passim*. Usener suggests that the *indigitamenta* of the old Roman religion were a survival of the ancient way of designating the gods among the pre-historic Aryans (p. 279).

the repetition of individual experiences, seems already demanded in the existence and development of these experiences. In other words the "gods of the moment" are conceivable as specific manifestations of a pre-existing religious consciousness, not as the elements or causes out of which that consciousness itself is evolved. To invoke an object as a god in the stress of momentary need is inexplicable, if you are not conscious of a relation to divine powers which extends beyond the moment. Nor is the theory urged on us by such evidences of the origin of religion as may be gathered from the study of primitive culture. And there is another point which must be kept in view. The social element in early belief is very strong, and not least in religion. What one man regards as divine is so regarded by the clan or tribe, and the religion of the social group is the religion of each of the members. Merely individual beliefs could not maintain themselves amid the shocks and disappointments of the struggle for existence: these beliefs persist in each because they are shared by all; they draw their nourishment and vitality from the social atmosphere. And this common belief, which is present in the dawning of the religious spirit, presupposes such a development of speech as secures an intelligible reference to a common object.

Judging by the thought-development which they demand, we are disposed to conclude that Spiritism, Ancestor-worship and Totemism are posterior to a simple worship of natural phenomena. They require a power to distinguish and interpret by analogy which argues an advance in intellection beyond the earliest stage. And certainly Totemism, where it implies the free use of generic ideas, appears to call for a considerable growth of language. I do not, however, believe that it is possible to fix the mode and order of origin of these phases of religion by an attempt to determine the degree of mental development which they severally involve. In the circumstances one could not expect any hypothesis formed on these lines to be convincing. So I will proceed to consider the general way in which thought functions in the period of primitive religion.

As already remarked, thinking is not so much revealed in determining the religious attitude and mood as in developing the world-view, within which religion works, and which goes to form its meaning. Its action at the primitive stage is naïve, not deliberate; and, unable to abstract and generalise, it can only avail itself of sensuous images and analogies. The animistic reading of natural phenomena betrays an unconscious use of the principle of analogy; for it is an instinctive projection of man's experience into things, a construction of them in terms of his own life. And the untrammelled activity of belief fashions a world which is the reflexion of human hopes and fears and needs. The content of this world is too fantastic and chaotic to be rationalised, inasmuch as thought is in bondage to the concrete and sensuous and builds on the most fortuitous associations. To us it seems a mad world, for its connexions are quite irrational and magical. A universe where what is conjoined in time is causally connected, where results can be produced by sympathetic magic, and a word or name is a real force, is very different from our own world. And yet the Spiritism of the lower culture was an expression of the meaning man read into his experience. Already he had begun to apply the key which he found within himself to interpret what went on without him. The West African negro who thinks disease a spirit that can be expelled by another spirit, and who attributes the tired feeling with which he wakes up to the fact that his soul has been fighting when he was asleep, is engaged in a process of interpreting which reaches very far back in human development.[1] It is not the case, I have argued, that the gods were in the first instance postulated to explain things; but that by and by they were believed to explain occurrences is doubtless true. On the whole the world of primitive religion—the world of Nature-worship and Spiritism—is one of naïve belief which man does not project in reply to questions, but which he instinctively develops under the impulsion of feeling and the urgency of need. The thinking process which underlies this formation of beliefs, and which is involved in the use of ideas and analogies, is not conscious and deliberate thinking.

The transition to the higher level where thinking becomes conscious is mediated by the operation of phantasy or imagination. The first stirrings of thought are revealed at the stage when men begin by means of myths to give a kind of explanation of the phenomena which excite their attention. Aristotle saw in myth the rudimentary spirit of philosophy: the φιλόσοφος was in a way φιλόμυθος, for both are the children of wonder.[2] Through mythology man seeks in a crude way to remove the strangeness of the world which encompasses him by telling stories about it, which bring it within a region that is more familiar to him. Mind has now begun its age-long endeavour to master the object, but as yet it can only strive through pictorial imagery to give meaning to experience. For the well-defined concept is not at its disposal; it can only use *Vorstellungen*, not *Begriffe*. The extent to which a race interprets its world through

[1] M. Kingsley, *West African Studies*, pp. 125, 180, 205.
[2] *Meta*, A., 982 b, 15.

myths depends on its degree of culture and its imaginative gifts. Low races, fighting for existence in an inhospitable environment, have naturally a more slender store of myths than those more happily situated. Mythology speaks the language which is native to the religious consciousness, and shares its personalising tendency. But it does not coincide with religion ; it often has no direct religious interest, for people tell stories about things which they do not worship or reverence. The rude and simple myth congenial to the lower culture may be illustrated from Australia. The sun is said to be a woman who sinks into a hole in the earth and travels underground to the east again in the morning. The moon is a man who, according to one tribe, originated in a bone thrown up into the sky by a boy, and "who now walks round by the south in the day time." Both in Central and South-East Australia the natives have myths of semi-human ancestors who created the first totem groups.[1] But the play of mythologic fancy in early culture is exceedingly wide. There are myths which are meant to explain facts in the development of civilisation, such as the discovery of fire, and myths which are designed to sanction features in the evolution of the cult, such as the substitution of animal for human sacrifice. In truth the scope of myth is as wide as the objects which interested early man and quickened in his mind a desire to explain them, whether these were phenomena of nature or facts in the social and religious life.

Significant from a religious point of view, and also from a philosophic, is the wide-spread myth of heaven and earth as the parents of all things. This seems to be the earliest form in which the human mind tried to give a meaning to

[1] Howitt, *The Native Tribes of South-East Australia*, 1904, pp. 427-430. Spencer and Gillen, *op. cit.*, p. 146.

the world as a whole. The story proceeds on the analogy of sex, and represents the all-embracing heaven as the father and the underlying earth as the fruitful mother of living beings. That the myth marks a natural stage of growing thought is supported by the fact that it is found in lands far apart, where the theory of borrowing is excluded and the hypothesis of a remote common source is very improbable. As a myth with a pronounced aetiological significance it cannot be absolutely primitive; nor does it as a rule enter into the focus of religious interest. But through the developed polytheistic systems the shadowy forms of the deities of heaven and earth can often be discerned in the background. A well-known variation of the story is found in New Zealand, where the Maoris have a tale of the separation of Papa and Rangi, the father and mother of all things. In Finland, Oukko, the all-father, originally had a spouse Akka, the earth goddess. The dim forms of Dyaus and Prithivi loom through the figures of the Vedic pantheon, showing us that the Indian mind had passed through this phase of thought. In Egypt Nut and Seb have the same meaning; they are ancient deities with no local cults. Alike in Asia Minor and in Greece the worship of the Earth-Mother was diffused, and had its root in the same primitive analogy.[1] And the contrast which runs through Greek religion between the Olympian and Chthonian gods suggests the two realms of the divine, the lofty heaven and the deep earth. But though the myth of heaven and earth served as a basis on which thought could go on to develop a cosmogony, it did not lie near enough to the

[1] Æschylus, *Prometheus*, 90, refers to παμμήτωρ γῆ, and in a fragment of Euripides we read, ἅπαντα τίκτει χθὼν πάλιν τε λαμβάνει. The various forms of Earth-worship, and their survivals in later custom are described by Dieterich in his instructive monograph *Mutter Erde, ein Versuch über Volksreligion*: Teubner, 1905.

centre of the religious interest for the religious mind to use it as a means of unifying the manifold deities of popular faith. Yet in the idea of the all-embracing heaven, the father of gods and men, there was the germ of a fruitful spiritual truth.

From what has been said it will be inferred that the present writer has little sympathy with the attempt made in recent years to revive the idea of a primitive monotheism. Further study confirms us in the opinion we had already expressed that it is against all psychological probability to suppose that animism and spiritism are a degeneration from a primeval theism. The theory postulates powers of thinking at the beginnings of culture which could not have existed then, and the evidences of belief in a "great god" among savage races in present or recent times come far short of proving the point at issue.[1] For the question is not so much the existence of a certain belief among contemporary savages, as whether that belief, after examination, can be taken as furnishing a clue to a state of mind at the origin of the religious consciousness among men. When the problem is so stated, the illegitimacy of the inference becomes apparent. The conception of a primitive monotheism is a bold hypothesis not necessary to explain existing facts, and that the facts should seem to yield such a conclusion to certain observers must be due to theological prejudices. The notion of a "great god," when it appears in the lower culture where the theory of borrowing is untenable, can be accounted for as a natural outgrowth of thought among those races. And it is probable that it was reached at a relatively late period in their history, when questions about the whence and whither of things, such as pave the way for cosmogonies, had begun to be asked. The

[1] *Cf. Studies in the Philosophy of Religion*, pp. 122–124.

native Australians have been instanced as a very low race which has a belief in a great god, and this belief, it is argued, is a survival of a primitive monotheism. Yet Spencer and Gillen tell us that among the twenty tribes of the North Central area there is no equivalent of Baiame or Daramulun, the "great gods" of the Eastern and South Eastern tribes.[1] And Dr. Howitt finds nothing in these deities which is inconsistent with the idea that they have been naturally evolved by the tribal mind. He sees in this anthropomorphic supernatural Being, who once dwelt on earth, but now lives in the sky, the embodied idea of "a venerable and kindly Headman of a tribe, full of knowledge and tribal wisdom, and all powerful in magic, of which he is the source, with virtues, failings, and passions, such as the aborigines regard them."[2] Nor is the case stronger with the Indians of North America. Here we have a higher type of savage culture, which developed cosmogonies, and where the notion of a Supreme Maker could naturally be evolved. Some writers find a monotheistic tendency in these peoples, though the term Manitu, sometimes rendered Great Spirit, rather stands for that which is mysterious or infinite than for a real personification of the divine. I may cite in addition the West African races, for whom a similar claim has been made. The Rev. R. H. Nassau, who was for forty years a missionary in these lands, in a recent volume several times asserts his opinion that a primitive monotheism obtained among these peoples.[3] And he finds here the vestiges of a primeval revelation which has been sadly obscured. In this case the writer's theological prepossessions have caused him to select a particular way of explaining certain phenomena, without previously en-

[1] *Op. cit.*, p. 492. [2] *Op. cit.*, pp. 500–501.

[3] *Fetichism in West Africa*, London, 1904. *Vid.* pp. 36–38, 52, 248–249.

quiring whether a simpler and more natural explanation is not possible. The idea of a "great god" who is Father and Maker is no doubt found here and in other parts of Africa also. He is a dim figure who is not the object of active worship. But instead of supposing that this is a remnant of an older and purer, if half forgotten faith, we can better interpret it as a genuine product of native thinking. The West Africans have their myths and stories of creation, and they could have arrived at the idea of a god who was a creator or maker of the world. That he is not actively worshipped need not mean that he has been forgotten owing to the growth of fetishism and magic, but may well signify that he was evolved as an explanation at a relatively late stage of development, and could not compete with the deep-rooted spiritism which was the immemorial religion of the race. If the theory is to commend itself to us which is simpler and more natural, which postulates less and makes fewer assumptions, then we may say with confidence the theory is not that of primitive monotheism.[1]

Through the mythological stage imaginative thinking develops into conscious thinking as a factor of the religious spirit. And this result becomes explicit at the polytheistic stage, where the gods are concrete and personal. At the beginning of this period, however, imagination has still much work to do. The personal gods are superior to the spirits by the possession of individuality and definite qualities. And the process in virtue of which they acquire the content which enables them to function as departmental deities is a process in which imagination is active

[1] Theologians and missionaries who detect evidence of an original revelation in the half-forgotten "great gods" of savages seldom realise the difficulties of their theory from a theological point of view. What providential value can be assigned to a "revelation" destined speedily to be forgotten and to exercise no practical influence on human conduct?

The basis from which imagination works is of course the developed individual character of man which is the fruit of the expansion and enrichment of his social relations. The establishment of a larger order of society brought about the transition from the tribal self to the individual, with a definite character and qualities, and special duties and obligations. And the world of gods had to be developed so as to correspond to the widened range of human needs. The work of expanding an elementary nature-god into a departmental deity with specific attributes was not, in its earlier stages at least, accompanied by deliberate reflexion. That the predicates which came to be attached to Indra and Varuna, Apollo and Athene, were originally a matter of conscious selection and inference can hardly be maintained. One must suppose that circumstances and associations, not to be traced now, stimulated the phantasy: but why Apollo, for example, was imaginatively invested with the character of a light-god, a god of healing and averter of ills, and a god of prophecy and oracle, we do not know. Imagination did not work at random, we may be sure, and some natural basis of suggestion and association must have existed. But what were the data which inspired its activity in given cases is shrouded in obscurity. One point, however, is clear, and that is the importance of the cult in the process. The personal development which had taken place made it essential that worship should be the expression of more elevated, varied and complex feelings; and this in turn required a corresponding development in the deities addressed. Through this necessary relation of the god to the cultus the arbitrary, or merely individual predication of qualities was guarded against. If a deity was imaginatively invested with certain attributes, or was accepted as the guardian and protector of a particular department of the people's life, his general recognition and persistence in such an office could only have been secured by his entering in this guise into the worship of a given social group. In this way fixity of form and community of belief were assured by the cult, which by and by endowed what was tentative at first with the spell of authority and the prestige of custom. The process by which a god becomes concrete and personal, with a variety of functions, is one which often obscures or altogether hides his original character. In cases like Zeus and Indra, Râ and Marduk the primitive basis is fairly clear: but in other instances there is great uncertainty, and a feature that became dominant at a later period is frequently far removed from the primitive character. For example, while the attributes and functions of Apollo and Athene are well defined in historic Greece, they give us no sure clue to the primeval nature of the god and goddess.

At the stage of fully developed national religion a conscious process of thinking comes into operation which is distinguished from naïve belief and imagination. Reflexion has a determinate task set before it. The problem which now occupies thought is pressed upon it by the needs of the social situation. For practical purposes the claims of the different gods require to be reconciled and order and unification brought about in the celestial hierarchy. Where material and utilitarian considerations prevail thought may refuse to embark on a speculative enterprise in the interests of religion. So it was in ancient China and Rome. Or polytheism may be transcended less through the activity of reflective thought than by the power of a vivid moral and spiritual consciousness, as with the Hebrews. But where the logical and thinking spirit is awake the religious problem directly invites its intervention. And the attitude of thought to religion at this juncture may be twofold : it may either aim at a rational reconstruction of religion from within, or it may occupy a detached standpoint and criticise it from without. In the one case the religious consciousness and thought have a common ground and are still in sympathy, in the other case a division has emerged and thought vindicates its independence. Naturally the process of religious evolution will be very different in the one instance and in the other. The best examples of these movements are found in India and Greece, and we may conveniently explain and illustrate them by considering in some little detail the religious development in these lands.

The case of India is most interesting, for it supplies us with an illustration of a religious evolution in which thought is the dominant and guiding factor. The course of the movement will be more intelligible if we keep in view two things : a natural genius for speculation in the Hindu mind on the one side, and a slenderly developed sense of moral personality on the other. The monistic tendency consequently had ample scope and brought about significant results Even at the mythological and practical period of the Vedas the germs of the speculative spirit appear : they can be traced in the formation of cosmogonies and in the manner of relating the many to the One. Kathhenotheism is the name which, after Max Müller, has been adopted to describe the spiritual attitude by which one god after another comes before the worshipper as supreme in the moment of worship, and is addressed with the highest epithets. And this easily passes into the more stable mood which sees in the many the forms of the One, and recognises a single presence in the manifold world of divine beings. The Vedas supply full evidence of this movement of mind. We find Agni and Indra, Varuna and Mitra all on occasion addressed in terms which would imply that each was highest and best, and the supreme source of things. In the Rigveda we read that Indra is exalted above the heavens and the earth. And then Mitra and Varuna are invoked as the "over-lords of the world," and "the mighty and supreme rulers of heaven." Agni is declared to be a power in earth and water, in plants and in men, a god who is one in diverse forms. "Thou, Agni, art born as Varuna, thou becomest Mitra when thou art kindled. In thee, O son of power, are all the gods contained, thou art an Indra to the sacrificing mortal." Thus early the character of thought, its impulse towards unity, is revealed in Indian religion, and significant indication is given of how the problem raised by polytheism is to be solved. The goal discerned from afar is an absolute monism. The path to the goal is marked by the idea of Rita, which appears in the Rigveda, and was originally the name for the rule or order of things, and grew into the notion of immanent and all-pervading law. Under the conceptions of Aditi, the infinite, Pragapati, who creates all things, and Prana, the vital breath, the Hindu mind was striving to express the idea of one underlying principle behind all appearances. The forms of the gods, already vague and melting into one another in the Vedic period, lost what little individuality they possessed under the solvent ot Brahmanical speculation. In this process two conceptions attained a great significance, Brahman and Atman. In the Rigveda they denote simply "prayer" and "breath," but in later speculation they become universal principles which are fused into one in the pantheism of the Upanishads. The development of this idea of Brahman or Atman, the universal life-principle and true being of things, is the characteristic doctrine of the Upanishads. "Just as the spider goes out of itself by means of its thread, as tiny sparks leap out of the fire, so from the Atman issue all vital airs, all worlds, all gods, all beings." The shadow of personality which was associated with Pragapati, the creator, has vanished in the notion of Atman or the world-life. And the fundamental thought of the Upanishads is the unity of man with the principle of all being. Their philosophy is an identity-philosophy. "Whoever knows this, 'I am Brahma,' becomes the All. Even the gods are not able to prevent him from becoming it. For he becomes their self." A further step remained to be taken. It was to explain the appearance of independence and diversity in the world and human souls. This was the problem which came to the forefront in the Vedânta, where the Hindu thinkers seek to expound systematically the relation of the supreme Brahman to other existences. Clinging firmly to the principle of identity, they had to explain these as illusion (Maya). Things only seem to be different. To the enlightened soul the veil of blindness falls away, and he recognises his identity with the One and indivisible Being. "That art thou," so runs the formula, and the man who knows it has passed beyond the region of sorrow and illusion. The mind filled with this higher knowledge rises superior even to the authority of the Vedas; for it knows itself one with the absolute reality. The Vedânta, as the name signifies, is the "end of the Vedas"; and it is the conclusion of the search for unity which runs back to the Vedic period.

One or two points are here deserving of notice. Thought working on the content of religion transforms it at length into a colourless identity, or rather strips away the veil of appearance from it and discloses what eternally is. And in doing so it effects a transmutation of the religious consciousness itself. The problem of maintaining a right relation to the gods through the ritual of worship gradually becomes a question of true knowledge. And as the old gods dissolve in the immanent one, so the soul looks not without but within to recognise the presence of the Supreme Being. The notion of a religious bond between the subject and the object falls away: salvation ceases to be either ritual or ethical but comes of insight. The soul that *knows* is delivered from the bondage of sorrow and illusion:

> "Once read thine own breast right,
> And thou hast done with fears."

So it was that in the hands of the consistent Hindu thinkers religion was converted into a form of knowledge, in which every difference between the worshipper and worshipped melted away, and the soul had no need to hope or strive: all that remained was to realise that itself was the One which had no second. Brahmanism is an illustration how, on the one hand, the thinking element in the religious consciousness makes for unity, and is restless till it finds a highest Reality which shall absorb all differences. But it also shows us that where thought entirely dominates the other elements, the personal values of life may suffer violence and the religious relationship be reduced to a fiction.[1]

Our illustration of the negative or critical attitude of thought towards religion is taken from Greece. Here thought attempts no inner reconstruction of the polytheistic system, but simply points out its defects and

[1] Of course speculative Brahmanisn neither is, nor ever has been, the popular religion of India. The faith of the common people is still entangled in spiritism and nature-worship, and does not rise to a subtle pantheism. Ancient Egypt, again, furnishes an example of a polytheistic creed, growing out of fetishism and animal-worship, in which the henotheistic tendency appears, and where finally, in the hands of the priesthood, the many gods are reduced to symbols of the all-embracing One. Here too the popular religion continued on the lower level, and pantheism remained an esoteric creed.

inconsistencies. The substitute it would provide is a philosophic religion, which does not grow out of the older body of beliefs but claims a validity of its own. And one can see a reason for this. Personality was never the shadowy thing for the Hellenic that it was for the Hindu mind. The Greek drew the image of his gods in sharp outlines, and his genius gave definite and permanent expression to their characteristics in fair artistic forms. Accordingly thought was confronted by a vigorous tradition and sentiment, which gathered round individual deities, and resisted effectively the fusion of the many divine figures into one real Being. Over and above this, Hellas was never a strong, centralised state where, to intellectual reasons, were added powerful political motives making for the unification of belief.

Under these conditions, then, we find thought in Greece working for the disintegration rather than the evolution of the traditional religion. The movement had its beginnings in the sixth century B.C., and arose out of the wonderful development of the reflective spirit which signalised the rise and early history of Greek philosophy. It took the form of a polemic against the popular theology. Xenophanes, the forerunner of the Eleatic School, was the first thinker to find fault with the current ideas about the gods. He censures the prevailing anthropomorphism, and points out that, if the animals had gods, they too would make them in their own image. For Xenophanes "one god is greatest among gods and men, neither in form nor in mind like to mortals." Aristotle, in his *Metaphysics*, tells us that Xenophanes looked on the whole universe, and declared that the One was god.[1]

[1] *Meta*, I, 5, 686 b, 10. The passage does not seem to mean that Xenophanes was the exponent of Henotheism, but that he sought to identify his one God with the world.

Anaxagoras, coming later, discredits the popular belief that the heavenly bodies are divine. The sun and moon are stones, he says, and the former is a fiery stone and larger than the Peloponnesus.[1] Having thus criticised the greater nature-worship, Anaxagoras set forth the theory that Nous, or Mind, orders all things. But Nous is still conceived materially, and, though it is said to be an external cause of order, it is by no means thought of as a divine person. Empedocles, the contemporary of Anaxagoras, like Xenophanes, criticises anthropomorphic polytheism, and he is well aware of the defects of the popular theology, though he does not replace it with a monotheistic idea of deity.

Turning for a moment to the religious attitude of the great dramatists, we note that Aeschylus and Sophocles allow the traditional polytheism to stand in its outward form, while they purify and elevate it by infusing into it a fresh ethical content. But Euripides is the child of the new spirit that had been growing, and here and there he gives significant voice to the doubts which were troubling the age. In a well known passage he puts the question whether Zeus be not a name for the necessity of things, or the reason which works in the minds of mortals.[2] As Zeller says, "These utterances prove that Euripides had wandered far away from the ancient faith in the gods."[3]

The Sophistic movement, questioning as it did the validity of knowledge and the traditional bases of

[1] οὗτος ἔλεγε τὸν ἥλιον μύδρον εἶναι διάπυρον καὶ μείζω τῆς Πελοποννήσου. Ritter and Reller, eighth ed., p. 120.

[2]
ὅστις ποτ' εἶ σὺ, δυστόπαστος εἰδέναι,
Ζεὺς, εἴτ' ἀνάγκη φύσεος, εἴτε νοῦς βροτῶν,

Troades, 885–886.

Cf. Iphig. in Aulis, 1034–1035.

εἰ δ' εἰσὶ θεοὶ, δίκαιος ὢν ἀνὴρ σύ γε
ἐσθλῶν κυρήσεις· εἰ δὲ μὴ, τί δεῖ πονεῖν;

[3] *Socrates and the Socratic Schools*, Eng. Trans., p. 18.

morality, materially contributed to the disintegration of the old theology; and when we come to Plato and Aristotle, we find enlightened thought silently setting aside the authority of the old polytheistic religion and replacing it with a philosophic conception of God. Neither of them thought it worth while to rationalise the ancient faith. And though Plato deals gently with the religion of the past, and recognises a value in it for the multitude who are incapable of deep reflexion (Laws, Bk. X.), he shows clearly enough that the philosopher understood its weakness and incoherency. The speculative idea of God is central in Aristotle's system, and his *Metaphysics* culminates in a 'theology.' But he has no interest whatever in bringing his conception of divinity into connexion with the gods of the vulgar faith, and is less tolerant than his master towards the myths and representations of popular religion. Henceforward in Greece the faith of the educated and the faith of the masses move on different planes. Stoicism and Neo-Platonism reveal to us the religious aspect of philosophy, but they are not speculative interpretations of the historic religious consciousness. The old religion lingered on in the life and custom of the common folk, but, unable to win the thinking spirit to its service, it sank into decay and was finally supplanted by a more vigorous faith.

The stereotyped forms of the Greek gods, always retaining something of a natural externality, proved an intractable material to a developmental process. And the religion of Greece, unable to adjust itself to the advances of reason, slowly perished. But it is by no means true that the negative movement of thought always brings about this result. The issue depends upon the intrinsic character and developmental capacity of a religion. Where a faith is possessed of inner vitality and responds to practical needs, it will endeavour to repel the attacks of criticism : or, if this is impossible, it will seek to meet them through reconstruction and progress. When a historical religion embodies values which the religious spirit would not willingly lose, it will always strive to maintain itself and live with the growing life of the age. The negative process of thought, assailing religion from without, only accomplishes the ruin of the stronghold when it is aided by weakness from within : the religion survives assault which is inwardly fitted to survive. Granted that a historical religion is still a centre of spiritual activity, those critical attacks which have a weight of growing knowledge behind them will induce a corresponding development in the object. The detached criticism of impartial thought will impel faith to self-criticism. This, in fact, is one of the important functions of thought as a minister to religious change and progress.

It is, of course, only at the riper and more highly differentiated stages of culture that the process of which we have been speaking manifests itself. But where science and philosophy have won their independence of religion, and evolve world-views of their own, action and reaction must ensue. This movement, inaugurated as we have seen in Ancient Greece, has been reproduced under changed conditions in modern Europe. I refer to the so-called conflict between Science and Religion. Into the details of this dispute there is no call to enter, but one or two points are worthy of notice. Here was a vigorous thought-activity and a powerful faith-life, resting on world-views which would not cohere the one with the other. The solution which is of the departmental order, *i.e.* where each claims validity in its own sphere, and neither has jurisdiction over the other, is not in the end defensible ; and for this reason, that Science and Religion, however sharply they seem to be contrasted, cannot be dualistically opposed, inasmuch as both have their ground in the undivided activity of the personal self. It is the one self-consciousness, reacting on experience, which develops both the religious and the scientific *Weltanschauung*. The unity of the self brings about the insistent demand that the attitude to experience be harmonious, and the claims of the scientific and religious consciousness be reconciled. Where modern science by its results induces change and development in religion, it will not be found, I think, that it does so by discrediting or causing a radical reconstruction of those spiritual values and ideals which are central in the religious life. The category of value really lies beyond the scope of natural science, which seeks to give coherency to experience through the principle of causal explanation. But out of the use of this method of causal explanation have emerged with growing clearness certain general views of nature and its development which have become, or are becoming, the property of all educated minds. Examples of these views are the Copernican astronomy and the theory of evolution. The historic religions, again, have all grown up in a pre-scientific age, and their spiritual ends and ideals have been set within a world-view corresponding to that age. To maintain the early and naïve standpoint in the face of modern science becomes more and more difficult, as we see in the case of Christianity. And though religious feeling was strong in support of the old conceptions of heaven and earth, of life and its origins, the pressure of the new ideas has become too wide and severe for successful resistance. The process of readjustment is promoted by the discovery that the essential religious values do not suffer loss thereby, but take their place in a new and enlarged setting. That in this reconstruction of the thought-environment religious ideas maintain an absolute identity of meaning can hardly be contended. The notion of God has not precisely the same significance for an enlightened Christian in the first and in the twentieth centuries. But what may fairly be said is, that all of spiritual and practical value in the idea can be conserved in the changed setting. Such a process of readjustment we are witnessing in our own age : and doubtless it has its perils due to misunderstandings and extravagant claims put forward by either side. But the process is inevitable, and is ultimately necessary for the vitality and efficiency of religion itself as an integral element in human culture.

The dispute between Science and Religion is not so much one between science and the religious spirit as between science and the theology which has grown out of religion, and which has pushed its dogmas into the scientific field. The tendency of the higher religions to produce a theology is a witness to the truth that the function of thought in religion is not an external one. To treat theology as a kind of degenerate outgrowth of the religious consciousness is to fail to recognise that it comes to natural birth through the activity of the religious spirit. Myth, legend, and cosmogony are the steps in a process which, on the level of clear and reflective consciousness, expresses itself in theological doctrines. The process is one in which thought attains an increasing mastery over its materials. Still, it is not the case that theology always appears when a certain degree of culture is reached. An intensely utilitarian spirit, as in China, may discourage attempts to formulate doctrines about the gods, or the gods may be too shadowy and abstract to bear the weight of dogma, as in the old Roman religion. But where the conditions are favourable, thought will make its claims felt, and a body of doctrine will be developed.

Theology does not originate in an abstract enquiry into the nature of the gods : it takes its rise from the cult, and retains a practical aspect throughout its history. It is at once a confession of faith and a system of truths to be taught. A developed cult is the basis of a theology, and the first essays of the theologian are attempts to formulate the meaning of what is done in the cult. The oldest elements of a religion are always contained in the ritual, and, compared with it, doctrinal construction is recent and belongs to the age of reflexion. The cult itself has grown up in a more primitive age, and the crude material view of things which it expresses gradually fades from the minds of men. The ritual of purification and sacrifice, and the immemorial forms in which the gods are addressed in prayer, must have a meaning, and when thought becomes deliberate and reflective it tries to formulate that meaning. So the increased definiteness which the forms of the gods receive, through the practical demands of the cultus, passes into the statement of specific doctrines in regard to their character and function. Theology explains and justifies what is done in worship. So, too, the founders of religion, and the exponents of a new religious principle, lofty figures deeply impressing the spiritual consciousness and forming living centres for the religious life, are made in turn the object of theological statement. This we see in the case of Buddha, and more markedly in that of Christ. Theology here attempts to expound, in a way that shall be universally valid, the doctrinal truths which are implied in the historic manifestation.

But theology, if it has its origin in an endeavour to assign a satisfying meaning to the acts of the cultus, by and by passes beyond this phase to embrace a larger material. And this is the body of spiritual experience which forms the living core of higher religion. It would be true to say that the formation of this living body of experience, practical and emotional, is the condition of any significant and impressive growth of doctrinal construction. And no other religion can compare with Christianity in the fulness and persistence of the experience which has found theological embodiment. Dogma here stands for an attempt to express in forms of thought the faith-experience which is the common possession of the religious community. Doctrine is only fruitful and valuable in so far as it coheres with and interprets practical religious experience. For then it is an endeavour, legitimate in itself, to set out in an objective and valid form the meaning of the spiritual consciousness of a religious society or church. And so long as religion represents a thinking as well as an emotional and practical attitude, the religious mind will want a theology. The advent of a systematic theology, however, is usually hastened by conflict of opinion, and by the existence of diverse doctrines for which the claim is made of interpreting religious experience. The practical needs of religion demand a common basis of belief, and to meet this an authoritative creed is evolved. In this process thought renders good service ; but the dogmatic system, which is the fruit of the thought of one age working on the content of religious experience, is apt in a later age to prove a source of difficulty and even of danger to the interests of spiritual religion. For under the sway of personal interests and conservative feelings a creed becomes stereotyped, and claims to absolute truth are made for it. It assumes a kind of independence of and superiority to the experience which is its condition and test. This is a situation fraught with peril in the face of advancing knowledge and growing spiritual experience. The way of truth and safety is to recognise that theology can never be a fixed and final product, but must be subject to change and development with the developing religious life of man. In the higher culture the self-conscious life of man becomes rich and complex, and each element within the whole is affected by the growth and expansion of the other elements. The religious consciousness cannot maintain itself unchanged alongside the evolution of knowledge and social ideals. So true is this, that even those who cling most passionately to "the faith of their fathers" can never read exactly the same meaning into the creed which their ancestors did. Each generation sees and evaluates the doctrinal heritage of the past through its own spiritual atmosphere. And in an ageing world which looks back on a long history of varying ideals and shifting standards of value, the conviction grows that dogma can neither adequately define nor exhaust the deep flow of the spiritual consciousness.

The outcome of the situation is the endeavour to adjust the claims of knowledge, faith, and spiritual experience through a religious philosophy. A Philosophy of Religion, the work of a developed and reflective culture, occupies a position which makes it possible to appreciate the function of thought in religion, as well as to recognise its limitations. Experience, it points out, is always richer than thought; and thinking cannot take up into itself the whole content of the religious consciousness, just as it cannot do so in the parallel cases of the poetic and artistic consciousness. In the circumstances the philosopher is unable to endorse the claim to finality put forward by the theologian. He points out that theologians have employed uncritically forms of thought which lay to their hand, and the result has been to detract from the value of their work. It may suffice to recall the use made by the patristic writers of terms

M 2

like οὐσία, ὑπόστασις, and πρόσωπον, and the part they played in the creeds of the early Church. Thereby was bequeathed a legacy of difficulty to those who strove in a later day to make theology a rational and consistent system. But the older race of theologians, when their matter proved intractable, left the refractory elements standing side by side with the title of authoritative truths, and so have earned the name of being "unscientific." Hence the religious philosopher, who tries to "think things together," is forced to a valuation of theology and its claims. An attempt in this direction was made by Hegel, and the Hegelian solution, if it does not enjoy the vogue it once did, has still representatives, and these too among thinkers who would not call themselves Hegelians. Hegel's view was briefly this. Theology, though reflective, has not attained to the concrete and systematic thinking of philosophy, and its dogmas still belong to the sphere of representation or figurative thought (*Vorstellung*). They must therefore be criticised and purified, in order to be raised to the form of the notion or philosophic concept (*Begriff*). The defect in this view is not so much the critical attitude taken up towards theological doctrines, as the assumption that religious experience can be translated into and fully expressed through philosophic notions. The study of religion in recent times has shown how deeply involved in it are the volitional nature and the feeling consciousness, and the attempt to absorb these elements in the thought-function is recognised to be impracticable. As little can the meaning of religion be exhausted in this way as the significance of a poem or a picture.

Another view has been lately put forward by those who share the opinion that theological dogmas are inadequate, while at the same time distrusting the power of philosophy to replace them by perfect forms. I refer to the attempt to substitute the idea of symbol for that of dogma. The symbol, as Höffding rightly says, makes clear the distinction between the original and special religious experience and the ideas through which it is expressed.[1] The latter, of course, are regarded as secondary and imperfect; while the vaguer, if suggestive, symbol is thought to be a fitter medium to bring before the mind the depth and richness of the spiritual reality. The Symbolo-fideism which is associated with the names of Auguste Sabatier and Ménégoz separates the faith state sharply from historical belief, and, instead of trying to express the experience in a clear-cut doctrine, has recourse to the less definite method of symbolism. For the symbol suggests the truth that transcends us. In this dislike of all reflective formulation of spiritual experience the impartial observer will discern a danger threatening religion from another direction. Divorce religion sharply from the reason, and you inevitably bring its objectivity into peril. And the symbol which sacrifices definition to suggestiveness cannot safeguard religion in this matter; for the content becomes shadowy and elusive, and the main stress falls on a subjective and indeterminate feeling-state. And though you made "working value" the only test of religious validity, I do not think that Symbolism would stand satisfactorily even this test. For faith will not *work*, either in the individual or the social whole, save on the assumption that its object is real and can be trusted. We cannot trust the object, if we believe that every idea we form of it must be more or less erroneous. The vague and indefinable reality to which the symbol points can hardly prove a ground of human faith or the support of human endeavour. No doubt man, whose life is cast *am farbigen*

[1] *Religionsphilosophie*, p. 184.

Abglanz, can never know as he is known. But the Supreme Being, to whom the soul relates itself in faith, must be the object of a spiritual knowledge which gives the worshipper the assurance that he is the source and realisation of the highest values and ideals. If this conviction is undermined and ruined, the religious life ebbs and dies. And to my mind it seems unlikely that Symbolism could maintain such a conviction in the average man.

The chapter may fitly close with a short discussion of the relation of knowledge to faith in the religious consciousness. This will complete our subject by bringing into the light the limits as well as the place of thought in religion. The first point to note is that thought, the function which systematises experience and connects its parts in a rationally articulated whole, is never the exclusive way in which the religious mind apprehends the object. The faith-element is at no time absent, and with faith there goes a judgment of value which represents an inner kind of knowledge that cannot be exhausted by reflective thinking. The thought-function is not suspended, but its office is subordinate to faith in the act by which the religious spirit apprehends the divine object. It is at the highest and self-conscious stage that the function of faith is most important. For here the spirit reverences a God who is at once unconditioned Being and Supreme Value, and who therefore cannot fall within the conditioned system of elements by which thought seeks to develop its explanations. Not, then, as an inference from the given world or any of its parts, but by an act of faith, the religious subject posits the divine object. It apprehends the object by an inward knowledge which is in terms of value, and is not capable of being adequately presented in notional form; for we cannot translate this faith into rational insight and also retain the spiritual character which the religious consciousness claims for the object. It is possible to proceed regressively from the facts of experience to a final Ground: but this process of reflexion, if it leads to the postulate of a Supreme Being, does not likewise give the Supreme Value the religious spirit demands. Speculative thinking, exercised on experience in order to bring out its ultimate implications, commonly reaches a Being that is the immanent unity or systematic whole of experience itself, and so has no transcendent aspect. And whether thinking develops the conception of a divine object which is the inclusive system of experience, or a conditioned element within the system, in neither case could the attitude to this object represent the attitude of spiritual religion. For the normal spiritual mind, if it recognises an in-dwelling of God in experience, cannot be satisfied with a Being who does not transcend in some way the imperfect mundane system. Nor is it an insuperable difficulty that the object of religious faith does not fall within the sphere of logical proof. The ultimate principles from which proof proceeds cannot themselves be proved. Even the speculative regress on a World-Ground is not a proof in the strict sense. For we cannot execute the return movement, and show how the Ground necessarily posits the world of experience. And accordingly, when we regard God as the unconditioned source of all values, our attitude is one of faith: it represents our practical demands and spiritual needs, and not a logical inference. No basis on which our theoretical argument might proceed could give this result as a logical conclusion.

It may be well to guard against a misconception here. It is sometimes said that faith begins where reason ends, and that faith and reason are two mutually exclusive attitudes of the subject. The result is to import a kind of dualism into the religious consciousness, which is supposed to follow reason up to a point and then to abandon it for a knowledge of a totally different kind. A method like this is wrong in theory, nor would it work in practice. Faith and reason, instead of being mutually exclusive, imply one another: in every phase of human experience both are involved, and the difference is only one of the degree in which either element is present. Science, for example, depends more on reason than faith, and religion more on faith than reason; yet in either case the two elements are there. The scientific man has faith in the power of thought to explicate the problem on which he is engaged, and he believes in the value of the hypothesis he is striving to verify. He also trusts what he cannot demonstrate, namely, that nature will exhibit in the future the uniformity she has done in the past. The religious man, again, trusts reason as an essential aspect of his self-consciousness, and when faith has made assumptions which reason shows to be inconsistent, he discards these assumptions. He recognises the claim of reason in his postulate that the world-view of religion must not be one that contradicts thought. *Credo quia absurdum est* strikes the note of fanaticism, and does not express a normal and enlightened religious outlook. But in the nature of the case the religious mind sees more clearly than the scientific, that for us there will always be a non-rational residuum in experience, and that the problem of rationality would lose its meaning if there were not always something given to rationalise. This residuum meets us both on the subjective and the objective side of experience, and its existence is implied in the character of human knowledge, which is always growing and never complete.

I cannot however accept the theory that reason is a purely secondary and superficial aspect of the religious consciousness, the submissive slave of feeling who finds reasons for what we believe on instinct simply "because it has to find them." The tendency which exists at present to identify religion with a supra-rational body of beliefs, which have their source and authority in the depths of the feeling-life, would, if generally accepted and acted on, prove fatal to the best interests of religion itself. Religions which are hostile to philosophy are unprogressive, as we see in the case of Mohammedanism. And if the argument in this chapter is correct, thinking is in a special degree the source of religious development. Self-consciousness, of which thought is an integral aspect, always demands to be in harmony with itself, and this is impossible if the content of religion contradicts thought. The very endeavour which the votaries of an ancient faith make to explain and defend it against the pressure of new ideas is an implicit acknowledgment of the principle. The work of thought on the content of religion is the great stimulus to progress, as it is the guarantee that a religion will neither drift into obscurantism nor lose its vitality under a dead weight of tradition. In other words the thinking aspect of the religious consciousness secures that religion will take a deeper meaning with progress in self-consciousness. For when a living religion finds itself at discord with reason, it sets to work to overcome the antagonism by means of a fresh and significant development.

CHAPTER VI

THE WILL IN RELIGION: THE DEVELOPMENT OF THE CULT

In a former chapter we have touched on the general psychological problem involved in the nature of the Will. We noted the objections which had been raised against the treatment of Will as a special aspect of the psychical life. These objections were founded on the fact that some form of will-activity is involved in all psychical process, while the activity cannot be directly apprehended as such, but is only reported to consciousness in terms of feelings and ideas. Admitting this, we nevertheless found that if psychology is to explain as well as describe it must deal with Will as an essential factor in mental experience. The obligation to follow this course is more patent on the highest levels of spiritual development where there is explicit differentiation of functions, and the Will is to a certain extent contrasted with Intellection and Feeling. And the distinction between the theoretical and practical point of view, if not absolute, has still a relative justification, and it must be taken into account in trying to understand the significance of man's spiritual development. Especially does the outwardly directed activity of the developed will react on the individual and social character, and the explanation of the latter phenonena must come more directly and intimately from the voluntary side of man's nature. Or, to put it otherwise, at the highly differentiated stage of personal life volition enters into relations of action and reaction with the other psychical processes which cannot be ignored if we are to offer something more than a merely external treatment of spiritual evolution. The rational, the mystical, and the moral attitudes in religion, as they alternately come to the front and recede in religious history, cannot be understood apart from the distinctive aspects of the psychological life and the personality which comprehends and sustains them. To appreciate them duly we must recognise that they connect themselves more particularly with the intellectual, emotional, and volitional sides of our nature. And whether you hold that the primacy belongs to Reason or to Will, you have to accept these three working factors, acting and reacting, if you are to gain an inward view of the development of religion. In other words the distinction is necessary in the interests of psychological explanation : its ontological validity is another question.

At present there is little danger of forgetting the practical side of the religious consciousness. The trend of philosophic thought in recent years has been to accentuate the volitional factor in human experience at the expense of the intellectual. The movement began with the primacy accorded to the Practical Reason in the Kantian philosophy, and it was helped on its way by the work of Fichte, and more particularly of Schopenhauer. From the field of psychology it received powerful reinforcement when psychologists came to recognise the active aspect of experience involved in selective interest and attention. Voluntaristic psychology is in the ascendant at present, and as a working method it has produced excellent results. Supported by the psychologist, th philosopher is making increased claims for the will, and seeks to draw into its sphere what once seemed securely within the domain of the intellect. Take, for illustration the following utterances of Prof. Paulsen. "On a large view of life and its forms we say the will is the primary and constant factor, the intelligence the secondary and variable." "What dominates the world of ideas is interest, which is will." "The understanding makes no ideals and has no feeling for them, value is a category of the will."[1] And these dicta are symptomatic of a general movement of thought. In the region of Epistemology the vigorous Pragmatist thinkers insist on translating the idea of truth into terms of working-value, and discard the intellectual solution :—

"Was fruchtbar ist, allein ist wahr."

And in theology the Ritschlian School, which has been active for a generation, is in strong sympathy with voluntarism, and assigns to practical value-judgments a central and all-important function in providing a basis for theological construction.

Though we cannot agree that reason is the second-rate and subordinate thing which it seems to be to some apostles of the new movement, this does not prevent us from recognising elements of value in the contentions of Pragmatists and Ritschlians. The notion of "working-value" is certainly of great importance to the religious consciousness, and in the early stages of religion it is the only criterion men have of the validity of their beliefs. In primitive culture the sole test of religious ideas must be the way in which they respond to man's needs and help him to realise his ends. The savage discards his

[1] Vid. *Einleitung in die Philosophie*, 1899, pp. 121–123.

etish because it will not "work"; and, to use a phrase of Dr. Schiller's, "Religion is the magic which works." Nor does the test of practical experience lose its value even in the highest form of religion. But in the fully developed self-consciousness thinking asserts its claims and reacts on the practical valuations. The worth of a religion for life is here modified by the degree in which it is consistent with reason; and that its value-judgments enter into a coherent world-view is an element in the total satisfaction of the self. The satisfaction sought, that is to say, is not purely and exclusively practical. No doubt a religion which works well will not decay. But a condition of its working well will be that it is not at discord with thought, and, if it works badly, the reason may be that it is out of harmony with the scientific knowledge of the age.

With these preliminary remarks I turn to the special problem before us, which is the part played by the will in the development of religion.

The religious consciousness is something inward, but it is an inward state which normally demands objective expression. In this it differs from an attitude of æsthetic contemplation which rests in the pure enjoyment of the object. To have value, says Tiele, a religious conception must proceed from an emotion and give an impulse to the will. A direction of the will is essential to piety, and a religion which does not express itself in acts loses its vitality: the constant interaction of inward and outward is implied in the growth of spiritual personality. The inner assurance that faith, as the subjective religious state, is in contact with reality depends very much on the degree in which faith transfuses itself with life and embodies itself in action. Even a mystical or contemplative piety cannot altogether dispense with an activity

of the will, though it be only in the negative directio
of repelling the intrusions of sense. And it is usuall
associated with some form of ascetic practice, som
endeavour to discipline the unruly desires which obscur
the higher vision.

The psychical effects of the activity of the will may b
conveniently regarded in three aspects: its effect o
feeling, on belief, and on the growth of personality.

(*a*) The influence of feeling on the will is, of course
more important in religion than the reaction of will
activity on feeling. Yet the latter point ought not to b
ignored. Psychologists have noted the fact that we ca
excite feeling by adopting the attitude peculiar to it.
And the dramatic art offers an illustration how an emotional mood may be reproduced, partially at least, through
the performance of the acts associated with it. In th
earlier stages of culture this feature is no doubt mor
prominent than in the later, where the feelings are to a
greater degree within the control of the self. The savage,
for instance, knows how to prepare for battle by dances
and mimic warfare, which beget the fierce passions that
carry him fearlessly into the deadly strife. Religious
feelings are engendered by active participation in the
ceremonies of religion, and in this way an individual
may be visited by a feeling-mood which he neither
expected nor perhaps desired. Nevertheless it would not
be correct to say that phases of religious emotion, such
as we have described in a former chapter, are created by
doing certain things. For the acts are the expression of
the feelings in the first instance; but at the same time
the energetic activity of the will reacts on the feelings and
intensifies them. The wilder emotions of savage or
semi-savage religion would otherwise be impossible; and,

[1] Höffding, *Psychology*, Eng. Trans., 1896, p. 332.

as in the case of the shaman and sorcerer, they are deliberately induced. In general, the effect of volitional activity is not so much to create as to strengthen and intensify religious feeling. A man's feelings prompt him to worship, but if he never worshipped at all the springs of spiritual emotion would dry up. Pious feeling is nourished by practical expression.

(*b*) The reactionary effect of voluntary activity on belief is important. The ordinary individual's beliefs are judgments on which he is prepared to act if need be; and, as a rule, it is true that beliefs which are not acted on in some way die a natural death. Belief in God, for example, which is never expressed in purposes and reflected in acts, is a name for an opinion that carries no living value. It cannot be doubted that the stated acts of worship and service, forming part of every religion, have gone to strengthen and develop religious belief: and the condition of half-belief in which an individual may participate at the outset naturally tends to pass into full belief at the end. The constant translation of the idea into act invests it with definiteness, and induces the feeling-tone associated with reality. As has been truly said, the decisive adoption and carrying out of a thought clears the whole mental atmosphere. If probability be not, as Butler held, the guide of life, still we may and sometimes must act on probabilities; but in the normal course of things these will grow into certainties if we continue steadily to act upon them. Men of action may not be men of intellectual power, but they are commonly men of strong belief. Prof. W. James has some suggestive words on this subject which are worth quoting. "We need only in cold blood act as if the thing were real, and keep acting as if it were real, and it will infallibly end by growing into such a connexion with our life that it will become real."[1] That there is substantial truth in this remark it would not be difficult to prove. For instance the steady performance of prescribed acts and the rigorous discipline of the will—*sicut cadaver*—in the Society of Jesus, have gone to produce an intense and powerful, if narrow, system of belief.[2] And it often happens that the priest who, at the beginning of his career, is troubled by sceptical doubts, as he grows into the life of the churchly system and faithfully performs its offices from day to day, finds his doubts slowly dissolve and ends as an orthodox member of the class to which he belongs. Such a process need not spring from self-interest: it may be a genuine psychological development where the activity of the will establishes a dominant interest, which, in its turn, defines and consolidates a real body of beliefs. In the normal man ideas bound up with practical activity can usually oust hostile ideas which are the pure product of reflexion. For the former have struck deep and wide-spreading roots in the personal life.

(*c*) The development of the whole personality is intimately connected with volitional activity. In the psychological history of the individual the consciousness of the self, as persisting through changing experience, is closely associated in its growth with the active interest which links the past to the present. Interest forms the abiding line of reference by means of which experience is ordered and valued, and the continuity of its personal history is realised by the self. In the production of this interest practical activity is essential; the ends which are involved are ends for the will; they would be meaningless were man not a being capable of purposive effort.

[1] *Principles of Psychology*, vol. ii., p. 321.

[2] With this compare a well-known saying of Pascal. Speaking of the use of holy water and the repetition of masses, he adds, "*Naturellment même, cela vous fera croire et vous abêtira.*"

Through the interest binding the past and future to the present, man develops into a being of large significance, whose mental life is encircled by a wide horizon. This growth in self-consciousness makes possible the activity of the reflective will whereby the self establishes order among the conative tendencies, and brings the impulses and desires into subjection to larger and more stable ends. So the will, by organising the experienced content of the self, achieves that increased definition in the form of experience which we term personality. Were man not an active being, not merely receiving experience, but in so doing reacting on it and moulding it to his purposes, he could not have taken the steps by which he advanced from the impulsive to the personal life. What is true of personal development in general of course holds true of the religious consciousness. Religion originates in practical needs, and it grows with the growth of these needs. The enlarged needs are the symptoms of an expansion of human nature. In this expansion man, restlessly seeking his own satisfaction, plays an essential part. And he contributes to his advance in spiritual self-consciousness by the practical organisation of his religious life. But the religious feelings and beliefs on which men act require a common centre round which to gather; and the identity which is implied in social and historic growth calls for an objective basis on which to work. Institutional religion is a presupposition of personal religion. It is through the organisation of religious practice in the cult, that religion secures a basis on which its development may proceed with the development of the social life. For the cult is the living centre of interest through which the historic continuity of a religion is made possible.

I take, then, the religious cultus in its varying

character as the expression of the volitional elemen in religion, as the manifestation of the religiou consciousness in action. I am well aware, of course that worship is not simply a revelation of will : it is als an expression of belief and emotion. And the truth is that no psychical factor is ever given in complet isolation from the others. But acts of worship ar primarily acts of volition, and in studying them w become best acquainted with the function of will i religious development.

Primitive religion in its acts reveals the genera features of primitive psychical life, a subject to whic reference has already been made. Emotional an impulsive features predominate, and the reflective wil which adjusts means to distant ends, and subdue momentary desires to a larger purpose, remains un-developed. Accordingly religious acts at the beginning of religion are simple and unorganised, the naïve expres-sions of the feelings which are uppermost in men's minds Prominent is the desire of the worshippers to lin themselves to the gods in a helpful communion, an so to secure the ends they seek. Sometimes this take the crude but dramatic form of doing what the god are supposed to do. When the god for instance i an animal, the savage, at the religious dance, will adop the gait and utter the cries of the animal to show hi sympathy with the deity. "In rites which are no strictly sacrifices, we notice men seeking to sympathis with their gods in what the gods are doing, and to tak a share in it by doing similar things themselves. Th Christmas and Easter fires in pagan times connected wit the worship of the sun are examples of this, and man other instances might be cited."[1] Of this character to

[1] A. Menzies, *History of Religion*, p. 67.

are the rejoicing and mourning which celebrate the birth and death of nature or the decay and resurrection of the spirit of vegetation. These motives underlie the cults of Dionysus, Attis, and Osiris, so widely spread in the old world. The rites themselves do not belong to a primitive age, but they express a conception of worship which is old and reaches back into early culture. They reveal that desire to be in touch with a life, large and divine, a desire which is found in the lowest as well as in the highest manifestations of the religious spirit. The Mass, for example, is a dramatic representation of the supernatural facts of redemption, designed to impart to the worshipping participants the spiritual memories and the mysterious efficacy of a divine sacrifice.

The importance of the cultus as a religious representation and means of expression naturally depends on its being organised; for only through definite and recognised forms can common feelings and beliefs find adequate utterance. Men soon began to organise their religious acts; and these, under the spell of custom, gained fixity and sanctity. In early religion it was the acts which counted, and the motives which prompted them were necessarily material. Plato, in the *Euthyphro*, defines the current idea of piety as a kind of science of asking and receiving.[1] The savage gives to the gods that he may receive from them, and the saying that "gifts persuade the gods" conveys a primeval belief. This idea is connected with one of the most important acts of the cult, the giving of sacrifice to the gods. That all sacrifice was, as the late Dr. Robertson Smith contended, in its primitive form a

[1] 14 D.
ἐπιστήμη ἄρα αἰτήσεως καὶ δόσεως θεοῖς ὁσιότης ἂν εἴη ἐκ τούτου τοῦ λόγου.

social meal which men shared with their gods, may not be true, though this was a familiar feature. But that some sacrifices were originally gifts pure and simple is likely enough, and corresponds to the motives which inspired savage worship. For whether the primitive barbarian sought to strengthen his fellowship with his deity by eating with him the sacrificial food, or offered to him a gift merely, in either case the object was the same, namely some good to the worshipper himself. Where totemism prevailed and the totem-animal was sacrificed and eaten on solemn occasions, sacrifice assumes a sacramental significance, and the idea of a participation by members of the tribe in the divine life is prominent. But though the sacrificial act had not always the same meaning, it was always the central and most sacred part of the cultus, where the contact between the human and the divine was closest.

The other main feature of early worship was prayer. The idea of communion with the gods can hardly be said to be present in primitive prayers. At first prayer was probably an appeal to the spirits in moments of stress and danger, and was not a stated form of worship. In the lower culture where deities are spirits, not personal beings, the magical element was closely associated with these utterances. Belief in the power of the word prevailed, and under the spell of this idea prayer became a fixed formula which was intoned and had a magical efficacy. The interpenetration of prayer and magic was exceedingly common among savage peoples, nor is there any hard and fast line of demarcation between spells, incantations and prayers. And where the greater gods have grown out of a soil deeply permeated by spiritism, the lower or magical attitude intrudes itself beside the higher. An excellent illustration of this is furnished by the prayers of ancient Babylonia, where at one time we hear the voice of spiritual religion confessing sin and at another the magic formula which has power over the gods. The Vedic poet, too, can say that "the faithful find Agni when they have recited the spells." The evolution of prayer from the sensuous to the spiritual depends on the progressive elimination of the magical idea and the growth of the notion of spiritual communion. Prayer and sacrifice, it may be added, are the most constant and outstanding features of worship.

The body of acts embraced in primitive worship was not great, but it served to move the feelings and to sustain belief. Feast and dance, sacrificial offering and prayer, these kept man in mind of the mysterious powers around him, and the religious acts which he performed helped to make the bond between him and his gods more real to him. The age of doubt was not yet: the performance of the acts was all-important, and each member of the tribe or group shared in the doing of them in virtue of his membership. The cult in which every individual had his part was a visible expression of common beliefs and feelings, and served to cement the social bond. This constant practice of the community, handed down from the fathers to the children, and acquiring the sanctity and authority of age, made the ideas embodied in the cult strong and persistent. The savage is naturally conservative in his beliefs; but even the civilised man is inhospitable to new ideas which contradict his consistent ways of acting.

The great social changes which led to a reorganisation of belief and the development of a conscious instead of an unconscious religion, or piety of custom, have been discussed. Personal gods demand a larger and more enlightened form of service, and the impulsive and ecstatic tendencies of primitive worship must give place to a more stable activity of the will. In a polytheistic system the gods possess individual character and attributes, and they have to be worshipped in ways that correspond to their character. Departmental deities, with definite qualities and spheres of activity, impose obligations on those who reverence them which are not possible under the rule of a colourless spiritism. Magic may control the capricious spirits, but a personal god who makes definite claims must be served in higher ways. A deity who protects the city will expect civic virtue in his votaries, and a god of war will demand valour in battle from his worshippers. The magical ideas associated with prayer and sacrifice, if they are not expelled, are still modified by the fact that the relations between the worshipper and the worshipped are personal, and the god commands as well as hears requests and accepts offerings. And in the piety which means obedience to divine behests the idea of religious service assumes a wider scope than ritual performance. Duty to the gods begins to widen out towards a way of life, and religion to become a loyalty to a divine bond.[1] But the focus and rallying point of religious activity continue to be the cult, which, however, develops features in harmony with the enlarged ideas of the gods. In national polytheism the gods break away from their immediate connexion with nature : and, though retaining traces of their naturalistic origin, they are at least partially raised above the world, over some aspect of which they are supposed to bear rule. Not in stream or tree but on the summit of cloud-capped Olympus the gods of Greece had their home. With the removal of the

[1] But here as elsewhere the persistence of the lower idea alongside the higher is noteworthy. In Greece, for example, during the classical period, to the common people piety (εὐσέβεια) still meant the careful performance of the ritual acts.

deity from the common haunts of men, the way of access to him grows less easy and the cult assumes more elaborate forms. Worship loses its early simplicity, and the media through which communion with the unseen powers is realised become complex. Temples and altars, places separated from the common world, are consecrated to worship and religious offerings ; and an image of the god within the hallowed precincts helps to lift the pious mind toward the divine object. The due performance of the ritual is entrusted to a priesthood, a select class qualified for their office by superior knowledge and sanctity. In this way the element of mystery which is essential to religion is deepened, while, on the other hand, the practical demands which religion imposes are increased. A well-organised and impressive cult thus becomes the means whereby religion strikes its roots deep into the national and social life. The cultus is the visible expression of the religious spirit in which all the citizens share, and through which they give utterance to their common hopes and aspirations. It is on this institutional basis that man rises to the consciousness of himself as permanently religious, and comes to recognise that religion demands a constant activity of the will.

There is one notion associated often with the religious cult on which we have not yet dwelt, but which deserves special notice because of its extraordinary influence in some religions. It is the notion of purity or holiness. The idea reaches back into primitive culture, and at first was merely external in its significance. Certain conditions of the body were supposed to disqualify the individual for the time being for religious fellowship, for participation in the rites and ceremonies of religion. More especially were the processes connected with generation, birth and death regarded as rendering the member of the tribe impure. By a natural association the idea was extended to certain substances as a source of defilement. Blood in particular was held to be impure, and contact with it involved a taint. The idea was magical, not ethical, and was rooted in animism and the belief in evil spirits. To meet this danger a cathartic ritual was evolved. "A dangerous spirit was supposed to reside in the impure thing and to be evoked by the unclean act; the potency which in the primeval stage of feeling had been perhaps regarded merely as something mysteriously baneful and 'uncanny,' now becomes personal and intelligible and can be dealt with and exorcised by certain efficacious rules."[1] This notion of ritual purity, crude and magical in its origin, was the germ out of which the important idea of ethical purity slowly developed. Yet the way to the higher idea was long and difficult, for out of the earlier belief grew in the first instance the conception of ceremonial religion, with its fixed rites of cleansing and rules for observance. The cathartic ideal was prominent in Judaism and remarkably so in the later Persian religion, where it enveloped the individual life in a network of regulations, to keep which must have been a severe discipline. The ritually important, which to our eyes seems trivial, blends with what is morally valuable, and is placed on the same footing. The Vendidad contains a multitude of prescriptions for the avoidance of defilement, as well as rules for penitence and self-mortification; and the weighty moral precept is set side by side with the purely ceremonial injunction. The universe under this system, as a writer wittily remarks, becomes "a battery of overcharged spiritual electricity," and the individual is threatened with harm from every quarter. Then most of us are

[1] Farnell, *The Evolution of Religion*, 1905, p. 103.

familiar with the "Touch not, taste not, handle not" of the Jewish Law, and the growth of the Law into a tyranny of sheer observance in Pharisaism. Judaism and Parseeism are ceremonial religions, but they may equally be termed legal religions; for the ceremonial system, composite in its origin, was in both cases referred to the divine Will as its source and authority. Mohammedanism, though it gives less prominence to the cathartic ideal, is also a legal religion where the will of God is divinely revealed in a body of rules binding on all believers. In Islam, as its Five Pillars indicate, obedience to the law is the main thing, and the performance of the act counts for most. Encompassed by divine commands the individual must become the instrument of God; and in repeating the carefully regulated prayers, by fasting and giving alms according to prescription, the soul mounts upward to everlasting bliss. The note of ceremonial and legal religions is a complex system of observances by which man and society discharge their religious duty.

Some remarks on the psychological significance of legal and ceremonial religion, and the part it plays in spiritual development, may be made. A notable feature is the extension of the cult with the strengthening of its influence. The careful performance of manifold ritual demands both separates the faithful from the profane world and acts as a strong bond of union. Moreover, legal religion promotes the conception of a more full and varied activity of the will in the service of the deity. For the prescriptions of the law extend beyond worship in the temple, and the rules of purity hold in the home and in the market-place. Hence the idea of religion is broadened to mean a service which spreads itself over the field of human life and an obligation that a man carries with him. And as one would expect in faiths so active and practical in their expression, ceremonial systems produce a vigorous and well-defined religious character and a strong if narrow form of belief.[1] The defects from which this type of religion suffers are the defects of its qualities. The stress is so laid on the external will-activity that the inner side of religion falls into the background ; and the mere doing of the acts, apart from the spirit, is credited with a value of its own. No ceremonial religion has been able to resist the fallacy of the *opus operatum*, the efficacy of the deed itself. Since the ceremonial acts possess intrinsic value, that value increases with repetition : the accent is on the performance rather than on the motive. With the decadence of the inner side of piety religion becomes formal and mechanical, and hostile to progress. The religious bond is externalised and so materialised. The relation of man to God is interpreted under the form of a contract, and in the fulfilment of the contract good works are valuable instruments on the human side. To balance the merit thus acquired on earth there is a corresponding reward in heaven ; while those who fail to perform receive the proper punishment. The whole domain of religion becomes impregnated with the atmosphere of commerce, and good deeds are construed under the form of religious assets. Hence the Pharisee computed his good deeds and proclaimed his desert, and the Persian knew to atone for his sins and keep his place secure in heaven by inflicting on himself the necessary number of stripes. In legal religions eschatology is prominent, and this is quite in keeping with their fundamental tendency. But the sensuous pictures of the bliss of the faithful and the doom of the unbeliever hereafter have

[1] The persistence of the Jewish and Mohammedan creeds, though it owes something to racial gifts, has also to be explained through the character of the cultus.

little to do with ethical justice. This triumph of the legal over the ethical, of the ceremonial over the spiritual, by ultimately mechanising religion brings about its dissolution. Progress can only come through a radical reconstruction by means of which the relation of man to God is spiritually conceived. Psychologically the religion of the externally directed will is a one-sided expression of human character, and suffers the doom of all that is abstract and partial. It ceases to satisfy the spiritual nature of man, and like Mysticism and Rationalism has to make way for some more complete embodiment of the religious life.

When the spiritual forces in a race are not dead, the religion of ceremony, grown mechanical, calls forth a reaction. Buddhism, early Christianity, and mediæval Mysticism show the human spirit asserting the claims of the inward life against a system of external observance. Often enough, as in many forms of mysticism, the reaction is one-sided like the system against which it is a protest: for the religion of mere deed you have a religion of mere feeling. In these cases the media of communion provided by the cultus lose their value, for the human soul, withdrawing into itself, finds itself "alone with the alone." Likewise when the idea of redemption, conceived as a deliverance from the bondage of the flesh, is accentuated the importance of ritual worship naturally declines. This is seen in Buddhism and Neo-Platonism where the way of salvation lies within, and chiefly demands a negative attitude of the will to the disturbing elements of sense. Piety becomes individual and ascetic. Here the realisation of religion as a living social bond, expressed in worship and carried out in service, is weakened. The monastic type of virtue prevails over that of a fruitful and helpful life.

The higher religious ideal demands an ethical will whose outward activity is the expression of inward principles. A complete religion implies a true union of inward and outward which gives meaning to life; for the details of conduct are organised by the central purpose, and the works reveal the spirit within. Hence the ideal given to the will, though it contain a negative element, must be positive and afford full scope to personal character by embracing the natural and social aspects of human nature. In other words, though man turns from this world to find his end and goal in a supramundane Good, he must return to the common earth and strive to bring his temporal existence-form into harmony with the divine ideal. Only through this complementary return movement does the religious spirit attain its full personal unfolding. Here the question might be put, whether at the stage of spiritual religion the cult can still retain its function and value. The substance of religion is just the spiritual life, so it may be said. Worship in the ordinary sense is now no longer essential, however necessary it may have been on lower levels of development. To one who fully accepted the Kantian view, that religion is no more than the recognition of moral duties as divine commands, the conclusion might seem natural. The adequacy of Kant's definition of religion need not be discussed at present. But it must never be forgotten that religion is not merely an individual vocation but a social bond. In all culture the individual and society develop *pari passu*, and the social aspect of religious duty can never be separated from the personal. Were religion universally construed as a purely individual concern it would soon cease to be a concern to the individual. The problem therefore is, whether the social aspect of religion can be maintained and made effective apart from the cultus, for, if not, the individual side cannot flourish. I cannot but think there is substantial truth in the following statement :—"As the scientific and moral so also the religious consciousness could not permanently maintain its specific character without a determinate method of giving it visible expression, and without the support received from the recognition of the community."[1] The religious cultus really flows from the nature of religion itself; and if we name the inner side of religion piety, then piety only preserves its vigour where it expresses itself in outward acts of worship. Religion is everywhere and always a bond of social union, and the common cult is the means whereby the collective spiritual consciousness comes to visible and definite utterance. For the higher spiritual life in the individual has its roots in the spiritual life of the community and grows out of it; and it is through the common spirit expressed in worship that religion in the normal individual is fostered and sustained. The organised cultus represents the religious feeling and ideal of a society, and by taking part in it the individual is made to realise his membership in a larger life and encouraged to faithful endeavour in the upward way. I venture in this connexion to quote the excellent remark of Höffding, the more noteworthy that there can be no suspicion of *parti pris* in the writer: "In the worship of the church the great drama of the race is represented, and the individual gains here a wide horizon for the contemplation and valuation of his own life."[2] To this we might add, he gains an inward quickening of the spirit and a practical impulse to the will which are equally important.

The problem in the higher religions is to make the material media of worship an adequate means of repre-

[1] Siebeck, *Religionsphilosophie*, p. 290.
[2] *Religionsphilosophie*, p. 318.

senting the ethical spirit. The cult is the most conservative side of religion, and in point of development always lingers behind the advance of spiritual ideas. Hence even in the most developed religion lower elements cling to the cult-forms, a heritage from the distant past. A progressive spiritual faith has to try to eliminate old sacrificial and magical ideas, and to bring the forms of worship into accordance with its own spirit. At the best indeed material media can be but imperfect instruments of the spirit : the line of progress will lie in treating them more and more as suggestive symbols, not as possessing intrinsic value or as efficacious in themselves. Sacramentarianism, although it claim a divine sanction, has in reality more affinity with the magic of primitive religion : it is in substance a survival, not a true development of the religious idea.[1]

The religion which is the most deeply inward and personal requires the fullest and most comprehensive outward expression. A hard and fast distinction between the sacred and the secular must give way, and the spirit which is active in worship must carry its activity into the wider fields of life. For piety reveals itself in large forms of service, and the spiritual will has to find content for the working out of the ideal in the manifold duties and relationships of human society. The religious will is in the fullest sense an ethical will : and yet it is something more, for it recognises that its source and goal are in a supramundane Good. This Supreme Value is made sure to it by faith. The standard of its valuations is not of the earth earthy, but, as Plato might have said, the pattern that is "laid up in heaven." The perfection of its working

[1] Sacramentarianism, it need hardly be said, does not belong to the origins of Christianity. A motive to its development lay in the needs and habits of thought of the pagan races who entered the Church.

will lie in the completeness with which it brings the highest ideal to bear on the common details of conduct.

It would be hard to over-estimate the importance of this volitional activity in building up and consolidating the spiritual personality. Character, it has been said, is a well-formed will, and this is true of religious character. They who do the divine Will, says Scripture, "know the truth of the doctrine"; and faith and practical life are ever in close interaction. The old controversy about faith and works loses its meaning when you realise that both are aspects of one process, the one the inward, the other the outward side of the spiritual life. On the other hand, the individual will, in developing a spiritual personality, is dependent on the religious will in its social manifestations. It finds there recognised ways of self-expression, and receives direction and discipline. The organised life and practice of a religious community at once corrects and guides the practical ideal of its members. And the individual who enters on the religious life as a member of a religious society has to advance to the free development of that life in action, that he may rise to the fulness of spiritual personality. Neither by vision nor contemplation can the soul attain to the possession of its religious birthright, and faith only lives and thrives by being acted out.

Of course there is a danger both in the individual and social development of religion that the volitional and practical side may be exaggerated to the detriment of that spiritual harmony which is the true ideal. Yet the danger is no greater than in the cases of feeling and thought. The possible evil is obviously the externalising and mechanising of religion, and the consequent drying up of the springs of faith and emotion. When these things happen, then religion persists in virtue of its institutional embodiments, but its adherents content themselves with the performance of what convention and tradition prescribe in the way of action. And the decadence of the personal side of belief and feeling brings about a divorce between religion and life which is fateful in its consequences. The restoration of spiritual harmony must proceed from the reassertion of the inner side of religion, of piety in the heart. Only thus can the outward forms regain that vital content which makes them spiritually significant. And then the practical aspect of religion will come to its due : religious service will be the utterance of the spirit within, and on this the vigour of the inner life essentially depends.

CHAPTER VII

INTERACTION IN RELIGIOUS DEVELOPMENT

In the present chapter I propose to discuss certain general features of religious development with which there was no opportunity of dealing adequately in the preceding chapters. We have hitherto been chiefly occupied with the psychological factors of the religious consciousness, and with the part they severally play in the evolution of religion. But it still remains for us to consider the general influences which stimulate religious progress, and to note how the psychological factors interact in religious development. The standpoint of the survey will not transcend the sphere of psychology; but in the endeavour to give a broad presentation of the facts in the light of the principles behind them, the way will be prepared for an attempt to read their ultimate or philosophic meaning. No one factor or element in itself furnishes the key to the development of religion: in the process various elements act and react on one another; and he who would understand must cultivate a comprehensive vision, and think together the things he sees.

Development, whether in the natural or spiritual sphere, is never a simple process, and cannot be reduced to the working of a single force. A living germ or a spiritual principle will not unfold in isolation: it demands an environment which contains diverse elements. Through the complex constitution of the surrounding medium the organism is stimulated in definite ways, and in its turn it reacts on the environment and uses it in order to promote its own life and growth. The term Evolution, as applied to biological development, is not the name for a single and sufficient principle of explanation. Darwin himself postulated accidental variations on which the law of Natural Selection worked, and supplemented his main principle by the principles of the Transmission of acquired Characters and Sexual Selection. And while Weismann and many other scientists try to eliminate the hereditary principle in this instance, De Vries, on the other hand, has shown reasons for holding that, in the origin of species, Natural Selection is qualified by a principle of mutation or spontaneous variation of the type.[1] For our present purpose, however, it is sufficient to note that Evolution, as an interaction of organism and environment, is a complex process which involves different elements, and is not to be reduced to a single law which controls all the facts. The fallacy into which many fall is that of regarding Evolution as the mechanical product of the factors involved. Given a number of organisms acting and being acted on in a certain environment, the 'struggle for existence' which is the natural outcome of the situation is supposed to explain the development that ensues. But it is needful to remember that the 'struggle for existence' is not a condition impressed on living things from without; it is the expression of their own 'will to live.' Save for the inherent striving of the plant or animal to gain favourable terms of life, it would never come into competition with other plants and animals. Natural Selection, that is to say, is not a

[1] *Species and Varieties: their Origin by Mutation*, 1905.

principle to which organisms are made subject, but a description of the way in which they come to limit one another through their own demands. And this central activity of the developing organism is apparent in another way. Each living thing exercises a continuous activity in order to maintain itself in life. In contrast to Natural Selection, where organisms compete with one another, and alongside of it, a process of Subjective Selection, to use Prof. Ward's phrase, is always going on whereby every kind of living thing extracts from a common environment the particular element it requires. Differences in type and a variety of elements in the environment are the conditions under which the principle of Subjective Selection is seen at work.

The importance of Subjective Selection appears in the fact that its range extends beyond the biological sphere. In psychological development the law of selective interest is of outstanding importance, and the idea of an evolution of mind caused by external forces acting upon it has not even a superficial plausibility. Knowledge is always a growth where the dominant factor is the active mind itself following the lead of interest. The problem becomes more difficult when we begin to apply the idea of development, as current language does, to special aspects or contents of the mind. For the tendency of speech is to endow religion, morality and art with a being of their own, and to regard them as having within them a principle of development apart from the mind in which they live and move and have their being. But we only need to put the question clearly to ourselves to realise that the principle of development does not lie in any given content of mind, in religion for example, but in the mind itself as a whole. For the particular content only lives as part of the larger whole, in this case the mind or conscious subject which comprehends and informs all its elements. If we are to speak accurately, it is not religion that develops but man as a religious being: consequently, the active principle in every form of religious development is man himself as a spiritual subject.

The question has been raised in an earlier chapter, how far it is admissible to transfer the notion of a dominant type from the natural to the spiritual world.[1] And we pointed out that the environment with which a plant or animal type interacts in order to unfold itself in a process of growth is not quite analogous to the relation which a certain aspect of conscious life bears to the other aspects. In the latter case the interaction is more intimate, falling as it does entirely within the activity of the one subject. The analogy of a natural type persisting through changes is suggestive, but it must not be pressed. A plant, for instance, can maintain its typical features despite a considerable alteration in its surroundings: and this degree of independence in one of the factors does not seem to exist in the case of interaction between two mental contents. As an illustration consider the way in which the moral and the religious consciousness interact, and note how the former influences the direction in which the latter evolves. The problem might be put thus: Are we to assert that a specific religion preserves a certain typical character through all the interactions to which it is subject in the course of its evolution? I do not think we are warranted in saying this, nor is there any good reason for maintaining that all features which emerge in the growth of a religion must have been involved in its beginning. In the cases of Egypt, Babylonia and Greece one could not point to any single factor controlling their long history from crude spiritism or fetishism to developed

[1] Chap. I., pp. 14-16.

polytheism or pantheism. No one epithet can describe, nor any single feature express, the character of an age-long growth of the spirit, where manifold influences have been constantly at work. The religions which come nearest to presenting a persistent type are those which owe their rise to personal founders whose life and genius left a deep impress on men. Such are Buddhism, Mohammedanism and Christianity. On the other hand, it is true that the genius of a people and the character of its culture give a colouring to its religion which lasts from generation to generation. The Greek's love of beauty, the ascetic temper of the Hindu, and the utilitarian disposition of the Roman are reflected in their religions. Still here we are not dealing with a definitely religious principle but with a broad feature of racial culture in which religion shares. If you search for a supreme and specifically religious principle which has continuously unfolded itself within that culture, and which explains each phase of its religious history, you are not likely to find it. On the contrary you will probably be impressed with the conviction of the complex character of religious growth and of the variety in the origins and values of the beliefs which it embraces. Hinduism, for instance, stands for a system which can find room for all degrees of difference between a crude polydaemonism and a refined pantheism. And the religion of every people presents to us the spectacle of higher and lower ideas embraced under a common name and appealing to diverse aspects of human nature.

In one respect the analogy of organic growth can convey to us a suggestive thought in regard to religious development. For organic growth is through a process of assimilation in which the plant or animal absorbs and transmutes the elements it selects from its environment. And religious growth, as distinguished from mere syncretism, depends on the capacity to assimilate. This capacity in its turn depends on whether a religion with a specific character has a living hold on the minds of men, and is the embodiment of a vigorous faith. Then it represents a vital structure of the spirit that can choose and absorb those elements with which it has an elective affinity, and which are able to enrich its own life. In this ability to select and transmute ideas and beliefs which did not originally belong to it, so that they come to form part of its own organic substance, a religion gives the best proof of its inward vitality. Where this characteristic life is wanting interaction only brings about a syncretism, not a real fusion of elements. As an illustration we can point to the way in which the Hebrew people, at different stages in their history, assimilated beliefs drawn from Babylonian and Persian culture.[1] By so doing they enriched their own system of belief. The same seems to be true of Greek religion, at least in the formative period of its history prior to the fifth century B.C. The figures of Artemis and Aphrodite, as they come before us in the Hellenic period, owe some of their features, especially in the latter case, to oriental influence; but they have been gradually purged of ruder elements and finally transformed by the spirit of Greek religion. So, too, the cult of Dionysus, originally an Asiatic worship, though orgiastic in its nature, was purified in Hellenic lands and had its wilder traits subdued. In somewhat marked contrast is the case of the old Roman religion. It never possessed the assimilative power to transmute foreign materials and set the impress of its own character upon them: and, being weak in constructive strength, it was correspondingly feeble in its capacity to

[1] The sources of the Old Testament conception of Creation and the Sabbath were Babylonian, but the raw material of these beliefs was worked into a form in harmony with the spirit of Hebrew religion.

resist the intrusion of alien elements. Roman religion from 200 B.C. presented the spectacle of a loose amalgamation, where gods imported from the East stood side by side with native Roman deities with which they had no affinity. Here was a religion which was susceptible of changes and additions, but which had not the inward vitality to reconstruct what it borrowed and develop by assimilation. In a broad way the capacity of a religion to develop with that whole of culture in which it is an element is a test of its spiritual fitness.

In dealing with interaction as a condition of religious development we have to note that the form and significance of that interaction vary with the stages of development. To put it otherwise, the assimilative process has not quite the same meaning and value at the lowest stage of religion as at the highest. A feature of religious development, as we saw, was the movement from instinctive to conscious, and finally to self-conscious religion; and this denotes an advance in importance of the subjective factor. The result is to bring the other elements which contribute to progress into a more intimate relation with self-consciousness and to make them more dependent upon it. Religion of course is never the outcome of external influences pure and simple; the mind's reaction on these influences is always essential. Still it is none the less true that in the lower culture the elements which work for religious progress, being natural rather than spiritual, have a certain independence and bear fewer marks of the activity of the subject. The lowest religions show the traces of instinctive reactions on man's part to impressions coming from without, when as yet he is unconscious of his own share in giving these impressions their character and value. Consequently the influences which make for development seem to belong to the outward order of things, and man appears to be moulded by them rather than to mould them. The strengthening of the subjective factor of necessity brings about a change, and with the growth of mind and reflective will man begins to play a conscious part in shaping his own destiny. He rises above the tyranny of circumstances and sheer terror of the unseen, and asserts his right to select the objects which are to interest his mind and to influence his conduct. With his rise above an immediate dependence on nature man becomes free to develop his higher faculties; and in the civilised life he surrounds himself with the ideal worlds of science and art, of law and morality. In this process of transformation the divine object is translated from the natural to the spiritual sphere, and man's attitude to it is less and less influenced by features and events in his external environment. The factors which are to affect the development of religion must now partake of an ideal character, and they are recognised by the subject to bear the impress of his own activity. It is not, for instance, at all likely that changes in habitation, mode of life, and external fortune will materially affect religious ideas and beliefs among the highly civilised nations of the world. The interplay of spiritual factors is of most importance, and slowly modifies the religious outlook. The forces which are influencing the religion of Western peoples proceed from science, morality and philosophy, all of which are closely related elements within the life of culture. And the problem of spiritual progress is the problem of their harmonious relation one to another. The constant and prevailing fact in this evolution is the psychological unity of the individual and the race, a unity that is revealed in all the stages of human society. On this postulate rests every attempt man makes to retrace in thought the history of the past and to appreciate its meaning. Progress demands interaction of factors; but interaction is only possible within a unity, in this case the unity of human nature which runs through all the vicissitudes of human experience. Take religion as it exists at any stage of culture, and you will find all the phenomena converge on the one centre, the common needs and desires of man,—needs and desires which are purified and elevated in the course of evolution but not fundamentally changed. Hence it is a true if not an exhaustive description of religious development to term it, as Tiele has done, a growth in self-consciousness.

After this general statement of principles let us turn to examine their working in the historical evolution of the religious consciousness. I shall confine myself to the consideration of the larger features.

The interactions which bring about development in the religions of the lower culture are mainly those which proceed from the physical and social environment. The need for change or modification of his religious beliefs came to primitive man through the stimulus of external circumstances, not through independent desire on his part. But the alteration in his surroundings impressed on him the necessity of such an alteration in his beliefs and practices as would secure their religious efficiency. Religious changes were precipitated by the migrations of primitive peoples and by the mingling of tribes. The local spirits and gods that were suitable in one habitation would require to be modified and supplemented in another, and an alteration in the relative pressure of the needs of life would work a like change in the relative prominence of particular deities. In the dim and unrecorded past these movements were in constant progress, and we know that all the historic races of antiquity migrated to their lands, where they mingled with the indigenous peoples. This is a process, however, which it is difficult to illustrate owing to the lack of materials for comparison. But in one instance at least we can indicate with some probability the influence of a new environment on the development of a race. The Aryan tribes whose religion is preserved for us in the Vedic Hymns were, at a period prior to the Vedic age, an undivided race with the Persians; and the two had continued one people after the separation of the other Indo-European groups from the parent stock. Linguistic and religious affinities make this clear. Yet how significant are the differences in the subsequent development of Hindu and Persian religion. And one can hardly doubt that the climate and life in India had much to do in changing the self-assertive spirit of the old Aryans—a spirit that is prominent in the Persian religion of conflict—into the quietism and mystical pantheism of Hinduism.

Especially must the interaction and blending of tribes have been provocative of religious growth. Contact with systems of religious belief and practice differing from their own undoubtedly exercised some quickening effect on the minds of primitive tribes, and made it less easy for them to rest with contented acquiescence in their own religious system. Against this we have to set the innate conservatism of tribal religion; but the religion of a conquering tribe in particular would acquire a prestige which helped it to penetrate the lines of defence. The conquest and absorption of a weaker tribe by a stronger meant a triumph for the religion of the conquerors, since the very fact of conquest pointed to the possession of gods more powerful or more propitious; and the myth that records the victory of one tribal god over another gives us a clue to the real circumstances out of which the story grew. Yet one form of belief seldom ousts another entirely; the religion of the victors is modified by that of the vanquished. In itself tribal religion has only the most limited capacity to evolve higher ideas, and the stimulus of contact with fresh forms of belief was needed to induce a developmental process. So one tribe acts on another, and belief, as the result of a fusion of elements, becomes more complex. This blending of cults was taking place at a stage in culture before the dawn of history; the process, we know, was in full progress in Egypt before the historic period. But the student of religion in trying to reconstruct this distant past has to depend largely on inference, for direct evidence is lacking. On general grounds, however, it is clear that only when the density of population brought about a constant interaction of tribes and peoples was there any significant development of culture, and so of religion. If the lands round the Eastern Mediterranean were the pioneers of culture, they were also the meeting place of races—and that at a date before the beginning of the Christian era greater than the space that separates us from it. Only now are we beginning to realise the movements of peoples and the inflow of conquering races which must have preceded the civilisations of Greece, Babylonia and Egypt. On the other hand, isolation is always unfavourable to the development of culture. "Where the nature of the country affords means of communication that facilitate this reciprocal action between nations, we see the civilisation of mankind fall earliest into a course of coherent progress; on the contrary, it has remained for thousands of years in the same uniform condition in regions whose boundaries, inhospitable and difficult to pass, have restricted the inhabitants to a constant employment of the same means to their ends and the same conditions of life."[1] Isolation then, whether caused by the nature of a country or the character of a race, is decidedly unfavour-

[1] Lotze, *Microcosmus*, Vol. II., p. 229. Eng. Trans.

able to any important development of the religious consciousness. The Australians, the Fuegians, and the Bushmen of South Africa are examples of tribes which have dwelt apart; and the poverty of their life is reflected in the poverty of their religious ideas. In the case of the individual it is important for his development that he should be brought into contact with new ideas and fresh social surroundings; and there is an analogy between the individual and a race of men. Fixity of habitation, aloofness, and scanty means of subsistence are usually more responsible for the low type of culture and religion we find in some savage tribes than defect in their original mental endowment.

Another factor which reacts on religious development is change in a people's way of life. The methods by which a group of human beings subsist exercise a controlling influence on their interests and desires, and so cannot but affect their religious ideas and actions. Hence a change in the mode of subsistence perforce induces a change in the religious outlook. The stage at which man gains his living by hunting is not compatible with any substantial advance in culture. For the life is uncertain, large spaces are needed in which to roam and search for food, and density of population is impossible; while the struggle for existence frequently brings about sanguinary conflicts between tribes. Under these conditions even a gifted race cannot emancipate itself from barbarism, as appears in the case of the Redskins of North America. The pastoral and nomadic life, though resembling that of hunters, yet represents an advance towards civilisation, inasmuch as it makes man less dependent on fortune and renders his existence more stable. The possession of herds and flocks modifies to some extent the primeval nature- and spirit-worship, and inspires man with a belief in the sanctity of the animals on which he depends. The nomadic background out of which the Persian religion developed is not obscurely indicated by the sacredness of the cow and the dog in the Avesta.[1] This reverence for domestic animals and a sense of their kinship both with gods and men are widespread among pastoral peoples. And, as the late Prof. Robertson Smith suggested, the pastoral stage may have brought about an expansion of the older totemism, where that obtained. "As the various totem clans began to breed cattle and live on their milk, they transferred to their herds the notions of sanctity and kinship which formerly belonged to species of wild animals, and thus the way was at once opened for the formation of religious and political communities larger than the old totem kins."[2] Be this as it may, it can, I think, hardly be doubted that a nomadic race, which connected its gods with the herds on which it depended for daily food, must have advanced towards the idea of its continuous dependence on divine powers. The more complete working out of this idea, however, belongs to a higher stage of culture which is established on an agricultural basis.

It is hardly necessary to point out that the knowledge

[1] Dr. Rivers, in his careful and thorough monograph on the Todas, points out that they must have migrated to their present home in the Nilgiri Hills. Their gods, he considers, were originally hill-gods, and they must have been brought with them to their present seats, which they have occupied for centuries. Here the Todas have become keepers of buffaloes, following the dairying industry, and developing a ritual in connexion with the work of the dairy. It is this ritual, in association with magical ideas, which has become the important thing, and the relation of the Todas to their gods, Dr. Rivers thinks, shows tokens of decadence. If this account be correct, and it seems intrinsically probable, we have here an interesting illustration how the development of a new mode of life may vitally modify, although it does not obliterate, an older nature-worship.—*Vid. The Todas*, Macmillan & Co., 1906, pp. 182 ff., 442 ff.

[2] *The Religion of the Semites*: A. & C. Black, 1894, p. 355. But there is no proof, it seems to me, that totemism was once universal, and therefore that pastoral religion was always superimposed on an older totem-worship.

and practice of agriculture, giving man a broader and more secure basis of life, were the condition of a civilised society. Agriculture makes it possible for a denser population to draw their food supply from a given area, and so contributes greatly to that intercourse of races which promotes the development of civilisation. Man's life now acquires fresh and more complex interests, and the gods are invoked to bless a new circle of human activities.[1] In recent years much has been written on the corn-spirit and the deities of vegetation; and though these gods do not play the ubiquitous part which is sometimes assigned to them, it cannot be doubted that they were prominent objects of reverence in communities which depended for subsistence on the fruits of the earth. The cults associated with the death, burial, and subsequent resurrection of the god, so common in Mediterranean lands, point to the sowing of the seed in the ground and the reaping of the fruits of the earth for their explanation; and probably the rites were believed to possess some magical efficiency.[2] This fresh cycle of human activity offers scope for extending the departmental sway of earlier gods and of adding to their attributes. The Earth-Goddess, a deity older than the agricultural stage, becomes now the fruitful mother, receiving the seed and bearing the fruits to nourish her human progeny. The wide-spread worship of Mother Earth represents man's consciousness of dependence on the produce of the soil, and expresses his desire to propitiate the spirit who may give or withhold a plentiful fruitage. And the immemorial

[1] The settlement of the Hebrew tribes in Canaan marked the transition from the nomadic to the agricultural life, and had a significant effect on their religion. The earlier Jahveh-worship became intermingled with the cult of the Baalim, or local gods of fertility, reverenced by the Canaanites. The predominance of Jahveh was finally secured by the rites connected with agriculture being referred to him as Lord of the land.

[2] *Vid.* Dr. J. G. Frazer's *Adonis, Attis, Osiris.*

customs connected with the sowing and the in-gathering of the grain show how intimately man linked his operations in the field to the working of divine powers.

The formation of the larger culture-groups is only possible on an agricultural basis, and the interaction of these groups is a fertile source of religious development. The conditions will be most favourable to development where a race comes into contact with another culture while its own religious ideas are still in the formative period, and have not yet hardened into a rigid and stereotyped system. For it is with a race as with an individual: there is a time when the spiritual character is growing and still plastic, and the process of assimilation takes place most easily. The presence of such quickening influences at the critical period is one at least of the causes of the richness of Greek religion: the absence of them is a cause of the comparative poverty of Roman religion. I venture to think the religion of the Aztecs of Mexico was suffering from a similar defect when the Spanish invaders first came in contact with it. Here a remarkable civilisation grew up, a kind of cultural oasis in a great desert of barbarism, and it had to pay the penalty of isolation. Religion was highly organised as an institution, but settled down in a narrow groove. The shadow of a great fear gathered over it, for the deity must be propitiated by the blood of man: it had become a fixed idea that every success which man desires must be wrung from the gods at the price of human sacrifice.[1] Had the Aztec civilisation been in contact with other civilisations and their beliefs, its religion could hardly have become stereotyped in this repulsive fashion.

[1] *Vid. Lehrbuch der Religionsgeschichte*, edited by Chantepie De La Saussaye, 1905, Vol. I., p. 38.

At a time not more than a generation ago the hypothesis of such interaction among the greater cultures of antiquity might have seemed venturesome, for the evidence in its favour was somewhat slender; but recent research has greatly modified our ideas of the character and extent of civilisation in the prehistoric period. The spade of the excavator has brought to light an Ægean civilisation which flourished two millenniums before the beginning of our era; and the civilisations of Egypt and Babylon are of course far older.[1] That great culture-systems could grow up within measurable distance of each other without mutual influence is inherently improbable; and there is evidence that such influence did exist. Then if we come down to the first millennium before Christ, we find traces of interaction between Egypt, Palestine, Asia Minor and Greece, Persia and even India. Our present knowledge does not enable us to determine the extent of this influence precisely, but common traits in belief and ritual point to a movement of ideas from people to people. As an example, we cite the related groups of beliefs which gathered round the cults of Osiris, Adonis, Attis, Dionysus and Mithra. The phenomena point to an active interchange of ideas, for it is incredible that religious conceptions and rituals so closely related could have been evolved in complete independence. Again, the simultaneous quickening of the religious spirit in different peoples might suggest a wave of spiritual influence moving from race to race. Such a thing is not impossible, though I do not say there is any conclusive proof of it. Nevertheless it is noteworthy that in the sixth century B.C. there should be a wide-spread uprising of the spirit in various lands. For this was the age of Confucius and Gautama, of Jeremiah and Ezekiel, of the Greek Mysteries and the Ionic

[1] *Authority and Archæology*, edited by D. G. Hogarth, 1899, p. 238.

hinkers. However we may try to explain it, a fresh piritual impulse seemed to come to birth in different lands bout the same time, and to inspire new interest in the eligious problem.

At the stage of spiritual development at which we have ow arrived, a new phase of interaction comes into rominence and remains an important feature of all higher eligion. I refer to the interaction of the personal and ocial factors in religion. The growth and differentiation f personality, which are the fruit of social development, nake possible an individuality and inwardness of spiritual ife to which primitive culture is a stranger. Man begins o experience religion as a personal consciousness which is ot of necessity the same in him as in his fellow-man. In he place of individuals who merely reflect the collective eligious consciousness, and are devoid of initiative, men f genius appear, men who feel the religious problem to be personal one and dare to think and speak for themselves. While continuing to be the children of their age, in virtue of their own spiritual experience they take up an ttitude of freedom and independence towards traditional elief and practice. They are ready to doubt and criticise, where men on lower levels of culture are content to accept he custom of their group because it is the custom. This eightened, individual consciousness acts as a ferment within the religious system, and brings about visible changes where aforetime change came slowly and without observation. Confucius and Buddha, Zarathustra and the Hebrew prophets are examples of persons achieving renewal or reform of religion through the strength and persuasiveness of inner conviction. This personal religious life is powerfully aided by the growth of the moral consciousness, in virtue of which man attains the perception of a realm of ends and values that claim his loyalty and obedience. In discharging this obligation the individua recognises that he enters into the possession of an inherit ance which is not to be measured by the things of sense and which gives his life a meaning of its own. And whe there is divergence between the traditional religion and thi awakened moral consciousness, the problem how t bring about a harmony of these conflicting worlds o value becomes urgent. The pressure of the problem i not felt by the mass of ordinary individuals, at least no keenly; it is the spiritual genius who experiences th strain, who recognises clearly that it is impossible to go o in the old ways; and on him necessity is laid to cry alou to the people the things he has meditated in secret and to quicken them to a clear consciousness of the grea issue. By his capacity to make the people enter into hi point of view and feel with him the prophet brings abou a revival or, it may be, a development of religion. And when a race reaches that stage of culture where men of spiritual leading and light can stand out from the average and common-place, it is in the possession of fresh forces making for progress. Large religious reforms and marked spiritual advances are not the product of the slow working of the common mind: they are initiated by gifted individuals who react on the common mind and lift it to a higher level. For ordinary intelligences can understand and follow where they cannot discover and initiate, and in so doing they give to a movement the momentum which ensures a triumphant result. I need hardly point out how important this interaction of the personal and social factors becomes in quickening the springs of spiritual interest and in ministering to the progress of religion. One mind, or perhaps several minds become the points in which the need of change is clearly focussed, and it is by them that the first steps are taken which lead to its accomplishment. On the other hand, the massive and slow moving social consciousness corrects the extremes of personal genius and preserves the continuity between the past and the present ; and from this source the reaction against a one-sided development draws its strength. The interaction of the personal and social elements is essential to the vigour and progress of ethical religion, and when the personal factor becomes feeble and ineffective a period of religious decadence ensues. The possibility of renewal depends on the power of the social system to produce spiritual leaders, who can discern the spiritual needs of the age and revive a drooping faith. "Where there is no vision the people perish." The activity of religious personalities, reacting thus on the common heritage of belief, breathes a healthful spirit into the dry forms of a religion, and inspires those changes which preserve its vitality against the hardening power of custom and the narrowing influence of tradition.

The development of religion is a history of the growth of spiritual personality. In primitive culture personal religion is a negligible quantity : in ethical and universal religion it is all-important. Or, to put it differently, the inwardness of the religious principle is a feature of the highest religion as distinguished from the nature-religions : spiritual values have taken the place of material goods, and man seeks in religion the satisfaction of the soul, and no merely external deliverance. Corresponding to this development of the inward and personal factor, the principle of interaction passes into a higher phase, and reveals itself in the active interplay of the different psychical elements. Feeling, thought, and will, as we know, are all involved in the religious consciousness, and the perfect balance and harmony of these elements are implied in the full realisation of the religious relationship. Progress, however, is never attained by the steady and equal growth of all three elements, but by the special development of one or other of them: this in turn calls forth a reaction which may lead to a readjustment at a further stage. In the dissatisfaction which every one-sided movement of the spirit sooner or later evokes there are active the demands of the larger self which already has the presentiment of something better and finally gives form to its aspiration in a conscious purpose. The ideal of a harmony that will satisfy the complete man is at once the incentive to progress and the corrective of a partial development.

A few words may be added to illustrate this interaction of psychical elements. At the reflective stage the activity of thought is prominent, and it becomes a chief concern of man to understand and explain his religious experience. The religious relationship, aforetime mainly a matter of feeling, is clothed in doctrines, and piety is cast in an intellectual mould. Thought pursues its engrossing task without, however, reaching a final conclusion. The excess of the thinking-element results in an impoverishment of the feeling-life, and to the soul craving for immediacy of experience, to present a dogma instead of the divine object is like the gift of a stone in the place of bread. The defining and explaining mind seems occupied with the shadow to the neglect of the substance. The claims of feeling become urgent, and assert themselves successfully against the dominance of intellect: Mysticism, with its contempt of reasoning and its rapt union with the Divine consummated in the fulness and intimacy of feeling, is in the ascendant, and offers to man a spiritual satisfaction he cannot find by the humbler method of reflective thinking. It is of the essence of thought that subject and object shall not coincide, but this estrangement melts away in the glow of mystical emotion.

If Mysticism thus triumphs for the time over Rationalism, its victory is not a permanent one. Feeling that despises thinking runs into excesses and vagaries, and its indifference to clear ideas renders it a weak and an unstable support to the practical religious life. Indeed, it is only in so far as Mysticism accepts the aid of ideas as interpreters—borrowing them from the existing theological system—that it succeeds in being practical in any serious sense. Meanwhile the demands of a regular and coherent religious life grow by reaction against the extremes of emotionalism, and men begin to realise that, if feeling is to be the only test of piety, the objectivity of the religious relation is placed in peril. Experience of the heights and depths of feeling—"the orison of communion" and "the dark night of the soul"—leaves the spirit athirst for a more sane and discerning outlook into the eternal world. And so it comes back to the view that man must not only feel in religion but also think and criticise: the reason aforetime rejected is now reinstated, although it may not be set on so high a pedestal as of yore. For the intervening experience always counts for something, and the readjustment which takes place is never merely the restoration of an earlier harmony.

Finally, take the case where religion has developed on the lines of a one-sided activity of the will. This is a phase which nearly all ritual religions pass through. For the tendency grows to lay stress on the right performance of details of the cult, and to attribute to the due performance of the prescribed acts an independent value. The secret virtue of the *opus operatum* is really a reversion towards the idea of magical efficiency which was so deeply intermingled with the cults of primitive religion. Where ritualistic formalism appears in a higher religion, it betokens an excessive stress on the scrupulous will to the detriment of the other psychical factors : for the accent is on the doing of the act, and a diminishing value is attached to the pious feeling prompting and the intelligent appreciation accompanying the act. The result is, as we have before pointed out, that religion becomes mechanical and decadence ensues. Well-known illustrations of this process are furnished by the later Jewish Legalism, and the work righteousness of the Romish Church at the close of the Middle Ages. Deliverance from this dreary formalism can only come through the reassertion of the rights of the neglected elements, in other words through the demand that man, in the exercise of his religion, shall feel and think as well as do. Yet the demand will only be effective if there exist individuals within the decadent religious system who are alive to the wider claims of the spiritual life, and can make the idea of a piety which embraces the whole man live in the minds of the people. But I think we must admit that the spring of such a reaction lies in ethical feeling more than in thought, and in the eyes of the prophet and reformer the claims of the inward and spiritual life are paramount. A Luther is not impelled to raise the standard of reform by zeal for a new theology, but by a burning consciousness of the moral corruptions of the Church. The broad fact remains that, unless a religion which has evolved in this one-sided way holds within it spiritual forces which can react successfully against the prevailing formalism, the path of spiritual development is finally closed to it. And, ceasing to develop with the developing culture of which it is an element, though it linger on in its institutional forms it ceases to be a living influence on the souls of men. If a religion is to meet the needs of a growing and complex human nature, it must not become stereotyped in any one direction, nor restrict its appeal to a single faculty.

Looking back on the process of interaction as revealed in religious development, we are led to the conclusion that the motive power which lies behind it is that concrete human nature which refuses to be satisfied with any partial fulfilment of itself. At the lower stages the elements which act and react wear an appearance of externality to the subject: they seem to determine the mind of man rather than to be determined by it. But here we have to bear in mind that things like natural environment and social change only exercise an influence on religion by the way they impress human spirits, and by the reactions they evoke from them. No belief, even the crudest, can be a purely passive state of the subject; it must represent an active attitude of mind. As religion becomes increasingly inward and self-conscious, the dependence of its development on such outward stimuli diminishes. By this is not meant that social changes do not continue to exercise an influence on religion in our higher civilisation; they certainly react in strengthening or weakening spiritual conviction; but they have no longer the old power in themselves to bring about the modification and reconstruction of religious beliefs. They may do so, however, by rallying round and giving impulsive force to other elements in the culture of the time, as for example the scientific or ethical spirit. Modern religion has become inward and personal, and the elements which most directly affect its progress bear the impress of the spirit. Science, philosophy and morality all act on the religious consciousness and affect the development of religion; but they do so because the mind, so to speak, finds itself in them and assimilates them. Hence the diverse aspects of culture which beget the religious perplexities of the present age are reflected in a division of the human spirit, and it is in the kingdom of man's soul that the stress of the contending elements is felt. The demand that religion be in harmony with science and morality—with the meaning mind reads into nature and with the norms to which the will subjects itself—is ultimately a demand for the human spirit to be in harmony with itself. This is the operative ideal which corrects the extravagances and errors into which religion runs, and on its working the health of religion depends. The ideal is personal, and it reveals itself in growing clearness with the development of personal life. Personal, however, be it said, not in the sense of an individual claim, but as the demand of the formed personality that lives and has its being in the society of persons. For the developed personality recognises its dependence on the social system, and it includes within the scope of its own highest good the good of the larger whole. This personal endeavour after self-fulfilment seems to me essential to the understanding of religious progress; and it is therefore only a qualified assent I can give to Prof. A. Dorner's interpretation of religious development as a dialectic process moving consistently to its goal.[1] So far as this suggests an immanent and necessary progress which uses human beings as its instruments, all that need be said at present is, that the history of religion gives little countenance to any such idea. On the other hand, so far as it suggests a concrete whole striving to correct partial developments, an ideal and spiritual nature in virtue of which a man

[1] A. Dorner, *Grundriss der Religionsphilosophie*, 1903, p. 413.

claims, and in varying degree achieves, a full in place of a partial satisfaction, the theory contains a substantial element of truth. To this extent, at least, Dorner's philosophical conception finds a psychological justification.

Up to this point in our study of religious development we have not raised the question of its ultimate meaning: our standpoint has been simply psychological. Our aim has been to show the successive phases the religious spirit has passed through, and to explain how, under the pressure of human needs, the religious relation has gradually developed from an external bond to an inward and personal communion. The conception of the divine object has advanced steadily with the spiritual growth of the subject, and the satisfaction which the soul seeks in religion has slowly assumed a higher and more permanent character. Nevertheless this age-long quest of man for God is marked by recurring disappointments; for when the old gods have ceased to satisfy, man has to seek and find new and better gods. He discovers after a while that these too are inadequate to his needs, and that again he must resume the quest. So the sting of disappointment becomes the spur to progress. And as the human soul embraces a larger and richer content, the things in heaven formed after the pattern of things on earth finally become too narrow for the scope of its aspirations; and so it breaks away from the old limitations and seeks a larger outlook. A feature of spiritual and universal religion is the rejection of a finite and mundane deity, and the progressive elimination from the conception of the Divine of those anthropomorphic qualities which are the heritage of the past. In the highest forms of religion the transcendent aspect of the divine object is recognised, and the supramundane nature of the human goal affirmed. There is something transient and fragmentary in all terrestrial experience, and the developed religious consciousness is driven to conclude that it seeks more in the religious relation than can be realised within this present sphere of sense and time. The two great universal religions, Christianity and Buddhism, in many ways far apart, have still this trait in common, that they realise the unsatisfying character of all mundane experience, and point man to a consummation freed from all material and sensuous fetters. The end in the one case is positive and in the other negative, but in neither case is it an earthly goal.

This supramundane aspect of religion is closely connected with the growth of the redemptive idea in the higher forms of religion. In early culture man sought deliverance through religion from external ills ; and now he finds the ills which matter most are closely interwoven with the personal life in its temporal existence-form. The problem of man's ultimate destiny does not appear capable of solution under terrestrial conditions, with which sin, sorrow and suffering are always deeply interfused. Hence the religious consciousness—especially in its Christian form—recognises that, while the good is immanent in experience, the completed Good is a transcendent Value. Or, as Plato might have said, the pattern which works on earth is laid up in heaven. It is faith which prompts this movement of the spirit ; it is faith which reaches out beyond this 'bourne of time and place,' and postulates the completion it demands in the unseen and eternal world. This 'venture of faith' is no arbitrary act, an impulse born of a vulgar discontent or a passing disappointment : if it were so it could have no inward significance. The movement is too wide and constant to be so regarded :

it seems rather to express the conclusion the human spirit draws when it follows to its issue the process of religious experience itself.

In the foregoing chapters I have tried to trace in outline the evolution of religion, and the point has now been reached at which the question of the validity of the principles involved becomes urgent. From the purely psychological standpoint the religious consciousness in its reference to a divine object may or may not be illusory; and psychologists who have studied it differ widely on the question of its truth. It is well, however, to remember that the religious mind always postulates the truth of its experience: apart from this postulate the experience itself would not survive, though it does not follow that what the religious subject is impelled to treat as true is therefore true. To apply the pragmatist maxim at this juncture would be to cut the knot in place of untying it; for if every idea is true in so far as it works, there is no religious idea which has not at some time been true, and possibly, for all we know, may become true again. And the individual who finds some private belief useful and satisfying might fairly claim truth for it. We do not seem able to reach an adequate criterion or standard on these lines, and a more catholic method of determining validity is needed. Rationality refuses to be absorbed in pragmatic worth; and a Philosophy of Religion, while it keeps an open ear to the claims of working-value, cannot ignore the demands of coherent thinking. The problem of the meaning and validity of religion and its development will always press on the philosopher and call for an answer. What success he achieves—and success at the best must be partial—will depend on his own personal insight into religion and the adequacy of his speculative principles. No philosophy, indeed, is final, but the philosophy of an age is its reply to the ultimate questions of life. So psychology, having done its work, hands over to philosophy the problem of religion, leaving it to say the last word on the truth of an experience around which gather man's fairest hopes as well as his darkest doubts.

CHAPTER VIII

THE MORAL IDEAL AND THE RELIGIOUS CONSCIOUSNESS

FROM the point we have now reached we might proceed to consider the validity or ontological value of the principles which are at work in the historic development of religion. But, before doing so, it seemed to us advisable to examine more fully the relations of the moral to the religious consciousness. The connexion between the two has no doubt been touched on from time to time in the preceding pages, but no detailed discussion was possible. And though the subject is old and perhaps rather worn, there are at least two reasons why something should be said about it here. Of all the phases of culture which interact with religion morality is the one which stands closest to it, and has the most important bearing on religious development. And, on the other hand, the problem raised by the relationship of the moral to the religious ideal leads naturally up to those metaphysical questions we have still to consider. On these grounds at all events the subject merits fuller consideration at this stage. Perhaps a word might also be said about the importance of the matter at the present time. The old idea of the subordination of Ethics to Theology is widely abandoned : and many who are not unfriendly to religion will be found agreeing that the validity of a religious dogma depends on the way in which it satisfies the ethical judgment, while its value can be none other than its practical service for the moral life. As a writer has remarked, in a former day, "no one hesitated to correct an ethical judgment by a religious text," but now the "relation is very nearly reversed." There are radical thinkers, however, who take a step beyond this. They argue for a divorce between Ethics and Religion, and claim a complete independence for the former. In the domain of ethical services and duties man, it is said, moves in a well-lighted region where he can see his way and is sure of the facts. But, when he turns to religion, he enters into a dim and mysterious world, where the clear light of truth never falls and all is hypothesis and conjecture. To suppose that Religion is the basis of Ethics is to mistake the shadow for the substance; the better way is not to be wise above our knowledge, and to unite over matters where agreement is at least possible. Why not leave this debatable land where strife is keen and tenure hazardous, and dwell together in quieter and safer parts. There is a certain plausibility in this, especially in an age in which religious dispute often runs high, and beliefs once closely associated with religion show visible signs of decadence. So the Ethical Societies which have sprung up in different countries seek to promote the ethical spirit apart from the sanctions of religion, and without reliance on any dogmatic creed. How far these societies are realising the purpose they have in view is a question that need not detain us here; but those who do not see their way to sacrifice the claims either of Ethics or Religion may well feel called on to give a reason for the faith that is in them. It may turn out on examination that the implications of Ethics are metaphysical as well as those of Religion; and it is possible that faith, conspicuously present in the one case, is by no means absent in the other. An enquiry of this kind will have to bring out the nature of the ethical as contrasted with the religious end, and will involve a discussion of the problem whether the two ends do not somehow coalesce in a higher idea, or whether the one does not find in the other its goal and consummation. The method to be pursued is, I think, fairly plain. The ground must be prepared by an examination of the development of the ethical consciousness in order to make clear the relations into which it has entered with the religious consciousness. The way will thus be opened for an attempt to grasp the true connexion of the one with the other.

The beginnings of Ethics go back to the customs which enter into the organisation of primitive society. An early group was feebly differentiated in its social structure, and embraced within a rudimentary form differences which were to become explicit at a later stage. In the custom of the tribe we detect the germs of ethical norms, laws, and religious usages. It has often been argued that morality is conspicuously absent from the origins of culture; and savage customs can easily be instanced which, to civilised eyes, seem the reverse of moral. Eminent anthropologists like Waitz and Tylor have adopted this view, and it still receives some support. Siebeck, for example, makes ethical action depend on the conscious exercise of freedom, and so finds it possible to say that the religious ideas of primitive men are practically destitute of moral content.[1] Höffding, too, declares that, at the lowest stage known to us, religion has properly no ethical significance, although, a couple of pages further on, he qualifies the statement by the admission that nature-religion has its ethics in so far as it makes definite demands on its adherents.[2] The fact that

[1] *Religionsphilosophie*, p. 250. [2] *Religionsphilosophie*, pp. 291, 293.

primitive religion finds expression in stated acts and customs is undisputed: the only point at issue is, whether we are to deny that these customs have any ethical significance. The question is largely one of the standard by which we judge. It seems to me that any custom which acts as a norm for the individual, and the breach of which evokes feeling, has implicitly an ethical meaning: and it is unfair to deny the existence of such a meaning because it does not coincide with the civilised idea of what is moral. The process of growth from the lower to the higher is continuous, and to draw a dividing line at a given point is an arbitrary procedure. The instinctive ways of acting by which the life of the animal and its species is conserved have taken form among primitive men in those immemorial habits which bind early society together. How constraining is the force of these customs on the members of clan or tribe is well known to all students of early culture. Such customs are nevertheless distinguished from non-moral instincts by the recognition that a breach of them is possible, however seldom it may occur in practice. The point is not the nature of the custom—to our eyes it may be repellent—the essential thing is the recognition of an obligation to do or to abstain from doing. And the man, however rude, who controls his momentary impulses and obeys a rule for his own good and that of his group, has taken his first steps on the path of ethical progress.

In the beginnings of culture religion is found connecting itself with the sanctity of the custom, and supplying motives for its scrupulous observance. By this it is not meant that in every case the savage finds the sanction for the custom in his religion; in some instances a conscious reason may not be present to his mind at all. "Whatever be the foundation for a certain practice, and however rivial it may be, the unreflecting mind has a tendency to lisapprove of any deviation from it for the simple reason hat such a deviation is unusual."[1] On the other hand, here can be no doubt that, on the lower levels of savagery, there is commonly a belief in magic interfusing tself with the operation of traditional practice, and endering any breach of the rule dangerous.[2] This is specially true where the wide-spread custom of Taboo prevails. A mysterious power is supposed to reside in the forbidden object, which acts with mechanical certainty in hurting or destroying the individual who, wittingly or unwittingly, touches or tastes it. Hence the natural respect for what is habitual is fortified by the dread of an uncanny power avenging the transgression of the custom; and this dread can bring about the expected result. But Magic is closely associated with Religion in primitive culture, and the boundary line between them is not hard and fast. Accordingly, alongside of the magical idea, and sometimes blending with it, we find transgression of the custom linked with the fear of offending a spirit which may somehow smite with disease or disaster. Under the reign of crude nature-worship and confused spiritism the divine object was too vague and characterless to supply any higher motives for conduct: and one has to admit the poverty of the human mind at the beginning of its development. Man was still at too low a level to conceive the custom as he expression of the will of a god. Not yet can we speak of religion as "loyalty to a friendly Power;" and he suggestion that simple and childlike trust preceded a downfall into selfish superstition has no warrant from recent anthropology. The condition of man at the

[1] Westermarck, *The Origin and Development of the Moral Ideals*, 1906. vol. i., p. 159.

[2] *Cf.* the interesting remarks of Mr. L. T. Hobhouse in his learned work, *Morals in Evolution*, 1906, vol. ii., p. 50, ff.

origins of culture was no genial 'state of nature,' as some eighteenth century writers dreamed: the life of the primeval savage was more accurately described by Hobbes as "nasty, brutish, and short."

The advance by which a more positive ethical meaning was infused into the custom of a social group was a religious advance. The unreflecting and half-instinctive observance of a tribal practice acquired a fresh significance when the observance was conceived to enter into the bond which linked the group and its gods the one to the other. For example, the natural tie of blood binding together the members of a clan received a concrete and visible expression in the totem; and the totem, regarded as divine, gave a religious sanction to the practices obtaining within the community. Religion, by thus connecting the observance of the custom with tribal solidarity, opened out a line of ethical advance which had great possibilities. The idea of obligation here contained reached a further point of development when the being from whom the clan or tribe derived its life was represented as an ancestor-god, who claimed a tribute of pious rites from his descendants. In some mysterious way the welfare of the society was bound to that of the divine forefather, and the prescribed acts by which the group acknowledged a common duty to the god took on the impress of religious loyalty. This loyalty to the bond, expressing itself in the careful observance of the custom, is the rude beginning out of which a conscious morality has grown. And such a feeling of religious loyalty develops whenever the god, whether conceived as ancestor or not, comes before the minds of the worshippers as a friendly Power, a protector of the tribe, a being whose help man can win. In obeying the custom of his society, and in regarding his obedience as an act of fidelity to his god, man was taking the steps that transformed an unthinking habit into the fulfilment of a divine law. Nor must we forget the educational value of norms of action supported by divine sanction. Through the self-control and conformity to a rule demanded by the due performance of fixed acts man had his early lessons in subduing his wandering impulses for the sake of a larger good. In the superstitious dread which prevented any violation of the custom lay the germ that was to grow into conscience, and in man's natural sense of kinship with his fellows and his god the feeling of moral sympathy had its root.

Slender differentiation, as already noted, is a feature of primitive society, and Ethics at this period is very far from having an independent existence or sphere of its own. It was only at a relatively late stage in social evolution that man distinguished clearly between a moral, a religious, and a political obligation. In early society morality has no being for itself apart from religion, and is therefore subject to all the limitations which naturalistic religion involves. It does not mean more than the outward compliance with the rule, and is not concerned with the spirit in which the acts are performed. The efficacy resides in the deed not in the motive, and it does not matter whether the individual obeys readily or reluctantly: it is of no consequence whether he likes to do what is enjoined or is impelled to do it by superstitious terror. Moreover the scope of obligation is limited just as the sphere of piety is limited. Each tribe has its own gods and follows its own customs, and what is binding within a particular group does not hold of the relations between members of different groups. In cases where the custom of the tribe would condemn the slaying of a fellow tribesman it would approve the slaughter of a member of a rival tribe. The goods which savage man strives after are material and sensuous; and the customs of his tribe, which are his only norms of action, simply express the stated ways by which he believes the material well-being of his group is promoted. The solidarity of primitive societies revealed, for instance, in such a custom as blood-revenge, is remarkable, but it is entirely dissevered from ideal motives or respect for human life in itself; and it can co-exist with such habits as the putting to death of the aged who have become a burden or the exposure of infants who threaten to prove an encumbrance.

The advance from a morality or piety of custom to a conscious morality corresponds broadly with the development of religion to the significant stage of national polytheism. The extension and further differentiation of society, introducing more complex motives and ends of action, are the means of bringing about a deepening of individual character, which is fraught with the most momentous consequences alike for Ethics and Religion. To this deepening of the individual consciousness must be traced the enlargement both of the ethical and the religious outlook. When various tribes with customs more or less diverse were merged in the nation, it is evident that the customs would require increased definition and a wider authority in order to function effectively in the larger system. So laws are developed which codify the customs—laws which are recognised as elements in the social well-being, and which are held to be binding on individual wills. Law is the custom generalised for the common good. By this means the feeling of duty, the sense of social obligation which leads men to limit themselves for the public weal, was quickened and sustained. Through the idea of law man made himself familiar with the thought that general rules of conduct were the expression of a conscious purpose, human or divine, and that this purpose was the well-being of the community. But even in the lower culture the custom could hardly cover the whole field of action, and this was true in a greater degree of a complex society in which the motives and ends of conduct were more varied. Men must soon have made the discovery that the law as universal sometimes presses hardly on an individual; that *summum jus* may even be *summa injuria*; and that there are acts, fruitful in weal or woe, which the law neither commands nor proscribes. It is at this point that morals begin to go beyond the *mores majorum*, whether as customs or laws, and assume an ideal character. So the idea of law receives a scope beyond what is merely given and established in society, and is made to express a good of a higher kind. The mind which consciously devotes itself to this good is recognised to possess an inward value, a value not measured by outward obedience to the law of the state.

This growth in ethical feeling has the most important influence upon religion, and is primarily responsible for the elevation of the gods from purely natural powers to beings with a moral character. The departmental deities of national polytheism are not mere copies of experience: they show traces of idealisation and reflect the values which move the minds of the people. Hence special virtues were attributed to particular gods in a special degree, and the virtues in turn received a sanction and consecration by being associated with the religious consciousness. It was a natural desire to bring religion into close relation with the common weal that often led a city to trace its laws to a divine founder, or prompted a race to regard its laws as divinely revealed. When ethical feeling recognised an obligation which transcended the positive laws of society, an obvious way of explaining this obligation was to treat it as a demand imposed by a divine law of higher authority. In Greece, for example, Heraclitus, in a profound utterance, declared that all human laws are nourished by the one divine law.[1] And Sophocles, it is well known, referred to 'unwritten laws,' laws in which the power of the god was manifest who grows not old.[2] The Hebrew prophet likewise could speak of a Law of God written on the heart of man. And for both Greek and Hebrew it seemed good to obey the dictates of the 'law within,' even when it bade them transgress the rule of society. This line of thought finds its natural conclusion in a Theological Ethics which construes the fulfilment of moral duty as obedience to the will of God, and treats immorality as a sin, or an offence against God. As the result of this movement the moral consciousness, which in the first instance reacts on religion and gives it deeper content, is finally consecrated by religion, and finds its place as an aspect of the religious life.

It is not, however, by any means necessary that the actual historic process should work out just in this way, and in fact the course of development is frequently different. For the loosening of the bond between Religion and Ethics, which inevitably takes place after the transition from tribal to national culture, instead of leading up by a gradual development to a new and

[1] Fr. 91:

τρέφονται γὰρ πάντες οἱ ἀνθρώπειοι νόμοι ὑπὸ ἑνὸς τοῦ θείου.

Ritter and Preller, eighth ed., p. 35.

[2] *ἄγραπτα κἀσφαλῆ θεῶν νόμιμα.* *Antig.*, 454–455.

μέγας ἐν τούτοις θεός, οὐδὲ γηράσκει. *Œd. Tyr.*, 871.

higher synthesis more often passes into some form of discord and antagonism. The reason is that the two phases of culture are not equally amenable to progress, and do not advance together. Religion is the more conservative and Ethics the more progressive phase. While the expansion of the moral consciousness is promoted by the practical needs of a growing society the pressure is less urgently felt by the religious mind, impeded as it is by an immemorial tradition fostered by sentiment. The religion which has its roots deeply fixed in the past is especially dear to the popular mind, which is of course less keenly sensitive to the claims of advancing knowledge. The result is that the old religious form, made rigid through the strain of conservative forces, refuses to develop to receive the fresh moral content : the old and the new stand in juxtaposition but will not coalesce, and discord and contradiction ensue. Thus an ancient but still living feature in the character of a deity may be quite opposed to fresh qualities which are ascribed to him ; a god on occasion may espouse the cause of the good without himself being good ; and, as in the case of the Olympians, persisting tradition may credit the celestial oligarchy with some of the worst vices of mortals. The line of development which best resolves the discord between the moral and the religious consciousness is that where polytheism passes through monarchianism to monotheism, and God is finally conceived as the Supreme Reality and the Supreme Good. On the other hand, the development of religion, even though it be in a monotheistic direction, may still be unfavourable to a harmonious relation with the ethical spirit. I refer to the case where a religion evolves a complicated and growing system of ritual ; for in this case religion undoubtedly exercises a depressing effect on the moral consciousness, and sets the moral values of life in a wrong perspective. Under the dominion of ritualism a trivial observance becomes as important as a moral principle, and the value of certain external acts is exalted at the expense of ethical conduct. The magical element intrudes to the prejudice of the moral. For ritualistic religion, wherever it comes to undisputed sway, means a recrudescence of those magical ideas which are associated with primitive religion, but which a progressive culture should strive to eliminate.

This slight survey of the historic development of Ethics and Religion is sufficient to show that the two have frequently been at variance ; and even when there is no open quarrel there may be absence of sympathy instead of fruitful interaction. Yet it would be wrong to suppose there is no bond of union between them lying deeper than these differences. When people disagree it is because they are concerned with a common object : and while Religion and Ethics have often been at issue, they are nevertheless occupied with the same problem of human good. And though they have come to regard this problem from different points of view, they have grown up from a common root in human nature, and are activities of that spirit of man which is one and cannot be finally at war with itself. Moreover, though Ethics and Religion do not progress equally, and sometimes even seem to move in different directions, a large view of the facts suggests a real interdependence. A radical degeneration of religion, betokening as it does a decadence of the ideal element in life, brings about a decadence in morality. Illustrations of this are the lowering of the sense of civic duty which accompanied the decay of piety in ancient Greece and Rome, and the rank growth of selfishness and oppression as spiritual religion faded in the church of the Middle

Ages. On the other hand, when religion makes a real advance, when the fire of the spiritual life burns brightly, the process reacts favourably on the moral consciousness, quickening man's sense of duty and inspiring him to fulfil his obligations. The rise of Christianity is a good illustration of this. So, too, a marked progress in ethical insight and practice, even if it fail to bring about the reform of an old religious system, paves the way for the ultimate acceptance of some higher form of faith. But while there is no good ground for speaking of a permanent discord between Morality and Religion, it is possible, without doing actual violence to the facts, to construe the relationship between them in different ways. On the one side it may be argued that morality presupposes religion, and finds in religion its explanation and goal; and on the other side it may be argued that morality is the fundamental fact, to which religion stands in a relation of logical dependence.[1] Kant is the best known spokesman of the latter view in modern times; but there are many to-day who would range themselves with Kant, without endorsing his precise theory on the subject. For example, it is urged that an ostensible advance in religion is always to be tested by the way it satisfies the moral consciousness, and progress in religion just lies in giving deeper moral content to the idea of God. Even more thoroughgoing is the conclusion drawn by Höffding, who asserts that, as regards its historical development and its motives, its content and its value, religion points back to ethical presuppositions.[2] The natural tendency of such a

[1] This is the view of H. Cohen, in his brochure *Religion und Sittlichkeit*, 1907.

[2] *Religionsphilosophie*, p. 298. The Dutch theologian Rauwenhoff, in his *Religionsphilosophie* (German Trans., 1889), finds that religion has its foundation in the unconditioned consciousness of duty; and what is enduring and central in religion is faith in a moral order. This does not, we are told, exclude faith in God: but it certainly does not make it essential.

theory, where it does not—as with Höffding—empty the idea of God of objective meaning, is to reduce the idea to a mere means, a *Hilfsvorstellung* which is useful in furthering ethical ends. One is constrained to ask if it is possible to construe the religious ideal in this way! Another school of thought contends that in and for itself morality is not intelligible, and when it stands alone it is condemned to sterility. Instead of being independent, the moral consciousness points back to and receives its inspiration from that deeper spiritual experience in which the life of religion is revealed.[1] This divergence of opinion is hardly to be settled by an appeal to historical facts, as it is usually possible to put different constructions on these facts without ceasing to be plausible. For instance, from the undoubted truth that man's growing moral experience has gradually invested the idea of God with higher content one thinker concludes that we have here proof that Religion is subordinate to and dependent on Ethics. Another says the facts only wear this appearance when regarded from the standpoint of historical and psychological development. The real presupposition of the movement is the divine Spirit working in and through the human consciousness; and so Religion, as a relationship of the human to the Divine, is prior to Morals in the nature of things. The only way to clearer light on the problem lies in passing beyond the region of history and reflecting on the nature of morality and the end it implies. The result of the discussion will perhaps make it plainer how the religious and the ethical ideals are to be related to one another. In offering some remarks on this theme I am entering on ground which has been the scene of many controversies; my object, however,

[1] The view of Eucken in his numerous works. *Vid.*, *e.g.*, *Kampf um einen geistigen Lebensinhalt*, 1907, pp. 277–278.

is rather to develop a positive train of thought than to engage in detailed criticisms.

In the main ethical theory has run on two lines, which may be broadly characterised as the Formal and the Teleological. In the one case the meaning of moral action is interpreted by the relation of the will to a norm or law which claims obedience. This is the so-called formalistic method, and it is usually associated with what may be termed the theological view of Ethics. In point of time it is the earlier theory, inasmuch as both custom and law were at first referred to religion for their explanation. The other method involves an attempt to interpret ethical action through the end to which it is directed, and the method is therefore named teleological. This latter view received its first and most important expression in the work of the great Greek thinkers. For Plato and Aristotle ethical conduct is such as tends to develop the true nature of man, and signifies that human powers are being realised in the line of the human end. That end is well-being in the fullest sense; and while Plato defined it as δικαιοσύνη and Aristotle as εὐδαιμονία, the two thinkers meant substantially the same thing, the harmonious fruition of human faculties in a rightly organised social system. The path to the end is mediated by virtue, as Aristotle insisted; and by this he had in mind the orderly and well-balanced realisation of capacities under the control of reason. And though Plato's and Aristotle's conception of the Good was not free from the limitations of their time—even Aristotle could speak of the slave as an instrument—it is noteworthy that both, by their insight and largeness of view, were saved from false abstractions. For, in the first place, they saw clearly that personal and social good were essentially interdependent, and must not be separated and opposed to each other. Or perhaps it

would be better to say, that the individual only had meaning and value in their eyes as an orderly element in th
social whole whose function was to realise the good. And
on the other hand, while they recognised that pleasure o
a noble sort would accompany the realisation of the good
they were perfectly aware that pleasure itself must neve
be identified with the end. In contrast to Platonism an
Aristotelianism ancient Hedonism worked with a thoroughl
partial conception of human nature; and the hedonisti
conclusions of modern Utilitarianism have been vitiate
by the false psychology which treated all desire as desir
for pleasure.

Religion lay in the background in the ethical theorie
of Plato and Aristotle, and had no decisive influenc
in forming their view of the end; but it again appeare
in the foreground in the ethics of Christianity. Th
Christian religion inherited from Judaism the conceptio
of a divinely revealed Law of conduct, which it wa
man's primary obligation to obey. With law as standar
action was defined, not through a theory of ends bu
by a doctrine of duties, and morality became obedienc
to the Law of God. By this change to the formal poin
of view the inward side of morality was accentuated, an
while the Aristotelian φρόνιμος was the master of a
balanced wisdom, the Christian found in faith and love
the inspiring and directing spirit for the fulfilment of
duty. The kingdom of heaven was not without but
within a man; so personality was set in the foreground
and the value of the individual life received for the first
time due recognition. I am not at present concerned
with the development of Christian Ethics at the hands
of the Church Fathers and the Schoolmen; but it is easy
to see that there are great difficulties in dealing with the
concrete and varied facts of Ethics through the general

onception of a divine Law. How is such a Law to be ormulated, and how when formulated is it to be consistently applied in detail? The rapid rise of casuistry ı the Scholastic Age was the natural consequence of the ttempt to answer the latter problem. It may suffice to emind the reader how Butler afterwards tried to solve he question through the idea of 'a rule of right within.' Conscience approves the good and is the inward monitor f God; but Butler also found it necessary to fall back n the principle of reasonable self-love, and the two rinciples he supposed on the whole to be in harmony with ne another. Beyond doubt the most impressive and nfluential endeavour to develop an ethical theory from he formal standpoint was that of Kant; and if it can be hown that his treatment of the facts of morality from he notion of law breaks down, the case for the teleoogical method will be greatly strengthened. In his pistemology Kant had concluded that the universality nd validity of knowledge were due to an *a priori* factor, o principles of judgment which the mind brought with t to the construction of experience; and in the Kantian thics the influence of the Kantian theory of knowledge s unmistakable. Kant approached the domain of ethics arrying with him the conviction he had won elsewhere, hat the specific character of experience is due to the universal. Hence for him the binding nature of a moral obligation could not lie in the objective end or in the consequences of an act, but must proceed from the universal law under which the will or practical reason acted. In other words obligation cannot be analytically derived from experience, but must be synthetically active in constituting experience; the difference between the theoretical and practical sphere being, that in the former the law determines what *is*, in the latter what *ought* to be. The subjective principle on which the will acts Kant termed th *maxim* of the will, and he formulated the moral imperativ thus: "Act in uniformity with that maxim, and tha maxim only, which you can at the same time will to be universal law." That is to say, the validity of the maxin or norm of the will lies in its universality, in its appli cability to all other wills. This is a topic familiar to al students of philosophy, and I will only deal with a singl point in the Kantian theory, and that briefly—the practica bility of such a norm. Now the salient fact which meet us here is that Kant, in order to secure the universal and *a priori* character of moral law, has reduced it in effect to the merely abstract conception of consistency. For a law of conduct is moral just because it can be universalised without inconsistency. Such a law, however, is powerles to create the concrete content of morality; at most i could only supply a possible test of an act whose morality was problematical. Lying is wrong, for you cannot uni versalise it as a maxim of your will without contradiction But the contradiction does not depend, as Kant implied on the nature of the maxim; it flows from the practica organisation of society, which could not hold together i all men were liars. Moreover, truth-speaking has no the inflexibility of an *a priori* principle, since cases occur where a deviation from the truth can be justified as the lesser of two evils. The emergence of casuistry is always the outcome of an attempt to lay down absolutely universal rules of conduct.

This defect in Kant's ethical theory has long been recognised, and I am not aware that any of his followers have been able to present the substance of his doctrine in a form free from objection. Windelband, for instance, insists that the consciousness of duty is *a priori*, and that the justification of ethical norms lies beyond the psychological processes by which they come to consciousness.[1] The fulfilment of duty, whatever the content may be, is the supreme end; but he fully admits that the idea of duty remains purely formal. Yet he argues that, from the formal conception of a mind directed to the fulfilment of duty, certain formal duties can be deduced which are universally valid,—*e.g.* Self-Control, Deliberation, Consistency. These, Windelband says, do not refer to the specific content of duty, but to the psychological conditions by which the discharge of duty is mediated. I fail, however, to see how obligations like self-control and consistency could ever be evolved from the abstract conception of duty: they are ideas which have been elaborated out of concrete moral experience, and they are recognised as virtues because they have proved themselves to be practical values. And an idea like consistency has a flexibility which indicates its dependence on social good rather than on an *a priori* norm. In face of the evolving content of morality and the frequent conflict of duties it is hard to suppose that particular duties are determined by any *a priori* norm. Reflexion on the facts shows that the direction and stress of any specific obligation always arise out of the structure and circumstances of a particular social system. And this serves to indicate that duties are defined by the end, not by a general law or rule.

The inadequacy of the formalistic method also appears in the fact that a reference to the consequences can never be excluded from the full moral valuation of an act. "If it is of no account whatever just what results in case of certain conduct of ours, then there is no maxim of any sort which could not be set up as a universal law."[2] Of

[1] *Vid.* the Essay *Vom Princip der Moral* in his *Präludien*, Freiburg, 1884.

[2] Lotze, *Outlines of Practical Philosophy*, Eng. Trans., 1890, p. 13.

course in valuing the agent it is necessary to consider the motive, for the motive and not the results is the direct expression of the character of the agent. Consequences are not a sufficient index of the will, because a man may have been unable to judge the consequences of his deed; and the complete results of any act cannot be foreseen. But even in the case where the motive is good but the effects of the act ought to be known to be bad—indiscriminate charity for instance—then we should condemn the act and the character that produced it. In fact, whenever we seek to arrive at an objective valuation of conduct we pass beyond the motives which prompted it, and consider it in relation to the social system and the general well-being. Hence motives as subjective principles of action come to be appraised by reference to the objective ethical end, and the individual act is valued in the light of the worth of this way of acting in general.[1] We cannot therefore agree with Westermarck when he says that "it is only from want of due reflexion that moral judgments are influenced by outward deeds," and that "the will is the only proper object of moral disapproval or moral praise."[2] Now it is true that a being destitute of rational will, and so uninfluenced by motives, is not an object of moral valuation: we can attribute no moral worth to an animal or a machine. But to separate the will from the outward act, to say that moral judgment has only reference to the will and consequences do not count, seems absurd.

Indeed it is only because the will brings about "outward deeds," that the question of moral valuation arises at all. Apart from the concrete ways in which it expresses itself,

[1] Sigwart (*Vorfragen der Ethik*, p. 10) has well remarked: "It lies in the nature of will that no single act can be regarded as perfectly isolated, so that reflexion would be directed only to the given case."

[2] *Origin and Development of the Moral Ideas*, 1906, vol. i., p. 247.

no will can be termed good or bad: we term it good when it acts on principles which subserve the realisation of good ends.

The question of the relation of ethical norms and motives to ethical ends might be briefly answered as follows. The standard or ultimate principle of valuation is the end conceived as some kind of social good, not an absolute moral Law. The norms and motives of action derive their positive value from the way in which they promote the realisation of the end. Norms are not abstract and *a priori* rules, but generalisations which grow out of the life of society and reflect the form and pressure of its ethical spirit. The product of a developing organism, they are themselves subject to development.[1] Their function is to define and simplify the line of action; and, becoming a general maxim of the will, they mediate between the motive, as subjective idea qualified by feeling, and the objective end. The value therefore of motives and norms is subordinate, and depends on their coherence with the end the realisation of which it is their office to further. The duties and obligations of man thus have their significance as steps towards the end, to work for which is the ultimate moral obligation.

It seems, therefore, that the attempt to develop a theory of Ethics by an analysis of the will inevitably runs into a formalism which is incapable of dealing with the concrete facts of moral experience. But the study of the subjective factor sets in a clear light the truth that the individual acts under the consciousness of freedom: ethical obligation is always construed as an "ought," never as a "must," and accordingly postulates in the individual the power to choose and determine himself.

[1] Here I follow Paulsen. I have also found the ethical works of Sigwart and Wundt helpful in connexion with the present chapter.

A specific feeling attaches to the "ought" and accom panies the exercise of moral choice, and this feeling it i difficult to account for simply by the relation of the wil to an end. For there may be purposive activity involvin the selection of means without the presence of this feeling The special colouring of obligation, it has been said is not due, as Kant thought, to the relation of the wil to a rule but arises out of the concrete character of th elements related.[1] I confess to some perplexity as t what is exactly implied in the phrase "concrete character." Does it signify that the feeling of obligation is a empirical fact which has simply to be accepted? Th feeling involved in the "ought" has certainly a qualit peculiar to itself: it is *sui generis*; there is nothing quit like it in the range of our experience. And though th feeling is subject to psychological development, its groun would seem to lie deeper than the region of psychology I shall refer to the point again, and meanwhile proceed t consider how far it is possible to give increased definitio to the ethical end.

I begin by another reference to the same penetratin critic. "Define the end as we may (and I shall not eve insist on the rigorous interpretation of its qualification a absolute), it appears to me that we cannot explain there from the actual concrete fashion of morality, and that th attempt to do so rests upon an inversion of the tru relation between principle and detail of moral practice."

[1] Adamson, *The Development of Modern Philosophy*, vol. ii., p. 111.

[2] Adamson, *op. cit.*, vol. ii., pp, 106–107. An attempt to rise from th empirical facts to the idea of the good or ethical end is made by Brentan (*Origin of the Ideas of Right and Wrong*, 1902). Brentano holds that, corre sponding to judgments which are true and self-evidencing, there are emotion judgments arising out of the concrete situation to which the quality rightness attaches. And when what is thus determined as right is also th object of the emotion of love, we have the good; and good finally takes form the end of human endeavour. But it is hard to see how the good can thus b

It may be granted that the first part of this statement has a substantial element of truth in it. After you have defined the ultimate end, you will not be able to show that this end is consciously before the minds of men at a particular time and place so as to guide their practice. More than this, the knowledge of the end, if it were present, would not account for the ethical situation as a whole. For knowledge of the end does not ensure practical consistency with the end and progress in that direction. Progress, we must remember, is no necessary process; and the moral life of a people at a given epoch instead of representing an upward movement may denote a failure to advance. It does not follow, however, that this betokens the collapse of the teleological method. Human action is purposive throughout, and moral action rests on an appreciation and selection of values. These values function as ends of human endeavour; and inasmuch as man is essentially a social animal, a πολιτικὸν ζῷον, whose well-being depends on others, these ends are determined as social. The social good which men set before them as the object of practical endeavour grows out of the ethical experience of society, and takes fresh and fuller form with the growth of that experience. The good which is willed by the individual can never be the Absolute Good as such, for that cannot be directly expressed in any single act: it must always be such a particular form of good as lies within the scope of his will and is realisable in the given social environment. But in a social system which is becoming complex, and in which there is a multiplicity of goods, if moral valuations are to be coherent and ethical practice is to be consistent, it is inevitable that a moral standard should be formed by

developed from the idea of right, for the term right as here used seems to involve the idea of good.

which the wills of individuals may be tested and directed to the larger good. And the standard, working through law, custom and public opinion, exercises a real influence on individuals even though they are not fully conscious of it ; it operates in bringing about a consistent direction of variously conditioned wills towards a common end. The justification of the individual end lies in its harmony with the universal end. The proof of the influence of such an end on social development does not depend on the capacity of individuals to formulate it explicitly : man seeks for more than he understands, and only the present shows how much there was in the past. The influence of the end is revealed where men are striving through the given forms of historic good towards something better. The words which Themistocles is said to have addressed to the Greeks before the battle of Salamis expressed the spirit by which, under the limitations of race and place, a society can move towards a universal good. The speech ran that, in all things pertaining to the nature and circumstances of man, there is always a higher and a lower, and they must choose the higher.[1]

How then are we to formulate the nature of this common end ? For social standards of value change, and if moral valuation is not to be purely relative, the standard must ultimately rest on an unconditioned end or ideal. This ideal will stand for the postulate on which Ethics depends; it is not a principle of explanation by which to give an adequate account of any historic phase of moral development. Now an attempt to formulate the ideal ought to have regard to the fact that the ideal must be at once social and personal : social, for there is no personal

[1] *Herod*, viii., 83. The account of the historic development of the Moral Ideal in Green's *Prolegomena to Ethics* will be appreciated by many who find difficulties in the metaphysics on which it is based.

development apart from society: and personal, for the good of society can only be a real good in so far as it is expressed in the consciousness of the persons who compose it. Some reference was made to the subject in the first chapter; and it may be well to repeat here what was said there, that, if we try to define the ultimate ethical ideal, we can only hope to do so in a formal way.[1] The content of the form is given through the good as historically experienced; and the good we have partially realised does not enable us to describe the living experience of the ideal good. The wisdom of age cannot be anticipated by youth, and the inner life of some far-off and ideal society cannot be forecast by those living in the present. When we try to give a consistent *form* to the ideal, we are led to think of a society of persons where the good of all is the good of each; where the individual life is a means to the social perfection, while society is equally a means to the full realisation of the good in its constituent members. In other words, the Ideal Good is one where personal ends are in full accord with the social end, and society in its turn subserves the complete and harmonious expression of personal powers. If the ethical ideal then can be designated the highest form of personal good, one can so far sympathise with the English School of ethical thought which has used the term self-realisation in this connexion. But I am prepared to admit with Dr. Rashdall, in his recent work, that the word as it stands is ambiguous.[2] Taken literally as the making real of the self which is, then no doubt the idea is contradictory, for the self is already real. On the other hand, this criticism does not apply, when we interpret the word to mean the making real in the personal life of the projected idea of a

[1] *Vid.* chap. i., p. 30.

[2] *The Theory of Good and Evil*, 1907, vol. ii., pp. 61–70.

higher self, through the effort of the individual wil
Regarded in this light the principle seems no more ope
to objection than the Aristotelian conception of εὐδαιμονί
as κατ' ἀρετὴν ἐνέργεια or ἐνέργεια ψυχῆς. And o
any view human good must be conceived as reached b
an activity of will which translates capacities into actuali
ties. Dr. Rashdall hardly does justice to the notion whe
he argues that the realisation of some capacity does no
distinguish between morality and immorality, for the ba
man also realises himself; and when he contends that th
realisation of all capacities is impossible, for to realis
some means to sacrifice others. Self-realisation, it seem
to me, is the form of moral progress, but I do not sa
that in itself it is a sufficient moral criterion: that wil
depend on the content or character of the projected self
Nor do I assert that every capacity of human natur
must be realised; under human limitations this is no
possible. An active philanthropist with artistic gift
might be justified in foregoing the realisation of th
latter in order to serve better the needs of his time: tha
would depend on the needs and the gifts in question
What self-realisation signifies is, that there should b
the fullest actualisation possible in the existing circumstances of those capacities which are consistent with
and lead towards the ethical ideal, or ultimate good, conceived in the form of a harmonious system of persons
When thus purged of ambiguity, the phrase self-realisation sets before us two characteristics of the moral
ideal: the ideal is a form of personal good; and it is
partially but progressively achieved by the ethical action
of persons. The term ought not to convey the thought
of an impersonal principle or idea which uses the human
will as a passive instrument to work out a predetermined
end. The process towards the ideal is rooted in per-

sonal activities, and it is gradual. Man advances by painful stages, and the goal in all its fulness is not before his eyes. His growth in ethical experience gives richer content to the ideal, but it likewise discloses the ideal in a region beyond the present, "on the limit far withdrawn." The goal moves with the traveller: at no point in the journey does he enter the land of promise, he only beholds it afar off. It is this fugitive character of the ideal to which Schiller refers in one of his poems :—

> "Ach, kein Steg will dahin führen,
> Ach, der Himmel über mir
> Will die Erde nie berühren,
> Und das Dort ist niemals Hier."

Yet this aspiration after the good, which never finds 'an earthly close,' seems to be bound up with the moral life as we know it, and we cannot think of a mundane order dissevered from the idea of endeavour and development. Progress implies a goal, but, the goal reached, an element of value in the process seems to have vanished.

At this point the question arises whether we can consistently think of the moral ideal embodied in a social system under present temporal and mundane conditions.[1] Subject to these conditions a state of society which nevertheless excluded change and development would not be desirable to us as we are now constituted. Without struggle and aspiration life would lose its interest, and in an earthly society where the actual coincided with the ideal the fashion of morality would have passed away. For the form of the moral life rests on the distinction and the difference of what *is* from what *ought to be*. On the other hand, if the moral ideal must be conceived as a

[1] Again *cf.* chap. i., p. 32 ff.

Supreme and Ultimate Good, it is impossible to think it under the image of a society in which the end is only in process of being realised ; because good presented in the form of a temporal development must always be conditioned, not absolute. In these circumstances some might deem it well to fall back on a doctrine of moral relativity, holding that the distinction between higher and lower values is valid, but asserting that the Absolute Value is an imaginative construction which changes with human change, and is not ultimately real. Yet if the idea of an Absolute Value is illusory, it is hard to see how the truth and validity of our ordinary valuations can be secured, since these depend for their coherency upon the standard. Moreover, any provisional standard you put forward must be based on an ultimate standard, and if this is illusory the whole system of value-judgments becomes unstable. As a logical consequence the certainty of objective good would be undermined, and every party and person might plausibly urge their claims to be the final arbiter of what was good for them. The natural issue would be the glorification of convention and the apotheosis of individualism. It was this sceptical conclusion, persuasively advanced by the Sophists, which became a great incentive to Plato to develop his Ideal Theory as a rational ground of thought and life. The Greek thinker conceived both theoretical and practical values to lead up to and have their source in a Supreme Value, the *ἰδέα τοῦ ἀγαθοῦ*, which was unconditioned, *αὐτὸ καθ' αὐτό*. And it is noteworthy that, in the *Republic*, he affirms that the metaphysical Idea of the Good must somehow transcend existence as given in man's temporal experience (*ἐπέκεινα τῆς οὐσίας*). The genius of Plato foreshadowed the truth which the latter-day moralist finds pressed upon him, the truth that the consequent attempt to think out the implications of the moral ideal takes us into the region of metaphysics, and involves the acceptance of some form of transcendency. For, as we have seen, the realisation of the Ideal Good under temporal and mundane conditions would be subversive of the spirit of the moral life.

Accordingly the thought lies to hand, that the failure to state the moral ideal in an absolute and finally satisfying form is not due to inconsistent thinking, but is the consequence of the fact that morality itself is neither final nor absolute. May the moral life not be the temporal form of a content which has its goal in the Supramundane and Eternal? Is it not possible that the ethical good is a phase, or, if you like, a stage on the way to a transcendent Good? To our mind, at least, a satisfying solution of the problem seems to lie in this direction, and the completion of Morality is, we believe, to be found in Religion. The ethical form is the realisation of an ideal self by the existing self: the religious ideal is the harmony and completion of the existing self through communion with a divine object. From the ethical point of view life is a vocation, where what *is* is ever confronted by what *ought to be*: from the religious point of view it is a temporal experience, through which the soul rises in faith to a divine fellowship and a peace which the world cannot give. Between the moral life and the religious consciousness there is no inner antagonism, nor is it possible to oppose them sharply to one another. A moral good is always an aspect of religious good, and a religious good is capable of being regarded from the moral standpoint. For religion is not only a matter of feeling and thought but also of will, and expresses itself as a "way of life." And in setting before men the life which "ought to be," it may be said to fall within the sphere of Ethics. On the other hand, regarded as the completion and ultimate destiny of personal beings, Religion, or fellowship with God, lifts the moral life beyond the realm of perpetual endeavour, and gives the soul, even intime, some foretaste of the harmonious completion which is its spiritual goal. The latter view, however, must be regarded as alone adequate, for to bring Religion entirely within the domain of Ethics inevitably leads to the interpretation of the relation to God as a means. But the God whom spiritual religion postulates, a Being who is Supreme Reality and Absolute Value, claims love and service for His own sake, and cannot without inconsistency be made a means to something beyond Himself. We cannot, I venture to think, sacrifice the absolute character of the Divine Object without our moral and religious valuations becoming incoherent, and our outlook on life sceptical. In Religion we have the personal assurance that those ontological presuppositions upon which Ethics rests are not illusory. The ethical spirit has its early growth under the guardian presence of Religion : and if by and by it goes its own way and claims to stand alone, still at the last, and as the fruit of reflexion on morality, we come to the conclusion that Religion in some form is the goal to which the moral life leads up. It may be worth while to make this dependence of Ethics on religious postulates somewhat clearer.

Ethics, in putting forward the idea of a universal end which it is the vocation of man to help to realise, makes demands on the real universe. For if the realisation of the end is primarily a human task, yet it is a task which depends on conditions that lie beyond the scope of the human will. Man's life rests on material elements which he did not create and can only imperfectly control ; and it is in and through a physical environment that he fulfils his spiritual calling. Were these conditions to become increasingly unfavourable to human activity, it is impossible to suppose the line of progress could continue open to the race. Consequently Ethics, with its doctrine of an ideal or universal end binding on human wills, must postulate that the universe will lend itself to the realisation of the ideal. To give a rational proof in justification of this postulate is beyond the power of the moralist, and this shows conclusively that Ethics as well as Religion involves an act of faith. The postulate itself carries with it the implication that the worlds which we contrast as natural and spiritual are inwardly related, and fall within the realm of a supreme purpose or teleological order. The rational justification of this conception, so far as it can be rationally justified, is the work of Metaphysics, and a theory of Ethics which develops its implications to their logical issue must involve metaphysical doctrines of some kind. Or to put it more definitely, if the worth of ethical ends is not to be imperilled, if we are to maintain that the material universe and the spiritual life are in the last resort in harmony, it is necessary to connect the ideal of humanity with the ultimate Ground of the World.[1] Now this is really what Religion does, though in a practical way and depending on faith more than on reason. For spiritual religion conceives the outward and the inward worlds, the worlds of facts and of value, to have their source and ground in God, who is the Supreme Reality and the Supreme Good. In thus linking the moral values of life with the highest object of his faith, the religious man finds their validity secured and his feeling of obligation towards them intensified. The importance of religion—and especially the theistic form of religion—in lending

[1] *Cf.* Wundt, *System der Philosophie*, 1889, p. 642.

the assurance of objectivity to the moral judgment must be kept in mind. For if morality is only a phase of human experience which is transcended in the Absolute, if moral distinctions have no meaning for the Absolute, it is hard to see how the validity of our moral judgments can be successfully upheld.[1] Our moral valuations derive their truth from their consistency with an ultimate End or Good, a Good continuous with the good in time but conceived as the final and eternal destiny of personal spirits. But if human good has no ground and counterpart in the Absolute, man can have no assurance that he is moving through the moral life to the fulfilment of his destiny in the universe. If the good we strive after under the form of morality does not lead up to and reach its consummation in a divine Good, morality loses touch with reality, and we might fairly refuse to stake vital issues on its truth. Moral uncertainty and slackness would be the natural outcome of the scepticism which Renan, in his later years, suggested was the portion of the wise. "There are many chances that the world may be nothing but a fairy pantomime of which no God has care. We must therefore arrange ourselves so that on neither hypothesis we shall be completely wrong. . . . *In utrumque paratus*, then. Be ready for anything—that perhaps is wisdom." An earnest and practical life cannot be based on such a shifting foundation, for this halting compromise is only fitted to puzzle the will, not to strengthen the hands. By accepting a divine vocation in life the religious man fortifies his moral decisions and gains confidence to follow what is higher. I do not assert or suggest that a genuine moral life depends on the acceptance of religious postulates : there is evidence that

[1] Dr. Rashdall (*Theory of Good and Evil*, vol. ii., p. 270 ff.) has some very relevant remarks on this point in criticism of Mr. F. H. Bradley.

practical devotion to the good may exist even where these are rejected. But on the whole such are exceptional cases, and can hardly be taken as a guide to the normal working of the human mind. In point of fact where there is a real and disinterested devotion to the good, there will be the demand that the idea of good have an ontological value that lifts it above the sphere of the shifting and relative : and religion is the response to this demand. Religion thus becomes the guarantee as it is the consummation of morality, and the moral life finds its place as an aspect under which the religious ideal is fulfilled.

It is, I think, in the light of the ontological postulates of the religious consciousness that the feeling of obligation must receive its final explanation. The content expressed by the word "ought" takes different forms at different stages of development, and is psychologically conditioned. Nor is the feeling itself an infallible index of the course to be pursued or an absolute rule of right. But the universality of the feeling justifies us in looking beyond temporal facts and psychological conditions for its origin. Its source must be sought in the nature of man as a free and personal being, a being with a destiny to fulfil in this universe in which he is called to choose and act. And between the individual and his final goal there must be some intrinsic bond of connexion. To realise what ought to be would thus be the free fulfilment on man's part of that which he has in him to become. The religious conception of a Divine Spirit by whom all spirits live, and to a full communion with whom it is their vocation to move, gives a reasonable meaning to that feeling of obligation which is a native heritage of the human soul. But the truth of this hypothesis will stand or fall with the theistic view of the world. At the same time, even though we accept this spiritual *Weltanschauung*, it is not possible to derive from it the idea of an absolute and divine Law to which all human wills should be subject. Under our present limitations any such Law formulated by us would not prove workable as a standard; and the laws which have been developed by historic religions bear the visible impress of a stage of human culture and cannot be treated as absolute norms. For human beings who grow in knowledge and spiritual experience, and in so doing outgrow the limitations of the past, the notion of a Law, whether human or divine, can only be provisional. It must be tested by the more ultimate category of End under which it falls to be subsumed.

A further word may be added in order to correct a possible misconception in regard to the nature of the human end or goal. This may be thought to lie only in the future, and its realisation may be supposed to imply an indefinite progress in time. Life, individual and social, certainly postulates time in which to work out the moral ideal. But we have already seen that the consistent statement of that ideal as ultimate is not possible in terms of our temporal and mundane existence; and from this we argued that morality itself is not ultimate. In confirmation it may be pointed out that, if a perfect society of persons on earth were the final end, this would mean that the great mass of personal beings must be treated as a mere step to a Good in which they were destined to have no share. The elect few in some remote age would possess the kingdom, while the many generations came and went, not even beholding it afar off. Here again the religious conception of the end comes to the help of the moral, and points a way out of the difficulty. The religious end can never be regarded as merely future. As the harmony and fulfilment of the personal life by fellowship with the Divine Life it is partially attained here and now, and is in a true sense a present possession. If we take the transcendent and eternal World to be the full reality which lies behind the temporal process, which is a lower grade of reality, it is possible to think of personal spirits as both developing in the historic process and yet reaching their consummation in a sphere which transcends that process. The conception has its difficulties, and it certainly implies the acceptance of some form of immortality. But we are guided towards this conclusion by finding that Morality leads up to Religion, and by bearing in mind that a social good must be an abstraction apart from the personal life-values in which it is realised. And if it is too much to expect Metaphysics to establish such a result, it may perhaps take us some way in this direction.

CHAPTER IX

THE ULTIMATE GROUND OF EXPERIENCE

We have hitherto been occupied in tracing the evolution of religion as an aspect of human experience. And we saw how development means a process of interaction between the different elements of the religious consciousness, and also between the religious consciousness and other phases of man's experience. Behind the whole movement, and giving it a unity, lies the human spirit with its perennial needs, advancing to fuller forms of satisfaction. For an insight into this process the study of the psychological nature of religion proved indispensable, and shed a needed light on features of the movement. At the same time it is evident that, if psychology is to say the last word about religion, religion is left in a highly ambiguous position. We have studied religion as a historic phenomenon and connected it with the nature of man ; we have estimated its place and function as an element in social life ; but the question of its ontological value, its ultimate meaning in the real universe, remains altogether in abeyance. The need of dealing with the problem in this case is practically urgent, for the religious consciousness makes an ontological postulate : it claims reality for itself and its object. You may indeed deny the validity of this claim and find the truth of religion to e simply its social working-value, but it is important to emember that the religious spirit itself could not main-ain its vitality if it shared your denial. Faith divorced rom reality, like the flower severed from its roots in the arth, is doomed to wither and die. By this it is not neant that faith depends on its every claim being ubstantiated: it does mean, however, that faith cannot ive on in the consciousness that its object is illusory. In he interests alike of truth and of religion, the student of eligion is urged therefore to embark on a higher enter-rise: the duty is pressed on him of testing the demands f religious faith in the open court of reason. We hall be told that the task of metaphysics is a profitless ne:—

> "Myself when young did eagerly frequent
> Doctor and saint, and heard great argument
> About it and about, but evermore
> Came out by the same door where in I went."

The fashion in metaphysics changes, as in other things; nd if a man live long enough, he may see the tenets vhich found favour in his youth fallen into disrepute. Even the metaphysician who refuses "to stake vital ssues" on the results of his profession is not perhaps ingular. Still, when all is said, we cannot get quit of netaphysics in some form: man cannot rest content with partial and departmental kind of knowledge, and is mpelled to seek the meaning of experience as a whole. Philosophy, as the systematic endeavour to read this neaning, is a constant problem, taking shape from age to ge with the growth of experience: the error lies in xpecting from it perfect certainty or absolutely final esults.[1] Experience itself is a stream still growing and

[1] Metaphysics, it has been well said, seeks to achieve the most complete and east relative knowledge of the world. Heymans, *Einführung in die Metaphysik*. 905, p. 1.

gathering in volume: the knowledge represented by th special sciences is ever increasing in extent and com plexity; hence the synthesis achieved by philosophy mus be provisional. None the less, philosophy, its outlool being synoptic and its method that of thinking thing together, has an indispensable function to fulfil. When i is faithful to itself it guards against a narrow specialisn which is bold to speak for the whole; and it points to unity behind all the diversities of experience, the counter part of the unity of personal life. Nor can the religiou thinker, on the plea perhaps of a theology historicall guaranteed, evade commerce with philosophy; for dogma which are metaphysical propositions must submit to th test of coherent thinking. A dogma, even when pu forward as embodying the fruit of reflexion on spiritu experience, must be discredited if it permanently refuse to cohere with the larger whole of knowledge: and th standpoint of the theologian who invokes reflexion t justify religious doctrine, while denying to reason th right to criticise it, is quite untenable. Metaphysics an Religion agree in postulating a Supreme Ground to th world; but the former seeks to connect the two b reflective thinking, while the latter posits the Object i response to spiritual needs and demands. Hence the on regards its goal as primarily Supreme Reality, the other a primarily Supreme Value. And while the religiou thinker cannot avoid intercourse with philosophy, as littl can the philosopher refuse recognition to religion. If th vision of the speculator is really synoptic, it must includ and study so persistent and characteristic a line of exper ence as the development of religion. He is not free t disregard the movement on the plea that its object illusory. For even the genesis and meaning of an illusio have to be explained. A philosophy of experience whic did not embrace a philosophy of the religious consciousness would be open to the charge of neglecting its catholic function, and of ignoring a significant body of facts. The ability to deal with all aspects of experience is a test of the soundness of a philosophical system.

In the present chapter the ontological problem involved in religion is approached by a discussion of the Ultimate Ground of Experience. The subject belongs to General Metaphysics and its treatment here is necessarily rapid and incomplete ; nor can it have the weight of an extended and detailed handling of the relative problems by one fully qualified. But some attempt seemed necessary for reasons already indicated, and in this chapter I offer the outline of an argument which may show the kind of answer that ought, as I think, to be given to the questions at issue. In the circumstances it appears admissible to bestow greater consideration upon those points which have special relevancy to the ulterior object I have in view. Hence some features in the Theory of Knowledge are examined with comparative brevity to allow of a fuller discussion of those problems where Metaphysics comes into close contact with Religion. The results reached will furnish a basis on which to discuss, in a concluding chapter, some ultimate problems of religious development. As to method I propose to take up first certain familiar solutions of the problem of experience, and show briefly where they seem to be defective. This will help to define the direction in which the present task lies and to prepare the way for developing a positive argument. I will begin with the naïve or common-sense attitude.

The ordinary man, innocent of science and philosophy, sees a solid and independent world without him, and over against it he recognises an inward world, a world of which he is directly conscious in thinking, feeling and willing. As part of that external world he finds other human beings who possess faculties like his own. The process of experience is no mystery to him, and knowledge is both natural and easy: things are there outside us waiting to be known, and as we know them so they are in themselves, whether we are there to observe them or not. The ordinary individual never dreams of doubting this, for other people, he believes, see the same things and treat them in the same way that he does, and where all believe alike they cannot be deluded. This natural realism, though it represents the prevailing attitude of the man in the street, can never be thorough and systematic and the observing mind cannot continue very long in this faith without coming across facts which bid him pause and reconsider his position. If things are just what we experience them to be, how come there to be errors and illusions, a fact which is obvious and practically important? The stick thrust into the water seems bent but cannot be so, the object which appears small in the distance must be a good deal larger than it looks, the person I was sure was my friend turns out on closer inspection to be a stranger. So everything is not to be taken straightway at its face value: correction of first impressions is sometimes necessary. The need of this was made very plain by the existence of certain illusions of sense to which all men are subject; and, as the origin of these illusions cannot lie in the object, which, it is assumed, does not change, it must be found in the conditions of sense-perception. Certain qualities we attribute to objects seem especially associated with divergences of judgment in different individuals, qualities like colour and temperature, taste, and smell; and a natural way out of the difficulty was to say that these qualities simply stood for impressions the thing made on *us* and were not really ocated in the spatially extended *thing*. Position, magnitude, and mass were in a different category and belonged o the object itself. So arose the familiar distinction between primary and secondary qualities which received its classical expression in the work of Locke. And though the theory quickly fell into philosophic disrepute, one can hardly doubt that it stands for a way of regarding experience common to a number of intelligent people, and especially to those with some scientific training. If you do not probe very deep, this seems a feasible way of giving its due to the external world, while also allowing that the senses have something to do in filling up the character of the object presented to us.

To Natural Science, at least in the earlier stages of its development, this theory had a distinct attractiveness. The man of science is commonly content to assume that the world extended in space and time, whose masses and movements he investigates, is a real world ; and if the organ of hearing gives us the sound, the waves of air are outside us and independent of us. Motion and mass, action and reaction, the conservation of energy, are real facts in the external structure of the world, and go to form that mechanical system which man neither makes nor mars. Space and time within which the world is set are themselves independent realities, and the universe with its boundless distances exists by its own right, and it was there when there was no human consciousness to perceive it. This was the scientific realism of Newton's time, and it was held by many men of science in the nineteenth century. But Natural Science, in the pursuit of its proper task, has tended to move away from this type of realism, and to substitute for it what has been called a 'transfigured realism.' While the independence of matter is not denied, the later investigations of the physicist have all gone to show that the nature and structure of matter are something very different from what the naïve empiricist takes them to be. In trying to analyse the ultimate elements of which matter is composed, the modern man of science goes far beyond what can be perceived or manipulated by the organs of sense. The moving atom or the vibrating ether cannot by any device be verified by the senses, and are only reached by a process of inference. To the chemist resolving a body into molecules, and these again into quantitative combinations of atoms, a material substance means something very different from what it does to the untrained observer. Indeed one might say that, under the examination of the man of science, the seemingly simple substance is gradually transformed into a complicated theory of the relations of ultimate elements. And this regress from the empirical fact does not come to a pause. It has been said that the movement of science is towards the explanation of the complex through simpler elements, but these seemingly simple elements in turn show themselves under analysis to be complex.[1] This statement is strikingly illustrated by the most recent theory of matter, the electrical, in which the once ultimate atom is resolved into a system of swiftly moving corpuscles. The corpuscle is a negatively charged unit or electron, and in the stable atom the negative electricity is balanced by the positive.[2] By the escape of corpuscles from the atom through their own excessive velocity or by a collision of the atom itself, the latter becomes unstable, and chemical combination, or the composite molecule, appears to represent the union of atoms which

[1] *Cp.* Poincaré, *Science and Hypothesis*, p. 173.

[2] I am aware that this theory—that of Prof. J. J. Thomson—is criticised in some points, and the existence of positive electrons is suggested. But the point is not essential to my argument, which is directed to show that brute matter becomes a complicated and invisible system of elements under modern analysis.

electrically balance each other. Electricity, in other words, binds the atoms into molecules. The electrical theory of matter opens out a way of explaining phenomena like Valency, the Periodic-Law, and Radio-activity. Sir Oliver Lodge has suggested that positive and negative electricity are due to a "shear" at a critical point of the ether, the continuous and incompressible medium which the scientist postulates as extending through the universe. And he would define matter thus: "Specks of electrified ether, isolated yet connected by fields of force, and in a state of violent locomotion"—these in great aggregates we call matter.[1]

Physicists, I suppose, agree that the electrical theory of the atom is a better working hypothesis than the vortex-theory associated with the name of Lord Kelvin. To say that it will be final is another matter, and we may note the judgment of Poincaré, who remarks, "It would be rash to say that the belief in electrons will not undergo an eclipse."[2] But I wish to direct attention to two points. On the one hand modern science has moved far from the standpoint of natural realism. And, on the other hand, the hypotheses which have marked its progress have one by one proved partial and inadequate. Where they justified themselves it was as good working methods of dealing with phenomena, not as full and satisfying explanations.

It is specially noteworthy that, within recent years, among some eminent men of science a new attitude has developed in regard to the significance of scientific method and the formulæ and hypotheses with which science works.[3] Writers of this school frankly abandon the

[1] *Modern Ideas of Electricity*, 1907, p. 341.

[2] *Op. cit.*, p. 165.

[3] Among those who identify themselves with the new way of viewing things are Karl Pearson in England, Boutroux and Poincaré in France, and, among German scientists, Ostwald and Mach.

position that scientific theories and laws are explanations in the true sense of the term : they regard them rather as a kind of "conceptual shorthand," as abridged descriptions or 'economical' statements by which man facilitates the process of manipulating nature for his practical ends. The physicist selects a particular aspect of the experienced world for study, and, neglecting the other aspects, proceeds to frame definitions and adopt conventions ; he then presents, in the abbreviated form of equations, symbolic descriptions of the way in which phenomena act within this sphere.[1] And sometimes the conventional and arbitrary aspect of the process is put so strongly that one is disposed to object that not every formula will work but only the formula which does justice to the facts. Nevertheless this group of thinkers give due emphasis to a very important truth, the truth that mechanism is only an aspect of nature, and a highly abstract aspect. They would have no quarrel with a philosopher like Prof. James Ward when he terms the time, space, and mass of dynamics abstractions.[2] When for instance you interpret mechanically the action and reaction of two bodies, you artificially isolate them and neglect a wealth of detail which cannot be irrelevant to a full understanding of the process. What Bacon said of the syllogism is precisely true of mechanism as a theory : it is *subtilitati naturae longè impar*. The limitations of the mechanical view come out clearly when we consider that quantitative relations can be thrown into the form of equations which express a universal functional dependence. From the independent variable you can proceed analytically to its functions, and from these return

[1] "Science is a body of signs invented by the mind to interpret things, and so make them subserve human purposes." Boutroux, *Science et Religion*, p. 241.

[2] *Naturalism and Agnosticism*, vol. ii., p. 66.

synthetically to the starting point. The process is a reversible one, and the mathematician employs both methods. But a dependence of this kind is quite inapplicable to the development of an organism, which is not reversible, nor has it any place in the sphere of human history.

It is not surprising that some scientists of the 'economic school' should abandon a 'transfigured realism,' and simply postulate sensationalistic data as the matter with which conceptual thinking deals. Prof. Pearson, for instance, regards the atom and molecule as "intellectual conceptions," and asserts that "matter, force, action at a distance are not terms which express real problems of the phenomenal world."[1] And Prof. Mach defines bodies as "compendious mental symbols for groups of sensations."[2] This comes near to Mill's conception of matter as "a permanent possibility of sensations."

The result is remarkable, for science under the leading of some of its chief representatives appears to have executed a complete *volte face*. Beginning in natural realism and following out its argument, it has finally arrived at the standpoint of idealism. The world which is presented to the mind is recognised to reveal in its fashion and texture the mind's work of ideal construction. And scientists have reached this conclusion largely because they have come to see the selecting, abstracting, and conceptualising activity of the human mind in the formation of scientific theory.

Natural and scientific realism thus break down as a theory of experience. Under the stress of criticism they are obliged so to revise their original assumptions, that in the end they have passed away from the position they

[1] *The Grammar of Science*, 1900, pp. 95, 276.
[2] *Popular Science Lectures*, Eng. Trans., p. 201.

occupied at first. But if realism is forced to make concessions to idealism, it remains to ask whether idealism with the means at its disposal is able to furnish a full explanation of experience. Idealism, however, is a large word, and I shall first examine briefly the type of Subjective Idealism which is usually identified with the name of Berkeley. The cardinal feature of Berkeley's earlier idealism—with its later phases we are not here concerned—was the assertion that *esse* is *percipi*. Matter is an abstract idea which has no counterpart in actual experience, and Locke's substance, the "support of qualities," is only a figment of the mind. If you press home the question what you mean by material substance, you find that it means nothing more than the perceiving acts of the human spirit ; and as an intelligible whole the impressions of sense form a kind of visual language by which the Deity communicates an orderly experience to mortals. From ideas or impressions of sense Berkeley distinguished notions, and he declared we had a notion of other persons which differentiated them from our perception of things. But for the modern philosopher the salient defects of his system are his failure to distinguish clearly sensation from thought, and his assumption that ideas are merely individual facts which can be arbitrarily related to one another. Without, however, lingering on familiar ground, let us consider shortly how far this type of idealism deals fairly with the world of experience. And to bring the matter more into line with present discussions, let us suppose the distinction between sense-perception and conceptual thinking drawn, and the organising and universalising activity of self-conscious minds recognised. In this case if you abstract from the generalising work of human minds, there will remain certain sensationalistic data or impressions of sense standing for the aspect in which things are supposed to be given to us. These data are not made by us but found, or if you prefer, necessarily experienced. The question therefore is, whether these affections of sense, in all their variety and degree, can be construed as the operation of a Divine Mind on our minds, and if the world of nature just means such an operation. A theological idealism of this sort, if offered as a philosophy of experience, cannot claim to be accepted on faith simply; we want if possible to know something of the way in which the Divine Mind impresses experiences on human minds. The analogy of intersubjective intercourse does not hold, for our minds act and react on one another through a sensuous medium which supplies a means of interpretation. If we are to suppose a sensation in the Divine Mind identical with the sensation in the human mind, the logical issue would seem to be that the mind of man is only a phase of the mind of God and pantheism is the outcome. To avoid this it may be said that God somehow causes the impressions of sense in men, but is not identical with them. This would mean that all the so-called "permanent possibilities of sensation," which we construe as an external world, represent fixed ways of acting on us by the Divine Spirit. The explanation of the seemingly independent world of things would be the constant operation of God, an operation which we do not will but receive. The permanency and order of the natural world just mean the uniform activity of God. The readiness to postulate divine Causality to explain the features of experience makes it difficult to refute this theory directly. Some of the points at issue will come up for treatment at a later stage, and I shall confine myself now to a few observations.

The distinction of outer and inner experience only

emerges clearly at the stage of conceptual thinking; but it is a universal, not an arbitrary distinction, and there must be a sufficient reason for drawing it. Can that reason be found in our receptivity to divine working as opposed to our self-activity? If we trust recent psychology, activity and receptivity are inseparably blended, and no clear-cut division of experience could be drawn on such a principle. Not even when our sense of passivity is pronounced do we necessarily treat the experience as external. The feelings are invariably regarded as belonging to the inner world, and yet a feeling of dejection or an emotion of fear may come to us independently of our own will. We do not on that account project them into the field of outer experience. Nor, as it seems to me, does the theory offer any satisfying explanation of the distinction man draws between his body and the surrounding environment on the one hand, and between his body and his mind on the other. The body stands for a group of experiences qualitatively distinct; and it is hard to see why, if this idealism be true, the body should be differentiated in any way from the world of outward objects among which it takes its place. For both my body and my environment are just ways of God's acting on my mind. Recourse might be had to the idea that the body represents a special and intimate mode of divine action upon the mind. So while my experience of another man's body stands for one mode of God's action, the man's experience of his own body stands for another, and my voluntary movement towards him would be an experience of a different sort altogether. Here we have assumptions rather than explanations, assumptions which you may justify by an appeal to divine omnipotence, but hardly by an appeal to human reason. Nor from idealists of this type does one clearly learn how the progressive forms of animal life are to fit into their scheme—how far, as Berkeley might have said, these exist as *ideas* or as *notions*. The artificiality of this idealism will always prove a drawback to its acceptance; and ordinary men and many philosophers will find it hard to believe that the house I see from time to time has no real persistence, but only denotes a series of divine operations upon my mind, renewed again and again as occasion demands.

Compared with the slender structure of Berkeley the Transcendental Idealism of Kant is a far more imposing edifice: and his system has the great advantage of distinguishing and relating perceptual and conceptual experience, and referring both to the unity of self-consciousness. Kant's merit is to articulate the formal aspect of experience, and to set in relief the universalising activity of self-conscious mind. At the same time, if we look to his ultimate analysis, Kant comes nearer to the position of Berkeley than to that of Leibniz, whose monad evolves the whole wealth of experience from its inner nature. To both Kant and Berkeley the experienced world is the outcome of a process of interaction,—in the one case interaction between God and human minds, in the other between the thing-in-itself, which is the ground of sense-affection, and the pure ego. The great difference is, that the orderly structure of experience is impressed on the subject by the (divine) object in Berkeley's theory, and is the outcome of the spontaneous activity of the subject in Kant's. There is much that is cumbrous and artificial about the steps by which Kant supposed the synthetic unity of apperception was realised; but, omitting any attempt to criticise details, let us concentrate our attention on one point. Is the Kantian effort to explain the connected and coherent world of objective experience from the side of the subject successful? Here let it be granted that Kant, if he does not always keep the fact in sight, still in the main drift of his argument relates the world of things in space and time to consciousness in general, and not to the particular ego. But admitting this, we have yet to ask if consciousness, as a general synthetic activity working through the functions of understanding and the pure forms of intuition (space and time) upon the manifold of sense, can give us the variously qualified world of perceptual fact. Now the thing-in-itself, regarded from the side of the object, is a thin abstraction, a mere fugitive ὕλη not capable of imparting concrete character and definiteness to the objects of sense-perception. One must conclude, then, that the determinate character and the setting of individual things are due to the form. Let us see how this works in the case of perception and conception. Now it is hard to see in what way a pure *a priori* form of perception, like the Kantian space, can be read into a non-spatial matter of sense at all: and even if it could, how are we to suppose that a mere contentless form should localise data of sense x, y, and z at A, B, and C, rather than D, E, and F? For in itself it can contain no ground why they should not fall into the positions M, N, P, rather than D, E, F, or A, B, C. The like insurmountable difficulty occurs in the case of time. So obviously there must be something in the datum of sense which determines it to be here rather than there, now rather than then; and the notion of a pure constitutive form of perception will not work. A similar difficulty emerges when we turn to the functions of the understanding. Take for example Kant's reply to Hume in the matter of causality. The gist of the Kantian argument is, that the category of cause and effect cannot be an experiential belief engendered by association, for it is already involved in the existence of experience. The apperceptive subject organises experience according to the principle of determinate connexion in time, this being the logical condition of experience falling within the unity of self-consciousness. Now it does not seem to be true, as Kant said, that we cannot think succession apart from causal connexion. Moreover, he had to make the significant admission that, while the general principle of causal connexion is *a priori*, the connexion of particular causes with particular effects is learned by experience. The formation of ice on a pool, for instance, is a change, and the proposition that this change must have a cause is a synthetic judgment determined *a priori* by the unity of apperception. But the connexion of this change with a particular atmospheric temperature is gathered from experience, and the synthetic function determines nothing in this regard. Now this position is extremely precarious; as is very evident when you bear in mind that causality is not a regulative but a constitutive principle for Kant. For it comes to this, that all the particular connexions of our given world are experimentally ascertained, and consequently must depend on the specific nature of the elements which are connected. And yet behind the specific connexions which make up all the changes in time is a thought-form which determines that causal relations shall exist at all. An *a priori* category, however, will not go to determine an orderly world if it simply prescribes that things must be causally related; for the rule would still hold good though the effects a, b, c were preceded indifferently by A, B, C, or by D, E, F, or by X, Y, Z. But experience on these terms would be quite incoherent, and if the *a priori* judgment is to work it must determine that A, B, and C shall have the succession a, b, and c and no other. This determinate succession is due to the specific character of the elements in question, and we learn it from experience. Empiricism, after the onslaught of Kant, begins to lift its head again !

It is important to remember that Kant was further hampered by a peculiar difficulty. For him the whole of an object A, which underwent change, was not embraced by the synthetic unity of apperception ; there was a residual x that was somehow given, an x which the Kantian philosophy could neither do anything with nor yet do without. So it seemed there might be a way out of this and other difficulties which attached to the Kantian work by discarding the thing-in-itself behind nature, rejecting Kant's extraordinary doctrine that the empirical self, as the object of inner sense, is not real, and raising the pure ego from an abstraction to the supreme centre and organising ground of all experience. This line of thought had its most impressive expression in the work of Hegel, and I shall now proceed to ask how far the Hegelian Idealism deals successfully with the problem that baffled Kant.

It must be granted that, by rejecting the dualistic and the individualistic elements in Kant, and developing the larger aspect of his idealism, Hegel and his followers achieved a far more consistent and systematic treatment of knowledge. For Absolute Idealists the organic structure of self-consciousness embraces all experience within itself, and the distinction of outer and inner only stands for the difference between a more abstract and a more concrete stage in the evolution of spirit. Nature, we are told, does not depend on the individual mind but on self-consciousness as a universal and fully articulated system. Ideas, not as psychical facts but as universal meanings, constitute the objective world : and " An idea always stands for something, is a symbol of something else than itself to the ego

hat has the idea."[1] This realm of meanings, it is
ırgued, though it sets out from the world of conscious
:xperience and refers back to it, is something more than
an be directly apprehended : and in its permanence and
ıniversality it has the character of objectivity. It used to
›e urged against some of the statements of the late Prof.
Green, that relations without something to relate are
utile ; and the same may be said of meanings. The
ystem of ideas is supposed to explain the seeming
ndependence of the material world as ground of possible
xperience, while it likewise guarantees that there is
ıothing in that world which is not the constructive work
›f intelligence. If the first statement is tested by the
econd, it cannot, I think, be regarded as sound.
Nothing is gained by calling nature a system of meanings
ınless you are prepared to admit that a meaning must
lways refer to something other than itself,—something
vhich has meaning, just as appearance points to some-
hing which appears. As little use is it to speak of the
bject as 'ideal construction' if you deny that this
neans a construing by the mind of a reality which has a
haracter and way of acting of its own, and which
nanifests itself to us in terms of sense. And when ideal
ontent is identified with existence, there must always be
omething inexplicable in the simple facts of everyday
xperience,—in the inevitable manner in which the objects
›f perception impress themselves upon us, in the unique
haracter and context of individuals, and in the way they
naintain themselves and persist through change. Setting
ut from the ideal and formal side of knowledge you
ıever reach what is specific and individual : hence even

[1] Caird, *Philosophy of Kant*, Vol. I., pp. 640–641. Prof. J. S. Mackenzie has
bly expounded and defended this view in an article in *Mind*, N.S. No. 59, entitled
'he New Realism and the Old Idealism ; and I have had in view some of his
atements in the criticisms I have offered.

the simple and elementary experiences on which ideal con-struction works must already be qualified by the presenc of a reality which is independent of the experient subject It may be argued that it is impossible to distinguisl sharply between consciousness and that of which we ar conscious. But to this one might reply that we are com pelled to distinguish the content from the object of know ledge where the object is another person. And in th case of a natural object it is not necessary that we shoul sharply oppose the thing to the consciousness of it. I would be more true to say that the character of the thin is revealed to us in the ideal construction by which w make explicit what is involved in our immediate con sciousness of it. Before passing from the point we ma remark that the theory under criticism derives a certai plausibility from the freedom with which it treats ideas a if they had an independence and vitality of their own On this supposition they are regarded as constituting significant system waiting to be consciously apprehended I confess I am quite unable to see how ideas can have th objective reality we ascribe to things ; for they are onl real in so far as they express activities of living minds Meaning no doubt is not private and individual merely but still it has not existence for itself beyond the activit of cognising subjects. And to speak of meanings a having a kind of being for themselves is only plausibl because, ignoring the mental process which develop them, you make them coincide with the realities whic yield meaning.

If we turn now to the subjective aspect of experience, w find Absolute Idealism is equally baffled in trying to giv a satisfactory account of the individual as distinguishe from the divine Self. Here again the truth seems to b that we get only the general form, not the uniquel qualified individual of experience. If the idealist is in earnest with the conception of 'consciousness in general' and its timeless structure as logical ground of experience, hen the personal self-consciousness becomes only an illusory appearance of the universal. The serious nature of the difficulty is clearly revealed in the intrepid but un-uccessful attempt which T. H. Green made to deal with t in his *Prolegomena to Ethics.*[1] The problem before him was to reconcile the timeless consciousness, the principle of unity in all experience, with the finite, changing and variously qualified self. And what he has to tell us is his. Consciousness as a gradual though interrupted de-velopment in time is a function of the animal organism, but notwithstanding it is somehow an Eternal Consciousness which makes the animal organism its vehicle. Yet this is not to be taken to mean a double consciousness but only wo aspects of an indivisible consciousness, which we annot comprehend in a single conception. Looking back on Green's theory after the lapse of a generation, few will be found to deny that here, as Sidgwick said, was a "fundamental incoherence." The difficulty of bring-ng the two aspects of consciousness into unity was not due, as Green thought, to our human limitations: it was owing to the incompatible nature of the terms to be united. Consciousness cannot at one and the same moment be in time and out of time, developing yet com-plete, human and divine, my consciousness and also the consciousness of all other selves.

The *impasse* to which Absolute Idealism brings us is due to its principle rather than to the details of its argu-mentation. For the cardinal article of its creed is, that the object has no reality save as known by the subject or

[1] *Vid.* Pars. 32, 67 and 68. *Cp.* also Sidgwick's criticism in *Mind*, N.S., No. 37.

self-consciousness in general. And we are confirmed in our conclusion that the unsatisfactory result flows from the principle when we remember that Plato and Aristotle by making the constitutive principle of real beings the idea or universal, became entangled in a like perplexity when trying to explain the individual. The problem of participation (μέθεξις), in other words the problem how the material thing could share in the fixed and eternal form, was a baffling one for Plato; and in the *Parmenides* his keen dialectic reaches an altogether inconclusive result in this regard. It seems hard to doubt that the great thinker is here criticising views which at one time he had shared, and that the master is anticipating the objections of his foremost pupil. With this we may compare Kant's failure to effect a complete and final synthesis of subject and object. Aristotle sought to escape Plato's dilemma by a more thorough correlation of the formal and material elements, the one being conceived not as beyond but *in* the many. Yet having accepted the doctrine of the form as real and constitutive, Aristotle was confronted with the task of showing how the εἶδος, which is common to the many, can give its concrete and individual character to the one among the many. Obviously the ὕλη in the end would require to mean something more than the privation of form, but Aristotle could not develop this view without seriously modifying the idealistic assumptions he had inherited from Plato. Hence he continued to cherish the thought that the form constitutes the individual. But Aristotle, with his scientific habit of mind, saw the perils of 'over-unification,' and he avoided the embarrassments of an Absolute Idealism by leaving an ultimate dualism in his philosophy: over against the elusive 'first matter' stands the abstraction of a Supreme Form, a thought which is its own content (νόησις νοήσεως)

Formal Idealism, ancient and modern, finally breaks down before the problem of individuality.

The stress I have laid on the inability of these types of idealism to do justice to the concrete wealth of the world of nature is, I venture to believe, essential. For the regress which reflective thought makes from the experienced world to its Ultimate Ground must depend, for its cogency, on a fair and unbiassed acceptance of the facts of experience at the outset. In this endeavour to do justice to experience, the counsel "back to Kant" will not help us, and especially when it is taken to mean that we are to fall back on the Kantian epistemology as it stands. If Kant taught us that experience is not a product mechanically impressed on the mind, if he helped us to recognise the mind's work of ideal construction in the things we know, his synthesis is nevertheless too exclusively intellectual in its character. For the synthetic activity is conative as well as intellective, and in the selective interest which goes to fashion our experience the will is essentially operative. Then, instead of assuming that the secret of knowledge lies in certain fixed and *a priori* forms of judgment, we shall rather look for light to the historic growth of experience which is the outcome of the interaction of living minds.

The present-day student who faces the question of the meaning and ground of experience finds the standpoint from which Kant proceeded to develop his answer unduly narrow. It is not enough to ask, What are the presuppositions of the experienced world as the object of the existing scientific consciousness? For experience is a growing process, and it is realised at very various levels, of which scientific knowledge is only one. Beneath man there extends a long series of animal forms possessing a being for themselves, able to react selectively on their environment, and maintaining an inner life which stands for an experience of some kind. Throughout this range of being action is not mechanical but purposive inasmuch as even the lower-grade organism displays powers of dealing with its environment in ways that help to maintain its life. *Suum esse conservare*, to use Spinoza's phrase, is a note of the living thing which differentiates it from mechanism. In the region of instinct this power of acting in order to conserve the life of the individual and the species assumes complex forms which, to beings accustomed to deliberative action, appear wonderful indeed. Here is evidence that conative activity may be purposive, and surely reach its goal, without rising into the region of knowledge and reflective will. Nor can there be any doubt that knowledge, which grows upon a basis of free ideas, at its earliest stage is simply an instrument for action and only lifts instinct to a higher level. There is no divorce between them; the more advanced phase of experience is prepared for by the lower and still carries with it instinctive elements.[1] Human intelligence is essentially a growth, a growth made possible by language, the medium of intersubjective intercourse and through language reaching conceptual thought. It is impossible to suppose that intelligence is a rigidly determined whole of forms: it has developed, and therefore has revealed the plasticity of every growing structure. The

[1] M. Bergson attaches too little weight to the evidence for continuity in development, when he speaks of the Life-impulse splitting organisation into the complementary forms of plants and animals in the search for an outlet to its explosive energy. Not finding this outlet in instinct, it has attained it in the intelligence of man by making a sudden leap upward from the animal. The only finalism Bergson admits is that of a unitary *vis a tergo*, a primordial life-impulse (élan originel de la vie). But even if a realm of meanings and values could be abruptly generated by the upward thrust of an impulsive life-principle, the principle must surely be something better than blind. *Vid. L'Évolution Créatrice*, 1907, pp. 95, 200–1 and *passim*.

experienced world at each stage has been the reflexion of the inner level of development of the experient individual. At the animal stage experience is restricted to percepts. On the level of primitive culture the causally connected world of science is unknown, and all causes are construed as living agencies. Civilised thought has evolved the conception of a mechanically determined world of things standing over against cognising minds.

In trying to think out the meaning of this developmental process, it is important to recognise that we cannot begin with a self and an independent not-self, and then proceed to ask how they come to stand in relation. The only fruitful path of discussion is to follow the genetic method, and enquire how they come to be differentiated. The question of the existence of a transsubjective object becomes definite only on the higher levels of experience, and it is only reflective thinking which can find it involved in the elementary forms of experience. The most rudimentary kind of consciousness would be a *continuum* of feeling, a felt whole in which differences are submerged. Progress is made possible by the awareness of qualitative differences in feeling which call forth appropriate reactions, and by the development of sensory organs which are responsive to various stimuli from the environment. There is no warrant for supposing that experience at any point begins with an incoherent matter of sense, a mere manifold of sensation which has to be coerced into order by the experient subject. The apperceptive self of Kant is really the highest term of a spiritual development, and its function must be connected with what has gone before it. As experience passes beyond feeling pure and simple and becomes differentiated in sense, it advances on an orderly basis of elements already existing. Coherency lies behind the growth of the subject and is not created by it. This comes out clearly when we consider the development of perceptual consciousness, with its presentation of sense-experiences in the form of things extended in space and persisting in time. We saw when dealing with Kant, that to read pure forms of perception into a manifold of sense independently given was not a possible operation. Consequently these simple and universal forms of order must be prepared for and made possible by the coherent constituents of experience itself. The world of coexisting things in space and successive events in time is not a subjective point of view but a valid interpretation. It is legitimate no doubt to lay stress on the ideal and constructive character of conceptual space and time; and there is truth in the dictum that "perceptions without conceptions are blind." But while this holds of a man's developed consciousness, it must not be taken to mean that the perceptual world is unreal. This is the world in which the higher animals live and move, and there is an early stage in the experience of the human individual which does not transcend perception. On this level objects are not generalised, and space and time are not abstracted from experience and conceived as infinite and all-inclusive wholes.

The development of conceptual thought by the help of language is the achievement of man, and generalised thinking brings about a far larger and more permanent idea of the world. Only at this stage are the relation and distinction of subject and object fully articulated, and the inner is set over against the outer world. Here again conceptual inference does not develop a conclusion without premises which have their roots in prior levels of experience. At the purely perceptual stage the individual has familiarised itself with experiences which it refers, for practical purposes, to its environment, and with others which are more intimately connected with its own body. Apart from this distinguishing capacity, the higher animals at all events could not survive in the struggle for existence. In the case of man, a step towards the evolution of the idea of inner experience was undoubtedly the primitive notion of soul or spirit provoked by dreams. A second and finer self within, which had the power to leave the body and return to it, became for the savage a means of explaining his illusions. This is the rude germ of the notion of consciousness as inward; but it was reserved for conceptual thinking, generalising impressions, gradually giving fixity in idea to groups of sensations connected with the not-self and marking them off as objective, to bring into clearness the conception of the subject as the permanent possessor of inner states. The mind long used to reflective thinking finds the universal distinction of subject and object simple and elementary: it is plain, however, that it is derivative, and that the outer and the inner worlds have evolved *pari passu*. The common world of universal experience in which civilised men move is the outcome of a long and continuous development, and has been reached through the lowlier forms of psychical experience,—through feeling, sensation and perceptual consciousness.

In recent years the conative aspect of knowledge has been emphasised, and it is true that selective interest and practical needs have played a large part in guiding and controlling the work of ideal construction. Man seeks to know in order to act, and he first attends to and develops those aspects of experience which are bound up with the wants of life. And we present an important side of the truth, when we speak of men organising the world of their experience after the pattern of their needs. But it is wrong to talk of the experienced world as being altogether moulded by the demands of appercipient subjects ; for the object, whatever its ultimate nature, is not a purely plastic medium but makes its own demands on the subject. The world often proves intractable to human wants and desires ; not every conception is found to work ; and the environment sets limits to selective activity. So the realm of universal experience, with its contrast of subject and object, arises as the outcome of interaction, and the result is never to be reached by setting out from either side of the antithesis. The broad generalisation of self and non-self which conceptual thought sets forth runs back to simpler forms, but at no point does it lapse into a flawless identity. The developmental process reveals a teleological unity, and postulates an inner adaptation of its factors. Thus the thought and will of the subject realise themselves within the objective world, and it is from out this objective world that man with his purposive activity has emerged. And this could not be if the elements of experience were not ultimately coherent, a whole co-ordinated and unified by an indwelling end.

In criticising Kant we concluded he was justified in holding that experience involves an activity on the part of the subject. This truth is very apparent in the sphere of conceptual thought, for every attempt to evolve such a process from the mechanical association of isolated elements has hopelessly broken down. The comparing and referring activity of the mind, and the movement by which it passes from one idea to another in the way of logical inference, cannot be expressed by any process of association or by an induction from experiences. In the matter of identity, which is the nerve of logical inference, this is transparent ; for the simplest form of induction already presupposes it, and the most elementary movement of thought, such as recognition, would be impossible without it. The self which ideally construes experience can only do so by distinguishing and referring differences to an identity; and if experience did not conform to this condition, it would cease to be our experience. For memory is essential to human experience, and memory is only possible on the basis of an identity which maintains itself and serves as a centre of reference. But logical thought may work with an identity which is purely ideal: the universal by which it mediates an inference may be a pure notion which has no counterpart in perceptual reality, as, for instance, any common mathematical symbol. Moreover, though perception provides a ground for conceptual process, the conceptions which are the outcome of selecting and generalising thought need not stand by any means for perceived objects. Nor, on the other hand, does thought make those real identities which persist as centres of experience. The friend I met to-day is identical in idea with the friend I met last week, but the ideal identity does not constitute his real identity as it is for himself. The recognition, however, depended on my power of uniting different experiences in one ideal and persisting content. And it would seem that this recognition of an identity in the object is only possible on the basis of a real identity in the subject. Recognition, as an act of the self, can only take place on the basis of memory, in other words, on the assumption that the self is conscious of itself persisting through its changing history. Apart from this persistence of the cognising self there would be no consciousness for us of the persistence of other selves or things. It is well to keep these truths in mind, in order to guard ourselves against the notion that the identity of the self, and of everything that can be an object to the self, is due to a process of ideal construction. We fully admit that the personal self of developed experience, involving as it does a continuity of interest and purpose and a variety of social relations, is an ideal construction; and it is never given in an immediate experience. But the process of ideal construing can only take place on the basis of a pre-existing identity. Without a conscious self which maintains its identity in different states of consciousness the process of construing could never have a beginning. And this fact is the guarantee that the process is indeed one of construing, and not the generation of a convenient fiction which has no warrant in the nature of things.

At this point some answer must be given to the general question of the regulation of conceptual thinking to reality. The drift of the previous discussion has been all towards the conclusion that the conceptual process presupposes a real world which it does not create but interprets. The activity of knowing always supposes something to be known, and the activity of reasoning something to be rationalised; and without this something given neither operation would come into play. It is, however, necessary to warn against a possible misconception. The reader may perhaps conclude that thought supervenes on a realm of substantial existences, and develops for itself a conceptual world: and this world, a kind of pale reflexion of perceptual facts, the thinking mind superimposes upon the world already given. This is not the conclusion I mean to suggest. But this conclusion is the natural consequence of separating and sharply contrasting the conceptual and perceptual process. There is not the slightest likelihood that, in the historic evolution of experience, the transition from the lower level to the higher was other than gradual and unconscious. What came to fruit at the higher stage was matured in the lower, and continuity was preserved. Hence there is truth in the view that the generalised world of intersubjective thinking is the result of a process which carries the perceptual world to a fuller degree of reality.[1] Thought and being are not identical, but thought is an aspect of reality, and the thinking view of things is just the more complete view of things. There is, it seems to me, right in this contention, but at the same time one must avoid certain fallacies to which the theory lends itself. Though thinking gives the higher and more complete world, it does not follow that reality is fully and perfectly expressed in thought. In fact, the conceptual process can never wholly absorb reality. For, in the first place, thought, expressing itself in judgment, always refers beyond itself, so that it can never be identical with the whole: and, in the second place, though thought connects and articulates the elements of experience, it has to do so by a method of abstraction and selection. And in this abstract aspect of thinking there is given the possibility that the theory it develops may be at discord with reality. But even where there is no obvious discrepancy, conceptual theories which satisfy men at one stage of history require to be revised and reconstructed at later stages, that they may work better and be less inadequate to reality. Reality, it is often said, is richer than thought; and this comes out in many ways. The self, for instance, must always be something more than the self in idea, for an idea is meaningless if it does not carry a reference beyond itself. The idea of ourselves, which we term self-consciousness, is only possible because the ego is more than thought —because it is also a living centre of feeling and will. On the side of the object the same superior wealth is found.

[1] M. Fouillée expresses the continuity of this process thus: "L'Évolution de la pensée n'est donc pas tout entière le résultat d'un système des choses extérieures à elle, mais un progrès intérieur par lequel la nature arrive à la claire conscience et à la possession d'elle-même."—*Le Mouvement Idéaliste*, 1896, p. 96.

We saw it was impossible to get the concrete thing, or the historical fact, in its unique setting and character, out of a general system of thought-relations. In one respect at least it is very necessary to bear this in mind. The necessity which we postulate to obtain between the elements of a conceptual system cannot be directly transferred to facts. Mathematics in its operations is an abstract conceptual system; but mathematical necessity is hypothetical, and the validity of the premises is assumed. There is no proof that in the vastly more complex realm of nature the same necessity obtains. The necessity which attaches to the action of a mechanical system is exactly in the same case; for the conception is decidedly abstract, as it disregards the qualitative differences of things in favour of their quantitative relations. Consequently the kind of repetition mechanical science assumes in its regulative maxim, "once true always true," is hypothetical rather than factual. The tendency to suppose principles of logical necessity to be somehow anterior to reality, rigidly determining its evolution, is a conspicuous example of *hysteron-proteron*. Such principles grow up within the system of reality and represent the ways in which thought works, but they are meaningless if regarded as prior to reality. The illegitimacy of the assumption has been very clearly shown by Lotze, and a sentence of his is well worth quoting in this connexion. "The real alone is and it is the real which by its Being brings about the appearance of there being a necessity antecedent to it, just as it is the living body that forms within itself the skeleton around which it has the appearance of having grown." [1]

At an earlier point in this discussion I emphasised

[1] *Metaphysics*, Eng. Trans., vol. i., p. 207. Prof. Adamson (*Modern Philosophy*, vol. i., p. 334) here agrees with Lotze against Kant. "There is no

the fact that the developed differentiation of subject and object could not be traced back to a point where difference lapsed into a pure identity. Even on the level of mere feeling the difference, which for conceptual thought is represented by the self and the not-self, must have existed as differences felt in immediate experience. These immediately felt distinctions became a basis for further differentiation. Ideal construction must have something on which to work, and if it develops and articulates our common world, it cannot create it. The crucial question now faces us, What is the nature of this something which each experient centre finds but does not make, and whose presence is reflected in distinctions within experience? An indefinable ὕλη, a pure thing-in-itself or any such characterless abstraction will not help us here. This will be very clear if you remember that the real we seek has to explain the individual and specific element in the object of experience. "What we require is a system of actual existences which are at least known as enduring, changing and interacting, and known as connected in the most intimate way with sense-experience. Matter can only be constituted by the qualification of such actual existences by the content of sensible appearance."[1] And here it is well to obviate in advance a possible misconception. The world of sensible appearance is not to be conceived as a kind of hybrid product floating midway between the self and not-self, and effectively concealing the nature of both. The Kantian work certainly suggested this doubling of existence, the phenomenal world intervening as an appearance between

more stringent necessity than that of actual fact," he remarks. To this one would assent, provided the question is treated as open whether facts present "stringent necessity."

[1] *Things and Sensations*, p. 7, by G. F. Stout, in *Proceedings of the British Academy*, vol. ii. The case for an independent not-self is put with great lucidity and force in this paper.

the subject and an unknowable thing-in-itself. But the essence of the present contention is, that this perfectly useless ὕλη, this fictitious *Ding-an-sich*, must be discarded altogether in favour of a system of actual existences having a positive character. And if we keep in mind the truth already urged, that ideal construction rests on immediate experience or direct interaction, we shall recognise that the thing as sensible appearance is an appearance of the thing; in other words, it is a revelation of the nature of the thing. For a thing is not concealed but manifested by the way in which it acts. This is, of course, very far from saying that matter as we know it is the independent not-self; but it does mean that in matter, as the object of common knowledge, the not-self is present as an active and constituent factor.[1]

The existence of a transsubjective element demands acceptance, if the philosopher is not to close his eyes to some of the simplest and most patent facts of daily experience. As the reader may have already inferred, to the present writer the most hopeful way of dealing with the problem is to follow the path originally opened out by Leibniz and further pursued by Lotze. The movement which Kant initiated, and which was so impressively continued by Hegel, leads to no satisfactory result; and however readily you admit that this idealism requires revision in its details, you will find yourself at an *impasse* when you try to deal with facts. To me, at least, the remark of the veteran thinker Wundt appears to be true, that the future of philosophy belongs to an ideal-realism which founds on the positive sciences.[2]

[1] With this the reader may compare what has been said further back on the relation of conceptual thinking to reality.

[2] *Einleitung in die Philosophie*, 1906, pp. 419–20. Wundt, however, is disposed to rate the contribution of Absolute Idealism to the future of philosophy higher than I should be inclined to do.

The postulate of independent realities whose nature is
ther than psychical imports a dualism into the heart of
xperience, and leaves the process of knowledge finally
nexplicable. Interaction of factors which are radically
ifferent in their nature is impossible, and commerce rests
n community of character. But if we conceive reality
o consist of individual centres of experience at very
arious levels of inner life, we escape the difficulty of
upposing that the self is confronted by an alien not-self
vith which it somehow interacts. Moreover, if you
ccept—and you can hardly refuse to do so—the principle
f the interaction of human selves in intersubjective inter-
ourse, there seems no good ground for denying that
vhat is admittedly true at one level of experience obtains
t lower levels; for experience is a continuous growth
rom the humblest form of conative synthesis to the fully
leveloped personality. It may be added that any work-
ble monadology must proceed on the assumption of
nteraction: the Leibnizian idea of a pre-established
armony, though it was the outcome of Leibniz's logic,
s artificial in the extreme. From the standpoint here
uggested, the qualities of so-called things represent the
nodes of action and passion in which individual centres
f experience manifest their being. It has been objected
o this theory that it makes consciousness a substance, and
hat this is nothing more than a bit of mythology, because
he unity of consciousness neither acts nor suffers.[1]
Now no doubt the conception of a centre of experience
s a substance has difficulties, and we must carefully
onsider our meaning in this connexion. The idea of
ubstance derived from the external world, the idea,
amely, of a constant substratum in which qualities in-
ere as attributes, is certainly inapplicable in this instance.

[1] *Vid.* Carveth Read, *The Metaphysics of Nature*, 1905, pp. 231–32.

If the word substance is used at all here it must b
understood to mean a living centre of experience whic
maintains its identity through its own changing state
The centre of experience is a self, or what corresponds t
a self at a lower stage of development. And if the se
or unitary consciousness neither acts nor suffers—an
it is hard to see how it can fail to do so, if it is to main
tain its identity through change—then the determinat
reference of states to a definite and persisting centr
becomes quite unintelligible. For specific qualities belon
to this individual and not to that, and do not float i
the void unattached and unclaimed. And if the qualitie
do not belong as states to a spiritual real which maintain
its identity in them, I do not see how you can accour
for the individual reference at all. If consciousness di
not involve this kind of conative synthesis, and wer
this synthesis not a feature of each centre of experienc
not even the illusion of individuality could be produce
And if individuals were not real then thought would b
helpless, since it would lack those bases of relatio
which are the condition of there being relations at all.

On our view the transsubjective object is not somethin
abstract and elusive, but in its ultimate nature is a syster
of existences whose being is psychical, and so akin to min
in ourselves. The superstition that perceptual and con
ceptual experience mean the creation of order out of wha
is essentially without character and order must be finall
abandoned. Space and time, as forms of serial orde
apprehended in perception and generalised in conceptio
must grow out of the system of changing existences, an
represent its qualification through the knowing process

[1] The space of non-Euclidian geometry is a system of conceptual implicatio
consistently developed : but the fact that conceptual consistency is here divorce
from possible perception would argue that hyperspace is not *bene fundatum* in th
way that perceptual space is.

The idea of empty space and time as independent reals is open to the gravest objections, and cannot, I venture to think, be consistently maintained. On the theory here adopted the ground of space would lie in the coexistence of spiritual reals which have a being for self, and this coexistence would be translated by the knowing process into terms of spatial order. Time again rests on the fact that all interaction must be reported in terms of inner changes in a psychical being. Change itself is a simple and elementary fact which thinking can never fully explain: and though you term it the category of 'becoming,' by giving it a name you do not make it more intelligible. Change is more ultimate than space or time, both of which in their developed forms are mediated by the fact of movement. For movement combines a spatial and a temporal series in a relation of one to one correspondence; and it is by the reference of the time-series to the spatial that man contrives to give determinateness and universality to his experiences of duration. And if you are to hold that change, on which time and space as ideal constructions depend, is unreal, you strike at the reality of consciousness itself which is only realised in the form of process or change.[1]

The core of reality is individual: it means to be for oneself in some way. But the nature of the real is only *developed* by the process of interaction with other reals. The isolated being is everywhere condemned to sterility, and it is owing to the active commerce between its elements that the world of experience grows in fulness

[1] I admit it can be shown, as Dr. J. E. McTaggart has done (*Mind*, N.S. No. 68), that change, as involving earlier and later and the being and ceasing to be of an event, throws us back on a time-series running from the past through the present to the future in order to become a universally significant process for us. But this by no means proves that change as a process of the real is constituted by time, or that contradictions which attach to the conceptual time-series carry with them the exclusion of time and change from any degree of reality in the universe.

and complexity. Progress in organic life is marked b increasing closeness and intensity of interaction betwee groups of elements, and variety of interaction correspond to growing complexity of structure. The same principl is revealed on the high level of development where huma consciousness ripens and expands. The human self i essentially a social self, and intersubjective intercourse ha been the indispensable condition of progress in self consciousness. The development of knowledge i secured by the active interchange of thoughts betwee living minds, and mental vigour is bound up with th process of giving and receiving. With the advance c civilisation the interdependence of units in the socia whole becomes closer, and the conspicuous advantage o culture over savagery appears in the capacity of civilise society to conserve every advance, and to make it part c the social inheritance. And just as interaction elicits in dividuality, so, in the higher social life, individuality i transformed into personality, which is the form for a ampler spiritual content. It is not too much to say tha the unfolding of personality is the revelation of a highe order of being ; for personal life is charged wit spiritual interest and purpose, and it relates temporal end to an ideal and eternal end. The inner life, with it fresh depth of spiritual experience, puts forward hig claims : it develops a realm of values which is contraste with the realm of facts and transcends the given worl This deepening of the inner side of experience express itself in the higher religious consciousness which conceiv the facts of life in terms of spiritual value, and ground all values in a Supreme Value. The result is remarkabl and deserves to be pondered by those who would tre experience as a merely mundane and temporal produc For in its higher reaches the spiritual content grows to arge for the purely mundane form: the pattern of the hings on earth is felt to be too narrow for the things in ieaven, and the religious spirit looks up to a transcendent nd eternal Good. Experience is thus a continuous levelopment from the lowliest life to the restless spirit of nan, whom the world cannot satisfy and whose thoughts "wander through eternity." This significant movement of the human mind is a fact to be considered by any one who wishes to gather the meaning of experience as a whole. He who excludes it from his purview in seeking a philosophy of experience is yielding to prejudice, not to the love of truth. A theory of experience cannot afford to disregard any of its aspects. If the goal to which the religious consciousness aspires were only "a fond thing vainly invented," the aspiration has still to be weighed and appreciated. So what we contend for on the part of the philosopher is the catholic attitude, the eye that looks steadily upon the whole and refuses to dwell exclusively on any part. Patient reason and upward soaring faith, judgments of fact and judgments of value, all enter into and give form and colour to that many-sided human history which the thinker tries to understand.

The speculative quest is then to reach an ultimate basis for that complex process of interaction upon which the development of experience depends. The movement will be regressive, and its goal a real ground for the commerce of real elements. The outcome must be a postulate, for the regress does not bear the character of strict proof. It is not possible for us to trace back the differences of the world to a principle of unity, and then to show how and why the unity passes into these differences. Starting from concrete experience we can only try to show the general nature of the basis it requires, and then test the result broadly by its value as a working explanation.

Moreover man, occupying a point within the proces of development, is unable to reach the speculativ eminence which offers an all-embracing vision of th whole. The dispassionate thinker is under no illusio about the finality of his speculations ; and his theory o the ultimate basis of experience simply stands for th most satisfying conception he can reach with the means a his disposal.

Lotze, in his well-known treatment of the problem o interaction, has justly laid stress on the unintelligibl nature of a so-called *transeunt* operation—*i.e.* the passag of an 'influence' from an independent being A t another B. For even if the illegitimate spatial image b discarded, a given 'state' could not pass from on centre of experience to another, because the act of passin means that it ceases to exist as the state of anything. I a group of independent reals be posited, then the fact o interaction is as much a mystery as a thing-in-itself whic we can think but never know. Suppose a number o reals A, B, C, D . . . . N, and suppose that a change i A symbolised by Aa is counterbalanced by D assumin the form Dd. Now if the existences are quite inde pendent there can be no reason why Aa should not b counterbalanced by Bb instead of by Dd, and the par ticular elective affinity becomes inexplicable. Further if the determinate change in A is uniformly to be con joined with the change in D, and not sometimes wit changes in B or C instead, there must be an inne connexion between A and D by which this correspondenc is secured and any other one is excluded. Moreover, th fact that B, C, and N refuse, so to speak, to take not of the change in A in the way that D does, mean that the negative attitude in the specific instance is onl intelligible on the ground of a positive relation. I other words this negative self-maintenance is determined by an affirmative character which excludes interaction in certain directions just because it accepts it in other directions. The conclusion thus lies to hand that the series of reals forms a connected whole; and it is this positive connexion, taken together with the determinate character of each given real, which decides that Aa shall elicit Dd and not Bb, and Bb shall elicit Cc and not Aa. But it should be noted that it is only a convenient act of abstraction which restricts interaction to two elements. In fact the interaction between two reals, in which they assume new qualifications, must induce responses in the other reals, although for practical purposes it is found possible to ignore them. The general conclusion is, that interaction depends on inner connexion, and the next step is to explain this connexion.

At this point Lotze, it must be confessed, becomes a hesitating and unsatisfactory guide; and metaphysical and ethical interests conspire to draw him in opposite directions. On the one side the all-embracing substance of Spinoza is distasteful to him for moral reasons, and he claims for human spirits a being for themselves, a detachment from the Absolute. But, on the other side, when confronted with the problem how individual reals interact so as to form one world, he suggests that so-called 'things' may be reduced to innumerable actions within the life of the one Being. Indeed at the critical point in his speculative argument he announces that pluralism must give place to monism, and the seeming multiplicity of individual states be construed as the states of one real Being.[1] Let M be the ultimate ground, A and B interacting things, and let R denote the remaining things, then M = f (A.B. R). If A passes into a, this is balanced

[1] *Metaphysics*, Vol. I., Eng. Trans., pp. 165, 225.

by a corresponding change of the other factors into b anc R′, and the equation now runs M=f (a.b. R′). Wha seems interaction is simply the immanent action of M or itself by which the equation is maintained. But strictly regarded the proof here offered by Lotze does not seem to be a proof how interaction is possible, but rather it reduction to an illusory appearance somehow generated by the compensatory movements within the one real Being Moreover, two questionable assumptions are made. It seems to be assumed that reality is a fixed magnitude and cannot be more or less than M. It also appears tc be taken for granted that within the states of M ar appearance of plurality is generated which has no valic foundation in the structure of reality itself. But if a connected group of qualities, which we construe as states of the individual A, are really phases in the life of an all-embracing M, what produces the apparent reference to A? The puzzle is how A should seem to function for itself while it is only a passing state of M. And of course the trouble is intensified on the grade of experience which is represented by human selves; and the continuity of development makes it arbitrary to say that individuality is real at this stage, but illusory at all lower stages.

I think, then, our position will be sounder, if we decline to treat interaction between individuals as nothing more than immanent changes within the one real Being. Centres of experience are real in the sense of having some degree of being-for-self; but they are not real in the sense of being absolutely self-maintaining and fixed in number. Each depends on interaction with others for its own development, and all depend on a living ground which brings them into responsive sympathy. And we are surely right in supposing that this bond of union is teleological in its working. That is to say, all centres of experience fall within an organising purpose, and have their meaning and place through the operation in each of them of an indwelling end which is the principle of unity and coherence in the system. By insisting on the teleological function of the ground of existence, it seems possible to hold that a principle of unity is present in the multiplicity of individuals without at the same time annulling their differences. Now in trying to determine more closely the nature of this bond of union it is plain that we can only proceed by the use of analogy: some principle at work within experience must furnish us with a clue to the connecting ground of experience itself. No philosophy, be it noted, can dispense with analogy in its ontological theory; the important point is to employ it in a legitimate way. It is always illegitimate to treat analogous principles as strictly identical, and here the scope and significance of the higher will far transcend those of the lower. Now one can hardly doubt that the only type of unity that is helpful in the present connexion is the type which is revealed in organic life. This is best described as a teleological unity; for a multitude of structural units are co-ordinated in the organism and brought into close interaction, while each is invested with a specific function and meaning in the economy of the whole. Every element has its life in and through the organism without thereby losing its definite office and character. Modern physiology has taught us to regard the cell as the structural unit of the body, the elementary organism which reveals in itself general vital phenomena.[1] What we call an individual is really an organism of organisms, and we cannot doubt that the cell under further examination

[1] M. Verworn, *General Physiology*, 1899, Eng. Trans., p. 48 ff.

will reveal itself to be complex. But all the units of the organism are comprehended in the process of inner change or metabolism, a movement at once negative and positive, by which the vital structure of the whole is maintained and each part is made to co-operate in the one life. The higher organisms furnish us with a type of unity in which each element, notwithstanding its close interaction with other elements within the body, retains a degree of individuality or being-for-self. Notably is this the case in what are termed the free-living cells (*e.g.* the white corpuscles of the blood); it is even possible for the individual units to develop an activity which produces pathological conditions, and thus to contradict their teleological function in the organism. And this suggests that the teleological principle is not absolutely pervasive, inasmuch as there remains a possibility of the elements resisting its influence and bringing about a process of disintegration.

The theory accepted in this chapter is, that the elements of existence are at root psychical, and that matter in the sense of the materialist has no proper being. It remains then to construe in terms of this hypothesis the phenomena of the organism, at least so far as is possible. The active and synthetic principle, or, if you please, the soul of the organism, the principle which makes it a unity, is will; not of course will in the form of volition, but as conation and directive activity, in virtue of which the organism exercises selection and strives to conserve its being. The idea of inward activity which embraces all the parts, or, to put it differently, the conception of conative synthesis, is a mark of life even in its humblest forms, and from simple reflex action up to reflective volition this unity manifests itself as purposive energy. This central activity overcomes the seeming externality of existences, and transforms a group of elements into a system of intimately interacting parts. It is not an argument against the reality of this unifying activity that we cannot think out the mode of its operation, for our conceptual thought always presupposes it as a prior fact. But beyond a doubt it does not work mechanically, and as teleological activity it may be termed will. We now take a further step and suggest that this principle of unity actually realised within mundane experience is analogous to the unifying principle which is ground of all experience. That is to say, the comprehensive Ground which connects all the centres of existence, and constitutes them a vital and interacting system, is a Supreme Will. We speak of life as an inner medium, which makes close interaction of parts possible; and the present argument is that this type of interaction, while realised in different degrees, is co-extensive with the whole system of existences. The universe is coherent because all its constituent centres of experience are sustained by the same ever-present Ground, a living Will which gives organic connexion to the multiplicity of spiritual reals and a place and function to each of them. This Will is the guarantee that the whole system is teleological, and the individual centre only realises its end in the interacting system. The interaction is real because the interacting individuals at every grade have a degree of being-for-self. But the being-for-self only becomes explicit within the system, and does not belong to an isolated existence. Interaction being made possible by the Supreme Will as ground, the development of experience which is thus realised is purposive in its character and reflects the nature of the ultimate principle on which it depends. One cannot suppose that the Ground of the world supplies by its activity the conditions for an upward development of life, yet in so doing prepares for the advent of a form of spiritual experience which has no counterpart in its own nature.

If interaction requires a sustaining Will for its ground, does the fact that interaction issues in intelligent and self-conscious experience justify us in concluding that the ground is also a self-conscious Will? This inference at any rate calls for explanation and defence, and competent thinkers in our own and recent times regard it as invalid. There is a tendency to treat the emergence of reflective consciousness as only an episode in the evolution of life. Thinking, we are told, is a serviceable function which is generated by the stress of the biological situation, but it is only a secondary and unstable product of the fundamental and persisting Will. Consciousness, it is pointed out, is at once the cause and the effect of movement, and it develops in the place of instinct just in proportion to the possibilities of hesitation and choice in the direction of movement. It is not the goal but the instrument of the life-process, and functions as a substitute for instinct. Then it is urged that the sphere in which intelligence shines is but narrow compared with the dark and vast region where only life and instinct prevail: and further, even when intelligence is revealed, it is only an inconstant product ever and again sinking back into the realm of the unconscious.

In reply it may be fairly argued that meaning and value do not depend on the circumstances of origin, and mind, if it is born in humble surroundings, must still be judged by what it has become. And it would be sheer perversity to deny that self-consciousness has proved to be the most important and far-reaching fact in the evolution of life. Thought has transformed the world of the brute into the world of civilised humanity. Nor is there much to be said for the idea that consciousness is a kind of by-product developed to meet an emergency. The outward occasion is a secondary matter; the most weighty fact is that unconscious conation has become qualified by consciousness and grown into intelligent will. No external stimulus could quicken the life-process to take an issue which was not the expression of the inherent possibilities of its nature. How conation could mechanically superadd to itself a new function in order to deal with the environment is a mystery, and equally mysterious is it how the appearance of continuity should be preserved. There are ample indications that every higher stage of experience was prepared for at a lower stage and was not externally superimposed; and the whole movement has the significant connexion which belongs to a teleological process. From our point of view the problem is how psychical elements, interacting as a system, at a certain point can be so quickened or intensified in their interaction as to form a unitary consciousness. For the degree of consciousness seems to correspond to the intimacy and inwardness of the interaction. To my mind the most satisfying answer to the question lies in the further postulate that the Will which is the ground of interaction is a self-conscious Will, and thus can be the sufficient reason for the development of a form of experience which is allied to itself. That self-consciousness emerges because the elements out of which it develops are qualified from the first by dependence on a self-conscious Ground, this, I venture to think, is a less "tremendous assumption" than the theory that self-consciousness, with all its associated values and meanings, is somehow the product of non-spiritual factors. It is not indeed possible to prove that the derivation of self-consciousness from something beneath it is impossible: at the same time it is impossible for any one to show by thinking how thought itself is the product of something else. Any existence to which psychical process supplies no analogy must remain for us unknowable. And if you are to say that the lower from out its own resources can produce what is qualitatively different and higher than itself, you cannot seriously look for continuity and meaning in development. In metaphysics no theory escapes objections, but the theory that the ultimate basis of experience is a self-conscious Will may fairly be termed the position of least difficulty. Any other derivation of the self-conscious spirit makes the problem of existence a more bewildering puzzle.

I shall conclude this chapter with the discussion of two further questions. In the first place I shall ask how far we are justified in attaching ethical predicates to the Being who is ground of experience. And in the second place I shall consider certain problems about the relation of God to the world and personal spirits. The two subjects have an important bearing on each other.

(1) Can we rightly call the self-conscious Being who is ground of experience good? Before trying to answer this question, let us be clear what we mean by it. The word good is used as a metaphysical and as an ethical category, and the two uses must be distinguished: the former denotes perfection of being or completeness of structure, the latter perfection of spiritual character. It is not admissible to conclude that, because you deduce the first qualification, this carries the second with it. The perfect structure of the Hegelian Idea, for instance, carries with it no necessary implication of moral goodness, and the Idea may be beyond good or evil. It has in fact been argued that the Absolute, just because it is perfect, transcends goodness, which belongs to the lower level of appearance. If we are to affirm that moral goodness is an

attribute of the Absolute Being, it must be on the ground of a judgment of value: and this judgment is not guaranteed by a purely metaphysical construction, for such construction does not touch the inner depths of spiritual worth. Nor can the problem be solved by a direct inference from the existence of moral goodness in human experience. For such inference, even if valid, could not give an absolute or supreme Good. But the truth is, the question cannot be settled on the line of an appeal to facts pure and simple; and just as validly as you infer goodness in God from its existence in the world, you can infer evil in Him from its presence along with goodness. The Manichæan heresy was an intelligible deduction from the facts of experience which it was meant to explain. Not in this way, then, is the goal to be reached: from no statement of the mere facts of existence can we draw the logical conclusion that the Supreme Ground of experience is also the Supreme Good.[1]

The position is more hopeful when one recognises at the outset that the good works in human life as a demand, as the claim of what ought to be in contrast to what is. The manifestation of ethical good goes with human freedom; and it is because man is free that he is conscious of a realm of values which stand for demands of the ethical spirit. The conception of a Supreme Value, or Ideal Good which connects and completes all ethical values, is a postulate or demand of the inner life. It represents the claim of the human spirit, that the values for which it strives are not illusory but have their ground in what is most real. This affirmation is not irrational in the sense that it conflicts with reason; in a broad way it might be called rational, since it is a normal claim of the

[1] Theologians who argue goodness in God from its presence in the world fail to see the one-sidedness of their premises, just like the teleologists of an older day who beheld only beneficent design in nature.

human spirit, and is consistent with the whole nature of man. But it is best described as an act of faith which embodies the deep needs and aspirations of man's soul. It is a faith on which men are willing to stake vital issues, for with it the higher significance and worth of life are bound up. The "venture is a noble one," as Plato might have said, and it expresses the confidence that the ultimately Real is the ultimately Good, that "the great soul of the universe is just." And while the content of this value-judgment has been deepened and purified by advancing experience, it is important to recognise that the judgment itself is the utterance of an enduring human need. If the Ground of all being were not also the Ground of all worth, if the moral ideal on which practical endeavour rests did not find living support in the Being upon whom all experience depends, a paralysing discord would be introduced into the heart of human life. Moreover, the value-judgments of the ethical must be taken in connexion with the value-judgments of the religious consciousness. These demands of the developed religious spirit present a body of spiritual testimony in regard to the character of the divine object which faith postulates. They utter in no uncertain fashion the inner assurance of the religious soul, that the supreme object of reverence is a spiritual Being in communion with whom its own spiritual life is completed and harmonised. God to the worshipper is a sustaining spirit who responds to what is best within him, and in whom his ideal of goodness finds a concrete fulfilment. This spiritual claim represents the felt conviction on man's part that the good he seeks, and is inwardly urged to seek, whether under the form of moral life or religious fellowship, has its source and goal in a Good which is most real. Neither the ethical nor the religious life could maintain itself on the assumption that the Supreme Good is a mere ideal projected by the human spirit as a device to mark out the way of progress. It is a postulate with which the validity and coherency of the developing spiritual life are bound up. The strength of the case does not stand or fall with the fact that in the historic process the content of the ultimate Good changes. It lies in the persisting demand that it shall be real. To sum up then: God cannot be proved to be good from the bare facts of experience; but the faith that he is good is justified by the form and pressure of the moral and spiritual life.

Our regress on the Ultimate Ground of Experience is thus along two lines, proceeding in the one case by judgments of fact and in the other by judgments of value. Or, to put it otherwise, the one path is that of reflective thinking on experience, the other that of examining the demands of faith and the needs of the inner life. Both ways converge upon the same goal, but each presents a view of the object which is not disclosed by the other. The two methods supplement one another, and neither of them by itself yields satisfactory fruits. An objection may perhaps be urged here. It may be said: "You have accepted two independent instruments of proof, and the very contrast of reason and faith precludes the assurance of anything more than an artificial coincidence in their results. Your case would be stronger if you held definitely to the one method or to the other. As it is, the Supreme Being and the Supreme Value are simply identified without it being shown that they cohere in character." In regard to the latter point I confess that this objection raises a difficulty against which philosophical thinkers often do not guard. They develop the idea of an Absolute, and then simply assume that certain ethical qualifications can be attached to it. Hegelian writers, for example, frequently attach a religious value to their Absolute which its metaphysical nature does not appear capable of sustaining, and students of Lotze will admit a like difficulty in his system. It is certainly an unsatisfactory method to develop the idea of the ultimate Reality in exclusive dependence on logical thinking, and then to take for granted that certain value-predicates belong to it. But the fault in question cannot fairly be ascribed to the method which co-ordinates the theoretical and the practical reason. When a discord ensues it is due to a neglect of this method or to a faulty application of it. The outcome of speculative thinking ought always to be tested and supplemented by reference to the demands of the practical and spiritual nature, for no conception of God can permanently satisfy us which is at discord with the value-judgments of the inner life. Moreover, the theoretical judgment and the value-judgment cannot be ultimately inconsistent. It is indeed impossible to resolve spiritual values into rational notions. A difference remains which is not reducible by our minds, and we recognise, describe and test our value-ideas by the way in which they work without being able fully to explain them. At the same time the difference, which corresponds to the difference of reason and faith, does not justify us in assuming an ultimate dualism. And it may be pointed out that the two spheres interpenetrate : the judgment of value implies an activity of thought, and theoretical ideas are also working-values. Besides, one has to bear in mind that both forms of judgment are normal functions of the human ego, which is a unity and cannot be finally divided against itself. Activities which are the consistent outcome of the unitary self cannot in the end be inconsistent. The assertion that the pure and the practical reason are at variance really involves a sceptical attitude towards the coherence of human nature—an attitude, be it said, which could as little be maintained in practice as Hume's reduction of the self to a fleeting series of states.

A systematic synthesis of the realms of fact and value under which experience takes form, is not then within our powers ; and the furthest point we can reach in this direction is represented by the teleological idea. The notion of end of course stands here for an immanent principle, not for a regulative conception. The two orders of judgment are inwardly adapted to one another because they are connected by a controlling principle or indwelling end. The coherence of facts and values rests in the last resort on the purposive unity of the universe out of which both orders of judgment draw their form and content. Human nature reveals the adaptation ; but its ground is deeper, and reaches down to that fundamental Will upon which the harmony and consistency of all experience finally depend.

(2) The value-judgments of ethical and religious experience have to be kept in view in any attempt to define more closely the relation of God to the world and individual spirits. A thorough-going pantheism, for instance, can find no room for these valuations, and this fact supplies a strong reason for rejecting such a theory. On the other hand, the postulate of the religious consciousness that the divine object is an ethical and personal Being, raises the question how far the ground of all centres of experience can be consistently thought as a person. For the demands of the religious spirit are not necessarily valid in the forms in which they are put forward : they may require modification alike in the interests of a higher spiritual satisfaction and of the unity of thought. The claims of reason and faith have to be adjusted, and, if

possible, justice must be done to both.[1] In facing this question the point has first to be settled, what do we mean by personality? The basis on which human personality develops is individuality, but in the personal life the individual basis is transformed into a unity of a larger and more ideal character. Through the function of conceptual thinking the person generalises, conceives his life as a whole permeated by a continuity of interest and purpose, and, through interaction with other self-conscious beings, defines himself as the possessor of rights and the bearer of responsibilities. The essence of personality appears to be the self as a centre of enlarged interest and ethical content, and the personal self is mediated by interaction with other selves. To the development of this personal consciousness the presence of a not-self, in the form of other persons and centres of experience, is necessary. As related to and distinguished from other persons and things the ego gradually comes to know itself as a focus of life and interest. Nevertheless the human self, though a growing, is never a perfect or complete personality. It does not contain within itself the ultimate ground of its existence; it is hampered in its progress by defects of knowledge and will; it is dependent for the stimulation of its energies upon an environment which always wears a foreign aspect, and which it can never fully penetrate and mould. Memory, with which the personal consciousness is bound up, is always more or less fragmentary: the illuminated spaces of life are separated by regular intervals of darkness: the more distant phases of our experience become blurred and faint, so that we cannot make them live again in the present, or fully appreciate the meaning they once possessed for us. To say, then,

[1] It is becoming clear that it was a decided defect in the Ritschlian theology that it based the idea of God exclusively on value-judgments.

that the ground of all experience is a person in exactly the same sense that man is a person would be inconsistent, and would spell weakness and imperfection.

It is sometimes contended that God is the perfect personality because he embraces all experience within himself, and is dependent on nothing external to himself. The characteristic limitation in the human personality is therefore done away with in the divine. Lotze has argued, and others have followed him, that self-consciousness does not depend on a not-self, but really arises through the inner act of distinction by which the ego contrasts itself with its changing states.[1] So it is suggested that all reality as experience may fall within the being of God, and yet God be a self-conscious personality. Human experience would only be different from the divine experience in so far as the Divine Self distinguishes itself from its own states. The reasoning, it seems to me, is open to doubt. It is true that the ego as a centre of experience cannot be created by its relation to the non-ego ; for the relation is only possible through an original position. But self-consciousness in man, as the reflexion of the ego upon itself, is always mediated by the presence of a not-self, and inner experience only rises to the level of a specific consciousness in and through the contrast which is developed between it and a sphere assigned to the not-self. Psychologically this is hardly open to question. The step of applying the human analogy without reserve to the Divine Being is of course a hazardous one, and the thought has weight, that the grounds of personality must lie wholly *within* the Supreme Self. Otherwise you are forced to regard the divine self-consciousness as dependent on limitations without itself, and therefore sharing the characteristic defect of human personality.

[1] *Microcosmus*, vol. ii., Eng. Trans., p. 678 ff.

Such an anthropomorphism accords neither with enlightened thought nor spiritual feeling, and imports a perplexing dualism into the heart of things. But it is at least open to us to suppose that the differentiation within human experience, upon which the development of self-consciousness depends, has its counterpart as an eternal fact *within* the Divine Nature. The object of the self, that is the region of difference in the mundane and temporal sphere, has its prototype within the being of the World-Ground, and mundane experience reflects in its temporal development the character which is eternally present in its source. In theological language, man is made in the image of God. This argument is not a proof, for proof in the nature of the case is impossible. Yet it is meant to suggest that there is a way of thinking the Absolute Ground in accordance with which it contains differentiation in its own being, and so can be regarded as perfect self-consciousness or a personality internally complete. The theory is at least less open to objection than that which resolves all centres of experience into moments in the life of God, and reduces human selves to states of the divine Self. One can sympathise with the objections which are urged by Personal Idealists against this thorough-going type of monism.[1] The Absolute cannot at one and the same time *be* the unity of all selves, and

[1] "Minds are not Chinese boxes which can be put 'inside' one another." Dr. Rashdall in *Personal Idealism*, p. 388. Here I am not unmindful of the phenomena of abnormal psychology, such for example as have been discussed by Dr. Morton Prince in his recent work (*The Dissociation of a Personality*, 1906). In the case analysed by Dr. Prince the disintegration of a personality resulted in alternating selves with distinct differences of character. The phenomenon, if established, that one phase of dissociated self can include the knowledge of another phase, while embracing a further knowledge of its own, may simply point to a region of sub-conscious memory open to the one and not to the other. Moreover, Dr. Prince's investigations do not prove that a lesser and a larger self can actually coexist as two consciousnesses, the one being part of the other. The condition of the activity of the one self is that the other remains in the background of the sub-consciousness.

these selves be *for* the Absolute. And the human self cannot be this specific consciousness, with its unique meaning and value, and also possess the quite different meaning and value which attach to a phase of the Absolute Mind. One cannot have it both ways: either the Absolute is a real self and finite selves are illusory appearances, or the finite selves are real and the Absolute is only a name for the impersonal system to which they belong. There is a certain consistency in Dr. J. E. McTaggart's bold identification of the Absolute with an eternal society of selves, and in his frank admission, that it is impossible to see how one self can be part of another.[1] Nevertheless, I believe his view of the Absolute fundamentally contradicts the normal religious consciousness, and makes the historical evolution of religion inexplicable. Metaphysics is always likely to go astray, if it pursues its lofty path paying scant heed to the value-judgments of human experience.

Yet some Personal Idealists, if I may say so, have been led into strange vagaries in their legitimate endeavour to avoid the *impasse* of pantheism. This remark, I think, applies to the type of idealism outlined by Prof. Howison, in his *Limits of Evolution*.[2] With a praiseworthy desire to conserve human freedom, he assumes the eternity of self-acting human spirits. Of this society of souls God is a member, and is only *primus inter pares*. He is the Perfect Type or Supreme Instance, and moves the world of souls, not as efficient, but as final Cause.[3] In the result we have a universe moved simply by human wills and in which Deity is not dynamically operative: and the human spirit is only dependent on God in the sense that

1 *Studies in Hegelian Cosmology*. Chap. iii.

2 See especially the Prefaces and the Appendices to the work.

3 There is a point of similarity here to the abstract Deity of Aristotle, who moves the world as object of desire (κινεῖ ὡς ἐρώμενον).

the particular instance logically depends for its definition on the Supreme Instance. If our argument is right, that individual centres of experience imply a Supreme Ground for their interaction, this theory must be rejected. And the notion that the human individual is eternal and absolute in his own right appears to have little or no justification from experience. This objection applies to the views both of Dr. McTaggart and Prof. Howison, but the latter is under the further disadvantage of having to defend the application of the term God to a Being who is one of a company of equals, who has no actual power, and upon whom men are in no real relation of dependence. Tried by the pragmatic test, this conception would be sure to fare badly. Prof. Howison is an acute and an ingenious writer, but Dr. McTaggart's theory is more consistent and logical.

On a fundamental issue, then, we see a keen dispute waged between the type of idealism which may be broadly termed Hegelian and certain forms of Personal Idealism. In one case, God is conceived as inclusive of the individual, in the other the individual is exclusive of God. And this sharp antithesis suggests the propriety of saying a few words on the vexed question of immanence and transcendence. The word immanent has acquired general currency, but beyond doubt it is often used, and more especially by theological writers, in a vague way, which, if convenient, is not satisfactory. God, we are told, is immanent in the world and immanent in human souls. In the case of a thinker who holds that God has no existence apart from the world and souls there is less danger of misconstruction. But in the case of thinkers who are concerned to insist also on the divine transcendence, one is frequently uncertain in what sense they maintain an indwelling of deity within the region of mundane experience. Where, as often happens, this view is part of a mystical attitude, the writers would no doubt urge that the fact was realised in the depths of the feeling-life, but was incapable of translation into terms of thought. And outside of Mysticism in the technical sense, the feeling of communion, of a spiritual presence of God with the worshipper, is supported by a body of religious experience which no sincere enquirer will care to treat hastily as an illusion. The Pauline testimony, "God worketh in you both to will and to do of his good pleasure" is a recurring note of spiritual autobiography. Yet when we try to be clear on the subject, we cannot, I think, suppose that the Deity has somehow a determinate existence in the mind of an individual; for individual knowing and feeling cannot at the same time be divine knowing and feeling, and a reality which is not an experience could not be in the individual at all. Our contention, be it noted, is not that the human mind is an impervious entity, but that there cannot in some inexplicable way be within the experiences of the self the experience which belongs to a divine Self. Still there is an element of truth in the notion of immanence, as I will try to show. It lies in the fact that God is the active and sustaining ground of all interaction between centres of experience, and, like the soul in the organic body, is an ever present and controlling influence upon the elements to which by his will he gives unity and coherence. The process of interaction upon which self-consciousness depends is made possible by the presence behind it of the supreme and self-conscious Will; and the whole conscious and sub-conscious region falls within the sphere of divine influence. I would therefore understand by immanence dependence upon divine activity and receptivity to divine influence; and it is open to us to suppose that this influence may be exerted in different degrees upon individuals. To describe the *modus operandi* of this activity is no doubt beyond our powers; but the same is true of the agency of the mind upon the body, and what we cannot construe into a theory we are constrained to accept as a fact. And an all-penetrative divine activity is necessary to account for the unity of experience.

The meaning we attach to the conception of transcendence will to some extent be clear from our previous discussions. All centres of experience have a measure of being-for-self, and maintain their individuality by the possession of an inner life. But with the development of self-consciousness there is a greater measure of independence over against the Ultimate Ground. The evil and error which intrude into the kingdom of persons are absent from the realm of animals and things:

> "They cannot err or go astray,
> But our immortal spirits may."

Absolute independence is of course excluded, for persons are members of the system of beings which is constantly sustained by the divine Will. God is transcendent, not as a Being far withdrawn from the world, but in the sense that his self-consciousness is not bound up with this mundane and temporal process, and his activity is not exhausted by it. The depths of the divine nature, or God as he is for himself, must always lie beyond our power to express through human images and analogies; and the Will which supports the whole system of existences cannot fall within the system as an individual member.

When the philosopher attempts to explain how it is that the Supreme Will 'plants out,' so to speak, a system of existences other than itself, existences which by their interaction generate this spatially and temporally qualified order of things, he is perplexed by the difficulties which beset this ultimate problem. The very idea of explanation means for us the establishment of connexion or continuity within experience, and here we are trying to understand the way in which this experience came into being. One is too prone to forget this, and to deal in figures and analogies which are only valid, if valid at all, within the region of our experience. Under this category falls the time-honoured conception of Deity as an architect and maker. Creation of the world *ex nihilo*, at a definite time, is a kind of explanatory *tour de force* open to grave objections too transparent to need argument. The idea of a Deity, suddenly impelled by a feeling of defect to create, is an anthropomorphism which can satisfy no one who has reflected seriously on the subject. It would be less open to criticism to say that the divine act of will which posits the system of individual existences is a timeless act—timeless at least in the sense that it does not fall within the human time-series of which it is really the condition. And the idea suggests itself that the internal structure of the Absolute, in virtue of which it is an eternally complete self-consciousness, is reflected in partial form in the self-conscious spirits which emerge within the world-process. The postulate here is, that the Divine Will can invest its content with a degree of otherness, while it continues to connect and sustain that content in the form of a system of existences which are individual centres of experience. These centres, by entering into more and more complex interaction, have been the basis on which the conscious self has developed. And conscious selves, in their turn interacting within the social system, have advanced to spiritual personalities, for whom their own life and history have become a problem. In thi momentous fact, in the world of spiritual persons, we fin the partial revelation of the Ultimate Source of things But, from its highest to its lowest form, all experienc points back to a Ground that sustains, connects an quickens, the Eternal Spirit through whom all spirit "live and move and have their being."

Der sichere Gang der Wissenschaft cannot be claimed fo the excursions of Metaphysics, and the sober speculato will recognise how far he comes short of that 'exactness which Plato desiderated in the highest matters.[1] But i Metaphysics achieved its task the metaphysician's occupation would be gone, and an engaging form of mental discipline would cease to exist. The prospect of such a consummation is remote enough, and the perennial problems will remain for each fresh generation to read and answer. Perhaps all that can be expected of an adventurer in this field is that he should suggest the solution which seems the most satisfying in the light of the knowledge of his age. But philosophy grows out of and depends upon the larger movement of Life, and Life as it flows onward induces subtle changes in the mental outlook and alters the valuation of things. Finality is therefore a dream ; no system will long survive without modification, and the most we can hope for any system is that it may be a stage to something better. The practical goal, one may repeat, is the speculative view which satisfies best : and the satisfaction is the satisfaction of the whole man, the personal spirit who thinks and feels and wills.

[1] *Repub.* 504 *E.*

CHAPTER X

SOME FINAL PROBLEMS OF RELIGIOUS DEVELOPMENT

In the previous chapter a speculative theory of the Ground of Experience has been developed, in a somewhat rapid and incomplete fashion no doubt, but perhaps sufficiently for the purpose on hand. It is in the light of this theory that we shall try to deal now with certain ontological problems which are raised by the development of religion, and to which our earlier discussions lead up. We were precluded from any attempt to treat them before this, for one cannot take them up without finding that, in the long run, they imply an answer to the question of the ultimate nature of experience itself. On the basis, however, of the results reached in the foregoing chapter we are in a position to handle these problems, and to show, so far as we can, the bearing of our results upon them. The problems to which I refer emerge naturally when any attempt is made to give a final interpretation of religious development and certain issues which are raised by it. The questions are indeed very old ones—at least two of them are so—and many controversies have gathered round them. But some sort of answer to them is expected, and rightly so, from any one who aspires to give a philosophical interpretation of religious development.

The three problems, then, which I propose to discuss in this connexion are: the Nature of Evil: Immortality:

and The Relation of Religious Development to the Idea of God. The subjects are somewhat closely related and the one leads up to the other. At the outset it may be well to state that I can make no serious attempt to deal with the historical evolution of these problems and the various phases of discussion associated with them. Even if the writer's knowledge were sufficient for the task, the task would require a volume rather than a chapter. My aim here will be to indicate the positive results to which the course of thought in the foregoing pages points, and to show how they bear upon our central theme.

(1) In every religion where the religious consciousness has reached the stage of reflexion, the nature and meaning of evil have become a problem and one of the most perplexing. The self finds itself hampered and baffled by the antagonistic forces proceeding from its environment as well as lying in its own nature. And it is compelled to ask whence these adverse influences arise and what they betoken. In the practical answer it gives to these questions a religion always reveals its characteristic nature. From polytheistic and dualistic religions a ready reply is forthcoming : war in heaven produces its counterpart on earth. But this idea ceases to be plausible when the unity of the world is apprehended and the claims of monotheism are recognised. Yet the facts are plain and they continue to provoke a solution. Both in the individual and in society a hostile element is at work constantly obstructing and interrupting the realisation of the religious ideal. Nevertheless evil seems intertwined with the existence of religion itself, which at one level promises man material deliverance and at another spiritual redemption. In the lower culture especially, the religious bond offers a means of dealing with the ills which oppress man and provides a remedy for them. Indeed neither morality nor religion could exist in the forms under which we know them, if the good

were not confronted with the evil. The process of overcoming the evil enters always into the practical life of spiritual religion. So we are confronted with the dilemma, that evil appears to be something which ought to be eliminated, and yet it cannot be eliminated without the form and character of religion being changed.

Any fruitful discussion of this topic must begin by drawing a distinction between natural and moral evil. By natural evils we mean all kinds of physical pain, suffering and loss ; and there also fall to be included under the same head failures (through ignorance or error) to realise our ends. The problem here, if not free from difficulties, is admittedly less difficult than in the other case. For it is possible to show that many natural ills are bound up with the structure of life, and are presupposed in the existence of pleasure and happiness. Physical death, for instance, is implicated in the life of earthly beings ; and the functions of generation and birth, with all that they imply, presuppose it. Pain, again, in certain forms is necessary to life ; it serves as a warning and a stimulus, essential for self-preservation, to all mundane creatures. Nor could there be the satisfaction of repletion apart from the pangs of hunger, and the joy of a purpose fulfilled implies a possible disappointment. Alike for sentient and for conscious beings uniformity in the natural order is necessary, and it is only on the ground of this uniformity that they can adapt themselves to their environment and use it for their subsistence. The process of learning, whether conscious or unconscious, depends on an order of things consistently maintained. And yet the working of this uniformity, which is good for the whole, may for individuals on occasion spell disaster, hunger or death. It may be further pointed out that a process of development is a feature in all organic beings, and with development there is presupposed an intractability of the material upon which the developmental process operates. No growth or progress is possible without reaction, selection and activity on the part of the individual, and in the natural order want and pain are essential to stimulate this activity. With every want satisfied as it arose, with no difficulties to overcome or pains to endure, a vigorous type of individual life could not be achieved. The quickening and concentration of energy demanded by the process of overcoming are necessary to the soundness and prosperity of individuals. Yet this intractability in the environment of the living being is perforce linked with possibilities of defeat and pain; hence that which, under one aspect, is a good, under another aspect may be an evil. But it is quite practicable to hold that natural evils of this kind, which seem incident to the process of life, are of a subordinate and relative character, and even, on the whole and in the long run, are a means to the good.

These remarks, however, must not be taken to suggest that all natural ills may be conveniently explained as involved in the realisation of the good, whether that good is regarded as expressed in a uniform and trustworthy order of nature or in the development of life. One might argue, though it would be difficult to prove, that the sufferings of the brute creation and of human beings are out of proportion to any beneficent purpose which could be achieved thereby. The exigencies of an evolutionary scheme surely do not call for a nature "red in tooth and claw," or for the ruthless extinction of the weak by the strong! Yet the range of human insight is too limited to allow of a conclusive answer on this point, nor can we return any sure verdict on the quantitative ratio of the pains to the pleasures of sentient beings. A more serious difficulty emerges when we come to consider the actual distribution of pain and suffering in the world, nd especially in humanity. It has been a very ancient ource of heart-searching why the righteous should be rought low and the wicked exalted ; and the observer o-day still finds cause to lament the inequalities of destiny, n virtue of which the good man often receives the portion f suffering and failure and his ill-deserving neighbour ealth and prosperity. It would be futile to attempt to ustify many of the harder facts of life on the plea that some igher good was being realised—to tell the honest parent, tricken down in the midst of his usefulness by disease, hat the discipline was a blessing, or the man of gifts, ondemned by misfortune to ignoble drudgery, that his haracter is thereby improved. So far as human judgment oes the inferences may be all in the opposite direction. The pressure of such facts has given vitality to the thought hat earthly experience is incomplete and issues in a life ereafter; especially does this idea appeal to those who herish the conviction that God is a Power that makes for ighteousness.

There is a further fact which has to be kept in view : he connexion of natural with moral evil. In the order f development the former is of course the earlier, and nly where there is reflective will can moral guilt come nto existence. It cannot indeed be said that natural evil s in itself the immediate cause of sin, but it furnishes the asis or condition upon which the latter comes into being. The natural wants, cravings, and pains form the sensuous round out of which sin emerges through specific reactions f the human personality upon them. It is true, no doubt, hat all sin is not of sense, just as it is true that every orm of sensuous satisfaction need not be morally wrong. But if you look at the matter from the point of view of evelopment, you will see that the physical pains and ravings, stimulating the ego to activity, supply those impulsive tendencies which the growing self-consciousnes may translate into acts of wrong-doing. Granted, there fore, the existence of a physical order in which evils ar involved, granted also self-conscious wills capable of choic supervening on that order, and the conditions are presen under which ethical evil can emerge as a fact in the universe The existence of moral evil in the world no one disputes whatever significance the thinker may attribute to it, o however he may try to account for it. The attempt t explain it really demands an answer to two problems : th psychological problem of its origin and development, an the metaphysical problem of its ultimate source an meaning. Of these the former is the simpler, and solution can be given to it which is so far satisfactory. A already suggested, the psychological conditions lie in th sensuous character and selfish impulses of the natural mar Supervening on these is the deliberative will, with a norr set to it by the custom, tradition or law which has bee gradually evolved by the social system. Consequentl the elements are there which make significant choic possible, and the choice may either be consistent with th norm or a transgression of it. When the acts of trans gression pass into habits and tendencies, evil as an anti social force makes itself felt. Within the social structur it has gained a place independent of any single will, an is become a constant danger to the developing persona life. When spiritual self-consciousness defines the law a the will of an ethical God, transgression is determined i its theological form as sin. Psychologically the conscious ness of sin develops *pari passu* with the consciousness c the good, and at each step the one constitutes the contras to the other. The soul in which the good is most full present is also the soul which is most keenly alive to th wrongness of sin. The constant element in this evolutio

s purely formal, the fact of inconsistency with a norm
or what ought to be : the content changes with growing
knowledge and spiritual insight.

The metaphysical question remains, the question of the
ultimate source and meaning of moral evil. The answer
nvolves the deepest problems of spiritual development,
ncluding the existence of religion in the form of a
edemptive process. No complete solution has ever been
given, and perhaps none can be given ; and a brief reference to the efforts which have been made will show where
he difficulties lie.

It may be noted at the outset that the stress of the
problem is owing to certain postulates we have made in
egard to the nature of the universe : the postulates,
namely, that all things are sustained by a Divine Will,
and that God, the ultimate Ground of things, is supremely
good. If you reject these postulates and say that the
Absolute is impersonal and non-moral, then the obstacles
o the solution of the question are no doubt diminished.
f, with Spinoza, we assert that good and evil are purely
subjective ideas of reflexion (falling under *imaginatio*, not
atio), then sin becomes a subjective illusion which does
not touch the real world at all.[1] And if, with Mr
Bradley, we relegate good and evil to the level of appearance which the Absolute transcends, it may be quite
possible for us to hold that " heaven's design can realise
tself as effectively in 'Cataline or Borgia' as in the
scrupulous or innocent."[2] Such theories offer a way out
of the difficulty just because they take it so lightly ;
and in consequence they have difficulties of their own,
many and serious, to overcome. But our conclusion that
he World-Ground is a spiritual and ethical Being forbids

[1] *Ethica*, Pt. IV., p. 64.
[2] *Appearance and Reality*, 1st ed., p. 202.

any attempt on our part to settle the question in this way
In his *Theodicée* Leibniz tries to reconcile the existence o
evil with the divine goodness by tracing back both mora
and physical evil to metaphysical evil. By the latter h
means the limitations which attach to all finite beings, an
the imperfections which are bound up with these limita
tions. The bad then is ultimately due to privation o
defect, and though, from a partial point of view, it seem
to be a discord, yet to an outlook divinely enlarged it ma
subserve the harmony of the whole. Leibniz's optimism
carries him to the conclusion that this is "the best of a
possible worlds," a conclusion however which rests less o
evidence than on the tacit assumption that this world mus
be the best because God has chosen it. Leibniz, a
Schopenhauer objected, does not show that the world i
good enough to be deserving of choice.[1] Under the sam
category of optimistic treatment may be set Hegel'
interpretation of sin, though it is characteristic of th
Hegelian method that the conception is more closel
connected with the idea of development, and thereb
gains in suggestiveness.[2] In this theory sin appears as
stage in the evolution of the self from purely natural an
immediate existence to rational and self-conscious freedom
Moral sin is indeed an act of will—here Hegel's insight i
sound—but he thinks it is involved in the dialecti
movement of the self from mere innocence to consciou
and self-determined virtue. In a sense the man who ha
sinned stands higher than the individual who is in blissfu
ignorance of sin, and he is higher still who has overcom
the evil and stands fast in virtuous habit. The gist o
Hegel's contention is contained in the familiar phrase, tha
"evil is good in the making." Now there is truth in thi

[1] *Vid.* Höffding, *Geschichte der neueren Philosophie*, Vol. I., p. 410.
[2] *Phil. der Religion*, II., 258 ff.

onception so far as it asserts that the moral ideal, when it levelops in the individual and society, always takes form s a contrast to the evil, and is ever realised through ersonal endeavour and conquest. On the other hand here are serious objections to the theory of Leibniz that noral evil is simply privation or limitation, and to the nterpretation of sin by Hegel as a means to the ealisation of developed goodness. The treatment in oth cases is too optimistic, and errs in ignoring he positive side of moral wrong-doing. If you are to ay that sin is only the discord that mediates a richer armony, the transitional jar needed to enhance the full oncord, then you cannot fairly accept the verdict of the noral consciousness which declares sinful acts ought not o be.[1] For they are explained and justified as a stage in he evolution of the good. And though at first blush his theory may seem to minister to our faith in the goodness of the world, it breaks down before the real facts of experience. There are sinful acts in plenty where the vil decisively preponderates over any possible good that an flow from them, acts which mar the life of the ndividual and hinder the progress of society. Instead of ninistering to a wider good they are antagonistic to it, and personal and collective development go hand in hand with the gradual elimination of such tendencies. And if the optimist were to carry his theory into practice and secure general acceptance for his ideas, the result vould be a slackening of spiritual endeavour and a decline

[1] The analogy of the discord in a musical movement is apt to be misleading. For here the discord is a necessary feature in the structure, and in a perfect omposition is demanded at that point in the development of the theme. And this s what moral evil is not, if the words 'ought not' are to have a meaning. It nay be true to say with Browning (*Abt Vogler*) that the discord "rushes in" hat "harmony may be prized." But it is one thing to say that the presence of in teaches us to prize goodness; it is another thing to say that sin is right in ts own place.

of the moral ideal. You cannot maintain the vigour o the fight if you are persuaded the foeman is really a frienc in disguise.

The other method by which theologians and philoso- phers have sought to explain the existence of moral evi is through the idea of human freedom. God made al things good, but man by the exercise of his freedon brought sin into the world with all its attending woes The truth in this view, as I shall try to show, is greate than in the other, but it does not shed light on all th features of the situation. To say that sin flows entirel from a misuse of personal freedom is to forget th connexion already pointed out between natural and mora evil. For choice in the concrete is never absolutel vague and unlimited, but operates on possibilities which are given by the actual situation. Hence the ground of temptation can never fall wholly within the will of the individual who is tempted and falls. His will is an indispensable factor in the process, not the whole of it. This becomes clear when we consider the actual way in which sin works in the world. Human experience supplies us with very many cases where moral degrada- tion is not accounted for by a series of deliberate acts of choice. A pre-existing evil environment infects the growing self, and wrong tendencies and habits are developed before the individual is fully conscious of their meaning. Did sin begin and end with the individual, the fact that it only attains power and intensity in society would be inexplicable. And it must also be remembered that the norm by which sin is defined, and the responsi- bility attaching to persons who conflict with the norm, are things which imply a social order, and they would be meaningless without it. The hardness of the task of redemption and moral renewal points to the truth, that the influences which generate moral evil are wider than the individual and call for corresponding influences to counteract them. It is the evil environment which makes every attempt to reform the single soul hard, and renders an individualistic solution of the whole problem impracticable. The moral is, that if you press the notion of individual freedom too far, you neither account for sin nor for obvious truths of the ethical life. Rigid determinism and so-called 'liberty of indifference'—if anybody believes in such a thing—are alike untenable.

Nevertheless I think that personal freedom, if it does not fully explain the vexed question of moral evil, yet casts a valuable light on it. Any conception of sin which ignores the fact that an act of sin must be a conscious expression of human will is wide of the mark. Under the reign of a mechanical determinism the notion of personal guilt is quite illegitimate. So much would probably be admitted by the upholders of the current doctrine of self-determinism, according to which the will is free because the self determines itself, although the act of choice between alternatives is never in reality an open one. It seems to me, however, the facts of the moral life postulate a limited if real amount of indeterminism; and in this connexion I would remind the reader of the contention in the previous chapter, that necessity is not proved to be embedded in the structure of the universe, and that in the sphere of mathematical inference the necessity is hypothetical. To say that it is absurd to suppose that either B or C may proceed from A is to assume it has been proved that necessity is inherent in things; and it is to forget that an act of will is something unique and cannot be expressed in a general formula. Nor is the question settled by an *ex cathedra* assertion that will is an expression of character, and therefore "figures but as one link in the endless chain of causes and effects." For human character, we repeat, is never perfectly unified and contains within it some open possibilities ; so it may happen that either side of an alternative can be chosen without the connexion of the act with character being broken.[1] These possibilities, be it noted, are not arbitrarily created : they arise out of the character of the self in its concrete historical setting, and there is no assertion that the individual is able to will anything or everything irrespective of what he has been. Indeed it is here admitted, that the more perfectly the character is unified in the direction of virtue or vice, the nearer do the open possibilities approach zero.[2] Two difficulties I have always felt stand in the way of a frank acceptance of what has been called 'soft determinism.' In the first place the judgment of regret, the attitude of repentance, on this view receives a strained and inadequate interpretation. For it simply denotes a change of feeling-mood in virtue of which I am out of sympathy with what I was in the past. It is indeed true that regret for past conduct betokens sorrow for the existence of elements in my character which rendered such and such an act possible.

[1] On the whole subject there are instructive remarks in Prof. James's paper on "The Dilemma of Determinism," in his *Will to Believe*, and in Dr. Schiller's chapter on "Freedom" in his *Studies in Humanism*. In a former volume I urged this argument, and, notwithstanding criticisms, I still believe it to be sound.

[2] The determinist would say that the appearance of indeterminism in a case of moral perplexity arises from the fact that the self does not know how it will act till the choice is finally made. In other words a psychological limitation at a particular point in the process is confused with a real contingency in the situation. It may be rejoined, that if to will or to abstain from willing is not an open alternative, and if my character together with the situation admits of only one choice, then the function of deliberation seems somewhat superfluous. And if it be said that in deliberating I only make clear to myself what I really want, and that I can strengthen a desire by bringing influences to bear on it from the background of character, one must answer that this surely implies some open possibilities latent in character in virtue of which I may make a better or a worse choice.

And it is likewise true that, if the act were not connected with my character, I could neither own it as mine nor feel regret for it. On the other hand, just as little would it be possible for me to repent of a deed if I were sure that, in the situation, only the one course was possible. The sting of regret seems to lie in the conviction that something better was then and there possible for me. And if one were convinced that this was an illusion, he might indeed designate the act as bad, but he would not cherish any penitential feeling in regard to it. Then, in the second place, if you deny to the self any power of making new beginnings in its ethical development, you must ultimately trace that development back to non-moral causes. For habits and dispositions have already formed out of the natural impulses and desires ere the ethical will can exercise a transforming influence upon them. In other words the rudiments of character precede moral choice, and a determinate development is already in process which excludes the emergence of open possibilities in its course. If the chain of cause and effect is to be preserved intact, there seems no help for it but to trace the evolution of moral character to non-moral sources. Confronted with this alternative it seems far better for us to accept, despite the undoubted difficulties and mystery which attach to it, the fact of a limited yet real amount of indeterminism in the growth of the moral self.[1]

Having thus stated our reasons for accepting a measure of indeterminism in human action, it now remains for us

[1] Kant, as is well known, tried to evade the dilemma of determinism or indeterminism by the unworkable hypothesis of an original act of choice on the part of the noumenal self which transcends the phenomenal series in space and time. In recent days Prof. Howison (*Limits of Evolution*) and Prof. Rogers (*The Religious Conception of the World*) seek to meet the difficulty by postulating the ultimate and eternal nature of the self. It is interesting to note that Dr. McDougall (*Social Psychology*, pp. 235-36) admits the force of this objection to determinism.

to consider the bearing of this conclusion upon the problem of moral evil. Our speculative theory, it will be remembered, was that personal spirits are all dependent on the Divine Will ; but that, along with this dependence, there goes a degree of being-for-self, so that human experience is not one and the same with divine experience. The real alternatives of choice which are open to these finite centres of will involve the possibility that they may conflict with the will of God, and thus contradict their own true nature, which is grounded in God. And this opposition of the human to the Divine Will is active in the generation of sin, and apart from the instrumentality of finite selves the reign of moral evil would not exist. Hence we are justified in saying that sin is not directly willed by God, and its presence in experience does not forbid faith in an ethical World-Ground. Yet we need not dally with the theological sophism, that a Being who permits the wrong he could have prevented is in no way responsible for it. If we keep in view the connexion of moral with natural evil, and also the fact that the whole process of experience has its final ground in God, we must conclude there is a sense in which all forms of evil as well as good depend on God. And an order of the world in which sin plays a part is in the end a divine order and fulfils a divine purpose. To our human insight the element of mystery is not lacking here, and the difficulty would be insurmountable if sin had to be taken as an enduring fact never to be conquered. The perplexity is diminished if we regard evil, which I think we may do, as a transitional phase of experience destined at the last to be overcome. If evil were embedded in the universe and its power ultimately insuperable, then pessimism would be justified. A brighter outlook is suggested by the practical truth that sin can be overcome in the individual and society, and spiritual progress is possible. It is not indeed true that evil is only "good in the making": let us repeat that the losses and failures which sin entails are not thus to be explained. But the reality of sin makes the moral life a strenuous struggle fraught with the gravest issues—a struggle in which the possibility of defeat is no illusion, but the hope of victory is also justified. There is dignity as well as responsibility in the vocation of the human spirit which is set the task of winning its way through temptation and conflict to fuller and richer life. It is well to remember too that the burden of all higher religion is, that this mundane experience is neither complete nor final but by its very imperfection points to a goal beyond. And if in this redemptive process man by faith gains higher help, none the less it is a process which is personally realised and calls for ardent endeavour and loyalty to the ideal :—

> "Gerettet ist das edle Glied
> Der Geisterwelt vom Bösen,
> Wer immer strebend sicht bemüht
> Den können wir erlösen."

But perhaps it may be objected that even this view is too optimistic. Human history does not show us evil being baffled and broken in a way that would suggest its final overthrow. Religion, despite its age-long development, has come far short of emancipating humanity from the thralls of sin and vice, and the bright hopes of a new reign of good on earth have time and again been doomed to disappointment. If the Christian Church, it has been said, has made so little progress in defeating sin after two thousand years, is there any assurance that its task will be completed after two hundred thousand? The difficulty which is here urged has already met us in our preliminary discussion of the Idea of Development in History. And, it will be remembered, we there saw reason to conclude, that, while the world showed signs of progress, the progress is neither constant nor uniform in its movement. If, to use the apostolic phrase, where sin abounds grace does more abound, still the defeat of sin is only partial and temporary, and it returns in a fresh guise to renew the conflict. Grosser forms of wrong-doing, if banished or driven underground, reappear in more refined forms of selfishness which may be almost as hurtful to the spiritual life. And beneath the veneer of modern civilisation there lurk savage and brutal instincts which, at some time of crisis when moral restraints are weakened, break forth and work havoc. Spiritual progress is a vocation which depends on the enlistment of human powers, and we cannot invoke any impersonal law which will ensure the universal rule of good in the world. In these circumstances the question recurs, whether this earthly experience in which the threads of good and evil are so closely interwoven, and in which the form of moral life presupposes this contrast, is after all a final experience. If this mundane history of ours were a phase in a larger process, if it were a stage to something beyond itself, the problem of evil might be in a better way to solution. For, as before observed, the problem is not soluble if we are compelled to accept evil as something final and ultimate. And if we are not justified in postulating the advent of a perfect kingdom of goodness on earth, are we warranted in believing that the present spiritual struggle reaches its consummation hereafter? Is it not possible that this temporal experience is felt to be incomplete and disappointing just because it is the prophecy of something higher? There is nothing inherently improbable in the thought that the path of earthly endeavour is only a stage in the journey of the pilgrim spirit of man and the final goal lies beyond it. The shadow of sin and suffering which broods over the world would be perceptibly lifted if man had any "sure and certain hope" that, when he crosses "the low dark verge of life," he goes to meet the dawn of a new day.

(2) In proceeding to offer some observations on the problem of immortality, I would remind the reader that we have already been led up to the subject in discussing the development of history and the realisation of the moral ideal. It there appeared that the acceptance of immortality in some form would help to free us from certain perplexities in which we found ourselves. But however practically helpful such a faith might be, we should be compelled to abandon it if it could be shown that the nature of the universe forbids us to cherish it. It has often been pointed out that the existence of a human desire does not guarantee the reality of its object, unless indeed it can be made plain that the object is at least possible and does not contradict the nature of things. The history of religion shows us many beliefs which were once deemed to have real objects, beliefs which in their day no doubt had a pragmatic value, but which in the growing light of knowledge were seen to have no counterpart in the objective world. There have always been those who hold that the picture of a life-to-come is the mere creation of desire, a *Wunschwesen* which it is impossible to justify and therefore best to set aside, a figment of a creed outworn.

> Nobis quum semel occidit brevis lux,
> Nox est perpetua una dormienda.

One who wishes to vindicate his right to believe in immortality must do two things: he must show that the doctrine of a life after death cannot be scientifically disproved, and he must bring forward evidence, either speculative or moral, tending to make it appear that the idea is possibly or even probably true. How far this can be done we may now go on to consider.

At the outset we have to keep clearly in mind that the validity of a belief can never be decided by the manner of its origin. Though the conception of immortality has developed out of spiritism and the belief in ghosts, this no more discredits it than modern astronomy and chemistry are discredited by the fact that they were evolved out of astrology and alchemy. The notion of the soul has its roots in primitive thought, and its persistence after death was at first quite unconnected with ethical ideas. At a later period, and under the influence of rudimentary moral notions, the future life was associated with the apportionment of rewards and punishments for the deeds done in the flesh. This has been a favourite field for the exercise of the religious imagination ; and those only learn to speak with reserve on this theme who are aware "of the feebleness of the human faculties and the uncertainty of the subject." Meanwhile the recurrence of the thought of a future life in early and later culture is a witness to a human need. This of course is not decisive, but the attempt to discredit the belief as a 'survival' is quite irrelevant.

If we interrogate science on the possibility of a future life, the answer at first sight might seem unfavourable. Scientific theory appears to indicate a functional dependence of mind upon brain. It is pointed out that with the advent of physical death the signs of psychical life always cease. In support of the idea of functional dependence the parallelism between intelligence and brain structure, between the convolutions of the cerebral cortex and the thinking faculty, is instanced. We are also reminded of the correspondence of certain areas of the brain with specific psychical activities ; and it is also shown how a defective blood-supply to the brain can induce mental disorders. So it is concluded the function cannot persist when its basis is gone, and the conscious personality must dissolve when the body dies. Yet it is easy to see that there is nothing in these contentions which will bear the name of proof. That thought is a function of the material brain never has been nor can be shown; and what is put forward as the hypothetical basis of mind really presupposes mind. No individual has an experience of his own brain, and his brain really stands for a group of possible experiences in a possible observer. These experiences are psychical facts, and the proposition "mind is a function of brain" logically reduces itself to the assertion, that one group of psychical facts is inferred to be a function of another group of psychical facts. You cannot pass outside the psychical and reach an independent variable beyond it. Nor, I think, does the theory of psycho-physical parallelism count in this connexion. For though the theory may be a convenient working hypothesis at the psychological level, it breaks down as an ontological postulate and must be replaced by the conception of interaction. According to the argument of the previous chapter the so-called physical is at root psychical, and it is on the basis of an interaction of psychical elements that the soul or self develops. The self is really the teleological principle which controls this interaction and so gives shape to the external structure. And the self-conscious mind can subdue and govern the bodily affections by an inherent right of rule. Hence it is at least an open question whether the existence of the soul is indissolubly bound up with that particular interacting system we term the human body. There is nothing contradictory in the thought that the soul, or formative principle, can fashion to its use a higher organism than the present one out of the elements at its disposal. Still a suggestive hypothesis is not a proof. I think, however, it is well within the mark to say that, so far as biology and physiology are concerned, the possibility of the soul's survival after death is by no means disproved.

But failure to disprove is one thing and positive evidence is another; and, when we ask definite grounds for belief in immortality, we are presented with a number of arguments, some resting on speculative and others on moral grounds. But before going further it is well for us to be clear how much an argument for immortality is actually designed to prove. For instance, thinkers have sometimes argued that the mind or spirit was eternal, not meaning by this that it was endowed with individual immortality. Spinoza speaks of the mind's eternal part: *sentimus experimurque nos aeternos esse*, he declares, and for this he proceeds to give proof. But the eternity is not that of a self which knows and remembers: it is only the soul's impersonal share in abiding reality. Schleiermacher, at the close of the second of his *Reden*, speaks of the immortality of religion as "a becoming one with the infinite in the midst of the finite, and being eternal in each moment." Yet whatever element of truth may be contained in these statements, it is plain that they are no argument for a personal survival after death, and they have been accepted by those who denied any such survival.

The older rational proofs for immortality were based on the assumed nature of the soul, and commonly presupposed the dualism of mind and matter. For instance the soul, though it had its seat in the body, was defined as a simple, immaterial substance; and so it was imperishable. This argument was discredited by Kant and is rarely urged now: nor, in the light of recent psychology, has the idea of soul as a kind of residuum reached by abstracting from the forms of psychical activity any plausibility. Modern thought, in so far as it offers a speculative argument for immortality, seeks to show that it is implied in the relation of the self to the Absolute. Dr. McTaggart, for example, gives reasons for holding that the Absolute is just the system of selves, and each self expresses an ultimate and fundamental differentiation of the Absolute. Consequently the self in its deeper nature can neither come into being nor pass away : it is eternally identical with itself, though this identity need not mean a continuous memory of existence. Indeed the latter qualification is indispensable, since the soul, being an ultimate differentiation of the Absolute, must always have existed, and yet the ego has no memory of such pre-existence. Dr. McTaggart thinks that all is not lost with the loss of memory, and what is of value may be preserved as well as transcended. Yet I imagine most people will find this doctrine of pre-existence, like Lotze, "strange and improbable." But the main objection to the theory is that it secures a certain immortality of the personal spirit at the expense of ignoring its weakness and imperfection, and also its dependence, in common with all finite beings, on a living World-Ground. The feeling of incompleteness so closely bound up with the religious consciousness must on this view be a mistake. We are told that the "whole is perfectly in every part," and "any hindrance to the development of any self would be a hindrance to the development of the Absolute."[1] But this must mean that moral evil is an illusion, and that the universe, seen *sub specie aeternitatis*, is perfect and complete throughout. A doctrine from which such conclusions follow has not much cogency. Again the philosophical

[1] *Studies in Hegelian Cosmology*, p. 52.

argument for immortality given by Professor Royce in his "Gifford Lectures" and his "Ingersoll Lecture," while differing in some respects very decidedly from Dr. McTaggart's, is still in agreement with it on this point, that immortality rests on an intrinsic and necessary relation of the finite self to the Absolute. The persistence of individual selves is guaranteed by the fact that each is the expression of a unique meaning, and "represents the totality of the Absolute in its own way." The Absolute is a self-conscious and completely integrated self, inclusive of all the various and interconnected selves which exist in time. The suggestive points in Royce's theory are, that he regards the true self of man not as datum but as ideal, a fulness of meaning to be realised. And, in the second place, he holds the essential feature of finite selfhood, as expressing the Absolute, to be purposive endeavour, teleological will, whose goal is to be a unique meaning, a perfect differentiation of the Absolute. Since this fulness of intrinsic meaning is never attained within mundane time-experience, the self must find its consummation in a larger individuality continuous with the individuality that dies. The self which thus attains perfect individuality in the eternal world is still distinguished from the Absolute: it is in a sense partial, for it must be supplemented by other selves; but, to use a mathematical image, it is "infinite in its kind."[1] The difficulty raised by this interesting train of thought is, that it is hard to understand how a being whose inherent relation to the Absolute necessarily guarantees its immortality can be consistently conceived to come into existence at any point in time. For that would sacrifice the necessity of the relationship. The only resource would be to fall back on some form of the

[1] *Vid. The World and the Individual.* Gifford Lectures, II Series, pp. 289, 298, 440 ff.

"strange and improbable" doctrine of pre-existence. Nor can it be said that Professor Royce makes it clear how an Absolute Self can include within it a universe of uniquely qualified selves. In strictness the finite self should be regarded simply as an expression of the Absolute's meaning, not as a self-conscious centre of feeling and will which distinguishes itself from the Absolute. Or, if the ultimate reality of individual centres be maintained, the Absolute ought to be conceived as impersonal process finding its concrete fulfilment in the system of unique selves. At the same time the thought is valuable that the human self has a developmental vocation in time, a vocation divinely laid upon it which requires a supramundane sphere for its full achievement. But I think the stress of this argument ought to rest on ethical rather than on metaphysical grounds.

If we are right in our speculative theory, the case for immortality is not likely to be furthered on these lines. For the nerve of the argument in the foregoing instances is, that the being of the individual self is so intimately and necessarily bound up with the nature of the Absolute, that its eternity is assured. On the other hand we found that, while finite things pointed necessarily back to a World-Ground or Divine Will, neither the being nor self-consciousness of God was necessarily dependent on the universe of things in space and time. To put it shortly, finite spirits are not necessary to God in the sense that God is necessary to them. They had a beginning and there is no divine necessity why they should not have an end. On this view immortality is not a logical necessity but an ethical goal, and its justification must lie in the moral and practical reason. That is to say, the personal life may have an inner meaning and value which are not exhausted in this earthly existence, and which point to a fulfilment beyond the present life. This was the line of thought which Kant opened out; and though the particular form in which he cast his practical proof may be open to criticism, it is still capable of restatement in a way that is helpful. The substance of the Kantian argument might be put thus: "The moral and spiritual life is the struggle to realise an ideal which demands fulfilment; but the temporal fulfilment is always partial and fragmentary, and so we must postulate some world 'of larger scope,' where the ideal and the actual approximate and finally coalesce in a perfect harmony. A universe in which the ideal makes such claims must in justice give an opportunity for their fulfilment; and the loyal servant of the law must have ample room for his service." This argument contains something of value, but the value can only be assured if this 'practical proof' is connected with the ethical character of God in his relation to man. Otherwise we have no guarantee that the universe will respond to the demands of the ethical personality.

There is one feature that is common to the forms of 'moral proof' which rest the hope of immortality on personal value, and it deserves to be noted. Taken strictly they do not suggest an intrinsic but a conditional immortality. For they rest on the idea of value partially attained and claiming to be completed, and therefore they do not apply to beings who have never entered upon, or who have utterly abandoned the higher vocation. On the side of spiritual religion, moreover, it may be fairly urged that it has no interest in claiming an absolute and unconditional immortality for every being that has borne the human form. The idiot, the infant of days, the half brutish ancestors of the race—all these, it may be said, having developed no personal life here, possess no claim to a larger life hereafter.[1] Nor does it appear that such

[1] *Cf.* on this point the remarks of Seydel, *Religionsphilosophie*, 1893, p. 323.

an exclusion contradicts any postulate of the religious consciousness.

Returning to the moral argument, it would be wrong, I think, to lay the weight on the notion of compensation, as has sometimes been done. The idea that the working of justice in this world must be supplemented by a system of rewards and punishments in the world to come has often appeared in the history of religion, and supplies a strong motive at a certain stage of development. But it is easy to see that it does not furnish an argument for immortality in the proper sense of the term. And in the matter of moral evil it is hardly doubtful that there is an immanent justice in this world ; the saint reaps inward gain and the sinner suffers inward loss. A moral proof which ignores this fact loses force in consequence.

There is still a difficulty which deserves mention. It is said that individuality is a limitation and a defect, and, far from desiring its persistence, the purified soul rather longs to be delivered from it and to be merged in some impersonal good. The thought of being bound down for ever to some form of personal life instead of being a joy is declared to be a burden : the prospect of immortality is a threat rather than a hope, and the idea is welcome that individuality has a final term. The East is more familiar with this view than the West ; but modern Pessimism endorses it, and points out in support that the human self is only an inconstant product of a vast and unconscious activity. It is argued that the advance of civilisation is marked by an increasing self-sacrifice of the individual for large and impersonal ideas, a movement which suggests that the higher self-consciousness seeks a supra-personal goal.[1] And Buddhism is often instanced as a religion which holds out to its millions of votaries the consumma-

[1] So Count Keyserling in his interesting volume *Die Unsterblichkeit*, 1907. p. 211 ff.

tion of Nirvana or passionless non-existence. In the face of such facts can we speak of man's universal craving for immortality? In reply it is right to say frankly that the longing for a future life is not always nor equally present in men. Many desire it eagerly, some expect it vaguely, and others wish for no world beyond the present. All perhaps we are entitled to say is, that the desire for a life hereafter preponderates in humanity, and is accepted by many as a solution of the imperfect and fragmentary character of this life. Nor does the race, as it grows older, become more inclined to narrow its hopes to this world. Buddhism, so far as it is a gospel of sheer annihilation, is an esoteric faith; among the masses of its adherents a positive hope of "some better thing hereafter" takes the place of a blank negation, and popular Buddhism even has its heaven and hell. From animistic nature-religion upwards to the higher ethical religions the existence of a widespread hope of a life to come is a normal feature in spiritual experience, however the hope may suffer eclipse in particular individuals, races and epochs.

We come now to the final question. If neither science nor philosophy can disprove immortality, can we justify the desire by making the truth of the belief a postulate of the religious life? If by postulate we mean something upon which the existence of the religious life depends, then immortality is not a postulate in this sense.[1] For a religion may exist and has existed where there was no belief in a future life. On the other hand, if we take the term postulate in a wider way to denote a hypothesis which gives deeper meaning and value both to religious and ethical experience, and which helps to reconcile contradictions, then the doctrine of immortality deserves

[1] *Cf.* Rauwenhoff, *Religionsphilosophie*, p. 576, and Lipsius, *Lehrbuch der Dogmatik*, p. 857.

the name of a postulate. As a postulate in this acceptation of the term, the idea of immortality falls to be regarded in two aspects: in its bearing on individual development and its bearing on social development.

(*a*) From the standpoint of individual development the consciousness of the worth of the soul gives weight to the hope of immortality. For the soul is the centre of value, and only in living and personal spirits are values realised. Is the conscious spirit then, in which the good is actualised, only a phenomenon in the world-process, appearing for a little and then vanishing? Men have often felt, and frequently given expression to the feeling, that, if physical and psychical evolution reaches its highest point in a spiritual personality, something seems lost which ought to be conserved if the doom of lapsing into nothingness overtakes that personality. The contradiction would be less palpable, the felt hardship less keen, if the soul in its temporal endeavour could count itself to have attained, if it had the feeling of inner satisfaction and completeness. Man would acquiesce more readily in the prospect of extinction, if he were conscious he had brought his powers to full fruit and had realised all he had it in him to become. But it is just a conviction of this kind which is conspicuously absent. The moral life is the struggle after an ideal which is never attained. And while religion solves this contradiction, in principle at least, by translating this struggle into a conscious communion with the Supreme Good, yet the communion at best is partial and interrupted, the foretaste rather than the realisation of a perfect fulness. It was asserted by the disciples of the Romantic Movement, at the beginning of last century, that religion made man eternal in each moment of the present, and that here and now he had his immortality. One who looks abroad on the religious life of men will not hesitate, I believe, to say this is the language of exaggerated enthusiasm, not of sober experience. The religious man feels that in spiritual communion with God he is indeed on the way to perfection, not that he is already perfect: the present is the prophecy, not the achievement of the goal. The spiritual life arises out of a temporal environment and makes that environment subserve its development; but the bearer of that life is conscious that it means more than any earthly vocation can realise. He hopes there is a fulfilment beyond the present, and he believes his sense of incompleteness would not be so real were it not prophetic of a future completion. But the ultimate source of this assurance is a faith born of inner experience and not a reasoned inference. I have already suggested why, as it seems to me, the speculative argument based on the relation of the soul to God breaks down. Nevertheless faith in God as the Personal World-Ground and the Supreme Good will always be the final and decisive principle on which a positive answer to this question depends. If the universe is not upheld by a righteous Will, there can be no confidence that it responds to man's deepest desires and hopes. If it is so upheld, there may be a legitimate trust that the children who cry for bread will not receive a stone. The God who is the Perfect Good must also be the conserver of values, through whom all centres of worth that deserve to be preserved and completed come to their fruition.

(*b*) But the problem has also a social aspect which should not be ignored, for it requires to be considered along with the personal aspect. We know that personal development is closely implicated with the structure of society. For all psychical growth is made possible by the interaction of psychical centres, and the personal life develops in and through the interaction of personal lives within a social system. The social good thus represents a larger good, to promote which individual endeavour is a proper means. That good, however, is only an actual good in so far as it is expressed in the inner life of persons; and if society gives an end to individuals, it in turn finds an end in mediating the development of higher and richer forms of personal life. When the individual sacrifices himself for the social good it is not for an impersonal end, but that the growing good of the whole may take shape in the enhanced values of the personal lives which compose it. We cannot judge the soundness of a society simply by its laws and institutions, and we have to test our social reforms by the way in which they react on the character of individuals. The conception of 'corporate immortality' has therefore difficulties, and those who favour the idea forget that society is a means as well as an end. Corporate immortality in the last resort must signify that the ultimate goal of all personal effort is the personal good of those who come after. But without denying nobility to this thought, one cannot see that a later race can claim to use the generations who have gone before as a means to its own good. And if the personal centres of value that constitute society have no hope of any persistence beyond the present life, the final extinction of all values becomes a likely or at least a possible result. To avoid this objection you may fall back on the idea that man has his eternal good in his present service: he is immortal "till his work is done." But this, one must repeat, finds no confirmation in our spiritual experience.

Any attempt to find man's final good in an earthly society brings us back to the old perplexity, how consistently to conceive a mundane goal to human progress. We found in our first chapter that neither a perfect social system on earth, nor a constant progress towards something better, could be coherently thought out as the ultimate end of man's spiritual development. The most satisfying solution seemed to be that the goal of personal development did not fall within this temporal process at all : it was supramundane and was not bound up with the perfection of any earthly order of things. It is because the highest good must be personally realised that we are justified in believing that society is fulfilling an ever-present end when it subserves the growth of personal spirits whose vocation transcends the world. Social development, instead of rendering personal immortality unnecessary, finds its final interpretation through it. I will only add that caution and reserve are indispensable in speaking of the future life. Those who seek to define and explain forget the limitations of human insight and court criticism by their material imagery. The theologian is more apt to sin in this respect than the philosopher ; and if theology is not to speak unadvisedly here, it must abandon definition and doctrine and be content to speak in the language of symbol. Nor do the spiritual interests of life demand any fully articulated eschatology. Man's last hope for himself and his fellows lies in the goodness of God ; and faith in the divine goodness means faith that God will not cast away but conserve all that is worthy to be conserved.

(3) We pass now to our final problem, the relation of the Idea of God to the Development of Religion. In the answer to this question are involved such ultimate conclusions as we can reach on the meaning of religious development. The foregoing discussions, psychological and metaphysical, have indicated how we conceive the nature of God and spiritual development, and we may proceed now briefly to suggest the results.

The whole system of interacting centres of experience depends on the conserving and connecting power of the World-Ground. And God, as the World-Ground, is the ultimate source of development in every form. The sustaining and interrelating activity of God is the condition without which the activity implied in development could not be. Evolution, whether it be termed material, biological, or spiritual, is therefore always a dependent process, the final meaning of which is not to be found within itself. But while God is the ground of development, he is also its goal, for he is perfect personality and eternally complete self-consciousness. Progress in the natural sphere has taken the form of the production of more and more fully articulated individuals, and spiritual progress lies in the direction of the growth of ethical personality through the interaction of conscious individuals in a social system. Personality forms on the basis of individuality. The study of human development, apart from ontological postulates, suggests that the formation, deepening, and enrichment of personality are its characteristic notes. It is in and through this growth in self-consciousness that man gains a deeper insight into the spiritual meaning of the universe and his own destiny therein. If the key to development always lies in the higher rather than in the lower phases of the process, then the key to man's development is the personal life. And the conviction that the ground of experience is a supreme and personal Will receives support from the character of the developmental movement within the world.

Taken in this connexion the development of the religious consciousness is very significant. For the common feature of all religion is that it grows out of a persisting need, a need which posits an object beyond the self which can satisfy the self. It is always by the establishment of some bond of connexion between the worshipper and his god that religion brings deliverance and satisfaction. The bond itself, as we have seen, is gradually transformed with the evolution of higher needs, and from a mechanical and half magical link becomes an inward and spiritual communion. From this universal impulse to religion in mankind two conclusions are to be drawn. In the first place, he is not a complete being who finds a full satisfaction in himself and his visible environment. And, in the second place, his nature must contain an intrinsic relation to a more perfect form of being which keeps alive in him the sense of imperfection, and impels him to higher and fuller forms of self-fulfilment. In the lowest stages of religion only the faint stirrings of this impulse are discernible, and to the unsympathetic eye primitive worship might seem only a rude device to secure the gratification of brute wants and to avert bodily ills. But when man rises above the tyranny of his environment this impulse takes purer forms and expresses its meaning more clearly. And finally it is disclosed as a spiritual desire springing from the depths of the soul, to be assuaged by no form of material good, and pointing to a transcendent goal. Religion is thus revealed as man's endeavour to realise his true destiny in the universe. This most significant movement rests on an inherent relation of the human spirit to the divine; but the relation is merely natural or implicit at the beginning, taking an external form, and it can become truly spiritual and self-conscious only through a continued process of religious development. By a long and toilsome way man rises to that spiritual consciousness of himself and the world, which is likewise the consciousness of his abiding relation to God. The working of God's spirit in man is the source of this persistent search, and he is also its final goal. "Thou hast made us for Thyself, and our souls are ever restless till they rest in Thee."

If God be conceived as both the source and the goal of religious development, we have still to consider more closely the significance of the process itself. And plainly the direction of spiritual progress does not depend upon man, but upon God. For man's spiritual nature, which is essentially related to the divine nature, is not determined by himself, but by God. Man may seek satisfaction and self-fulfilment in various ways, but he only finds them when he seeks them in the line of his divinely implanted end. The direction and the goal of his true self-realisation are given by God. Hence religious development will always be distinguished from mere change by being an advance, or a means towards advance, in that spiritual knowledge and experience of God which are the final end of all personal spirits. In this light a movement in religion which, taken in isolation, seems one-sided and defective will still fall within the developmental process if it brings about by reaction a fresh advance. So there may be progress where it is not superficially apparent. But certain philosophical interpretations of development, the reader will remember, we saw reason to reject. The end is not eternally realised, nor is the time-process mere appearance. For this takes the heart out of human endeavour and undermines the reality of all human values. Nor can we admit that all religious history is an immanent and necessary evolution in the line of the end. The unprejudiced student of the facts does not find this even superficially plausible, and it leaves no room for human freedom and sin. Within limits, spiritual evolution reveals a degree of plasticity, and movements are initiated which seem to issue in failure and loss instead of ministering to progress. And so it is in religion.

Human souls are not unresisting materials like bricks or stones, each to be fitted into its predetermined place in a rising structure. The spiritual life is a real test where all possibilities are not foreclosed : and though our spiritual vocation is fixed, we may fulfil or fail to fulfil it. In the religious life there are real gains and losses ; and it cannot be otherwise if the higher calling is to be a genuine proof, and faith itself an act of freedom. The same holds true of society. Under spiritual leaders the religion of a people can be reformed and enter on a larger life. But the opposite may be the case ; and a religion once living may fall into decay and become a hindrance and not a help to human progress. The failures and disappointments, the felt discords and the acts of sin which are part of man's religious history, are evidences that he is not merely the passive instrument of divine purpose. Rather is he the potential fellow-worker with God, who can fulfil or come short of his spiritual mission.

Yet here, too, there are hopeful signs. The discord and dissatisfaction which enter into the evolution of religion could not be experienced so vividly if man, through all his wanderings, did not retain some consciousness of his relation to God. It is this permanent affinity with God, dimly felt it may be, yet never wholly lost, which makes man conscious of his shortcomings and forbids him to rest in a partial satisfaction. So the task of spiritual advance is laid upon him : in a higher form of religion he seeks deliverance from the contradictions and disappointments of an older one, and as the fateful journey proceeds he gradually realises how great are the demands of the spiritual life and how high are its hopes. The interruptions, the deviations and the retrogressions which mark this history flow from the limitations and imperfections of human nature. The soul of man is not a complete and perfectly balanced system, and society reflects the instability of its constituent units. Hence in the interaction which goes to the development of religion the adjustment of the elements is never perfect, and some one becomes dominant. In the spiritual life one-sided movements are constantly arising, which in their turn call forth a reaction : out of this conflict the way is opened towards some larger form of faith. The distinctive psychical elements in man, interacting with the environment and responding to its stimuli, are the active factors in religious development. In our previous discussions we noted how thought, feeling, and will can each bring about a one-sided movement of the religious spirit which, in virtue of its limited character, cannot maintain itself and has to be transcended. As Eucken has said, there is "a dialectic of life," and spiritual progress is only achieved amid struggle and disappointment, amid oppositions and revulsions. The historian of religion leads us through a scene of bewildering complexity, and faiths have grown and passed away whose contribution to man's spiritual development we can only faintly conjecture. But elements of value in a vanished religion may have been absorbed by another, and so continue to work for good although no historic insight can now trace and disentangle them. Yet whatever losses there may have been, to the eye with a large outlook the outlines of a real progress are visible, and man is seen to have struggled upward from the sensuous to the spiritual. The highest religion to-day immeasurably transcends in spiritual content the meagre creed of primitive man, and the end is surely better than the beginning.

God is not only the ground of religious development, he is also a directing influence working within it. He is the constant Will that ever tends to bring human wills to the realisation of their true end. Religious progress is a dialectic one, at least in the sense that its movements ever require to be supplemented and completed, and the human spirit cannot rest under the burden of a felt defect. This need of harmony and completeness depends on man's inner relation to God, the perfect Person, and it is no human discontent which will not suffer him to abide in any narrow faith. It is in answer to the presence and pressure of divine influence that he seeks a deeper spiritual experience. When a religion has run into the extreme of Mysticism, or sunk into a mechanical Ritualism or a barren Rationalism, the uprising of the spirit demanding deliverance and fuller self-expression is really man's response to God's working. Hence in all religious development there is a mingling of divine and human elements. If man sets out to seek God, it is because the spirit of God is with him to prompt the search; and if through many wanderings he rises to greater heights of spiritual communion, it is not without the leading of the Father of Spirits. No religion, however poor and narrow, has been without some breath of this heavenly impulse, and our faith in the divine Source from which the inspiration proceeds is also our confidence that the human spirit will not come short of its goal.

If the view repeatedly urged in these pages be right, the goal of man's religious development does not fall within this present order of things. And if the process has its issues in a transcendent sphere, then the perfect comprehension of its meaning is denied us. We are like the spectator witnessing the earlier acts of a drama, aware that he will only grasp their full significance when the final act has been played. But the postulate that personal spirits find their consummation with God in a transcendent world is needed to remove the contradictions which beset the idea that man's spiritual development can come to its completion under earthly conditions. To turn this postulate of faith into a clear and sharply defined doctrine is not practicable ; it can only be attempted by carrying the ideas and images of sense into a region of the spirit where they are no longer relevant. It may be granted, however, that there are difficulties in supposing that the supramundane life of the spirit is one from which any notion of further development must be excluded. For it is essential that there should be continuity between the lower and the higher stages of being, and human spirits pass from this world in varying degrees of incompleteness. There is something contradictory in the thought that the personal life can be at once made perfect apart from its own movement. The possibility remains that religious progress under this earthly time-form is only a phase of a movement larger and more comprehensive, a single stage in a great development of souls.

In drawing this discussion to a close I do not wish to convey to the mind of the reader the impression that our theory of the relation of God to religious development is a complete solution of the problems raised by the subject. It is only fair to acknowledge that there are difficulties about which I have said little, difficulties which it is better, however, not to pass over in silence. It may be asked how, since you refuse to admit that human consciousness is a phase of the divine consciousness, is it possible to hold that man's whole spiritual development lies within the compass of divine knowledge ? Does the fact that man is a personal centre of experience which others do not share, not argue a limitation in the divine knowledge ? Beyond doubt a Deity who influenced the spiritual development of humanity under the disability imposed by partial ignorance, and therefore from whose acting error and failure were not excluded, would not satisfy the religious needs of men. Faith would be crippled by a paralysing uncertainty which extended to ultimate issues. Forms of idealism which insist on the complete exclusiveness of psychical centres of experience seem to lay themselves open to this objection. But the theory adopted here is that, while psychical experience is unique and individual, the centre of psychical experience is also a centre of interaction. God is the fundamental Will, the ground which sustains and the activity which connects all individuals. Hence he is not subject to the limitations which attach to individuals within the system; and every experience must mean something to the ground that makes it possible, as well as to the experient centre itself. In this intimacy of connection between the ground and individuals, the condition seems to be present for a knowledge which is all-penetrating and perfect. Moreover, the alien and impervious aspect of the object, which always remains for subjects within the interacting system, no longer exists between the individual centres and the self-conscious Will from which they proceed and upon which they depend. The manner of divine knowledge no doubt transcends us, and our knowing can at the best only be a feeble reflexion of the divine intuition. For man knows after a fragmentary fashion by laboriously establishing continuity between elements of his experience; he is denied that perfect insight into the parts which rests on a comprehension of the whole.

Another, and perhaps a more perplexing question, remains. How, it will be asked, does this development of personal spirits, a development reaching its highest form in religious progress, affect the being of God? It is a process which has its ultimate source in God and expresses his Will. Are we to suppose that God attains a greater perfection as the universe becomes a more perfect embodiment of his spiritual purpose? Thinkers have sought to evade this disconcerting difficulty by boldly proclaiming the unreality of time and change, and affirming that the real universe is a static whole, perfect and complete in every part. For reasons already given the attempt to solve the problem in this way breaks down. Time, as an ideal construction elaborated by intersubjective thinking, may have only a degree of reality; it cannot be illusory if spiritual values are to be conserved. The real universe, conceived as God and the whole range of individual spirits dependent upon him, cannot exclude change and increase in goodness. The difficulties in this conception may be serious, but its rejection involves difficulties still more serious. To God himself the development of souls must have the value of a purpose increasingly fulfilled. But we are not entitled to say that it signifies a progress in self-consciousness for God, as it does for man. Perfect self-consciousness in God is the constant condition of spiritual development in time, not its outcome. We must remember also that the value which attaches to a fulfilled purpose of man, who labours under limitations of knowledge and power, of fallibility as to the proper means and stubbornness in the material, cannot apply in exactly the same sense to God. If we are right in holding that the goal of spiritual progress lies in a sphere that transcends this mundane form of existence, its full meaning cannot be expressed through any earthly images and analogies. Yet, constituted as we are, we cannot avoid employing these figures in the endeavour to read the meaning of our life and destiny. Used with discrimination they are helpful, but they are never adequate.

One such symbol has obtained a wide currency; and few will deny its deep suggestiveness, even though they are constrained to deny its fitness. The Christian religion has made us familiar with the thought that God is Love, and as Love is working for the deliverance of men and their union with Himself. To some, no doubt, this will seem the language of exuberant optimism; and yet Christianity cannot be charged with passing lightly over the evil and sin that are in the world. And Dante, fated to wear "a sorrow's crown of sorrow" and to eat "the bitter bread," could still in his final word proclaim that Love is enthroned on high:

L'Amor che muove il sole e l'altre stelle.

But the secret of this optimism is its largeness of view. They who cherish it do not take this earthly order as a final fact: they see it as a stage in the development of spirit, the temporal beginning of a progress whose issue is in eternity. And if this attitude to the universe calls for faith, it may be said that faith lies behind the exercise of reason itself. Fundamental human needs find living expression in the trust that a God who is Love brought finite spirits into being, and by the path of spiritual progress leads all upward-striving souls to a full fellowship with Himself.

INDEX

INDEX

THE END

R. CLAY AND SONS, LTD., BREAD ST. HILL, E.C., AND BUNGAY, SUFFOLK.